VIRTUE ETHICS IN THE CONDUCT AND GOVERNANCE OF SOCIAL SCIENCE RESEARCH

ADVANCES IN RESEARCH ETHICS AND INTEGRITY

Series Editor: Dr Ron Iphofen *FAcSS, Independent Consultant, France*

Recent Volumes:

ADVANCES IN RESEARCH ETHICS AND INTEGRITY

Series Editor

Dr Ron Iphofen *FAcSS, Independent Consultant, France*

Editorial Advisory Group

Professor Robert Dingwall *FAcSS, Dingwall Enterprises Ltd and Nottingham Trent University, UK*

Dr Nathan Emmerich *Institute of Ethics, Dublin City University & Queens University Belfast, UK*

Professor Mark Israel *University of Western Australia, Australia*

Dr Janet Lewis AcSS, *Former Research Director, Joseph Rowntree Foundation, UK*

Professor John Oates *FAcSS, Open University, UK*

Associate Professor Martin Tolich *University of Otago, New Zealand*

ADVANCES IN RESEARCH ETHICS
AND INTEGRITY   VOLUME 3

VIRTUE ETHICS IN THE CONDUCT AND GOVERNANCE OF SOCIAL SCIENCE RESEARCH

VOLUME EDITOR

NATHAN EMMERICH

*Institute of Ethics, Dublin City University &
Queen's University Belfast, UK*

United Kingdom – North America – Japan
India – Malaysia – China

Emerald Publishing Limited
Howard House, Wagon Lane, Bingley BD16 1WA, UK

First edition 2018

Reprints and permissions service
Contact: booksandseries@emeraldinsight.com

British Library Cataloguing in Publication Data
A catalogue record for this book is available from the British Library

ISBN: 978-1-78714-608-2 (Print)
ISBN: 978-1-78714-607-5 (online)
ISBN: 978-1-78714-993-9 (Epub)

ISSN: 2398-6018 (Series)

Printed and bound by CPI Group (UK) Ltd, Croydon, CR0 4YY

ISOQAR certified
Management System,
awarded to Emerald
for adherence to
Environmental
standard
ISO 14001:2004.

ISOQAR
REGISTERED

Certificate Number 1985
ISO 14001

INVESTOR IN PEOPLE

CONTENTS

NOTES ON CONTRIBUTORS

Sarah Banks is Professor in the School of Applied Social Sciences and Co-director of the Centre for Social Justice and Community Action at Durham University, UK. She researches and teaches in the fields of community, youth and social work, with a particular interest in professional ethics, community development and participatory action research.

Helen Brown Coverdale is a Teaching Fellow in Political Theory at University College London. She holds an Arts & Humanities Research Council funded PhD in Law (London School of Economics) which applied the ethics of care to the theory of punishment. Helen is a legal and political theorist, and has taught political thought in the Philosophy Department at King's College London and the Government Department at the London School of Economics.

David Carpenter works at the University of Portsmouth where he lectures in moral and political philosophy and researches in the broad field of research ethics. David is currently engaged as an ethics adviser to a DFID-funded project in South Asia. He is a long-standing Chair of an NHS Ethics Committee and regularly contributes to the work of the Health Research Authority in training and research projects. He was Vice Chair of the former Association for Research Ethics, which is now part of the Association for Research Managers and Administrators. He is a member of the British Psychological Society Ethics Committee.

John Elliott is Emeritus Professor of Education and Lifelong Learning at the University of East Anglia, UK and a Fellow of the UK Academy of Social Sciences. His most recent publications include '*Reflecting Where the Action Is: The selected works of John Elliott*' (2007), and '*Curriculum, Pedagogy and Educational Research: The Work of Lawrence Stenhouse*' (with Nigel Norris Eds 2012).

Rachel Forrester-Jones is Professor of Social Inclusion, and Director of the Tizard Centre, the leading UK academic group working in learning disability and community care, at the University of Kent. She has more than

170 publications and is the recipient of more than 45 research grants. Rachel is the founding director of a new Research Cluster for Applied Research Ethics and Integrity at Kent and is a recently qualified Barrister (NR) and chair of the Research Ethics and Governance Committee at Kent.

Martyn Hammersley is Emeritus Professor of Educational and Social Research at The Open University, UK. He has carried out research in the sociology of education and studied the role of the media in reporting research findings. He has written several books, including: *Methodology, Who Needs It?* (2011); *What is Qualitative Research?* (2012); (with Anna Traianou) *Ethics in Qualitative Research* (2012); and *The Limits of Social Science* (2014).

Richard Kwiatkowski is a Senior Lecturer in Organizational Psychology Development and Learning in the Cranfield School of Management at Cranfield University. He is a former Chair of the British Psychological Society's Ethics Committee and Vice-Chair of the Cranfield University Ethics Committee. He is also a Chartered and Registered Occupational Psychologist and Counselling Psychologist.

Kath Melia is a sociologist and Emeritus Professor at the University of Edinburgh. Kath's most recently published work is *Ethics for Nursing and Healthcare Practice* (2014). Her current interest is in the relationship between ethics, sociology and the law in the context of clinical practice.

Jason Z. Morris is an Associate Professor (currently chair) in the Department of Natural Sciences at Fordham University. He earned his Ph.D. in Genetics at Harvard Medical School. In addition to his work on the genetic regulation of Drosophila development and behavior, he has published ethics articles in *The Journal of Medicine and Philosophy* and *Research Ethics.*

Marilyn C Morris, MD, MPH is an Associate Professor of Pediatrics at Columbia University. Her research focuses on regulatory and ethical aspects of human subjects research. She is a past IRB chair and current IRB member at Columbia University Medical Center.

Nicole Palmer is Research Ethics and Governance Officer at the University of Kent and is currently pursuing a PhD in Research Ethics and Integrity at Kent. Nicole has responsibility for the University's research ethics review processes, developing policy and procedure on good practice and misconduct. Nicole provides training, advice and guidance to staff and students. She is co-founding member of the Applied Research Ethics and Integrity Research Cluster in the School of Social Policy, Sociology and Social Research at the University of Kent.

Anna Traianou is Reader in Educational Studies, in the Department of Educational Studies at Goldsmiths, University of London. She has carried out research into the nature of teacher expertise and, in particular, the ways in which knowledge (including research knowledge) are implicated in policy-making and professional practice. Her publications include: *Understanding Teacher Expertise in Primary Science: A Sociocultural Approach* (2006) and *Ethics in Qualitative Research: Controversies and Contexts* (with Martyn Hammersley, 2012).

ABOUT THE SERIES EDITOR

Dr Ron Iphofen, FAcSS, is Executive Editor of the Emerald book series *Advances in Research Ethics and Integrity* and edited volume 1 in the series, *Finding Common Ground: Consensus in Research Ethics Across the Social Sciences* (2017). He is an Independent Research Consultant, a Fellow of the UK Academy of Social Sciences, the Higher Education Academy and the Royal Society of Medicine. Since retiring as Director of Postgraduate Studies in the School of Healthcare Sciences, Bangor University, his major activity has been as an adviser to the European Commission (EC) on both the Seventh Framework Programme (FP7) and Horizon 2020. His consultancy work has covered a range of research agencies (in government and independent) across Europe. He was Vice Chair of the UK Social Research Association and now convenes their Research Ethics Forum. He was scientific consultant on the EC RESPECT project – establishing pan-European standards in the social sciences. He has advised the UK Research Integrity Office; the National Disability Authority (NDA) of the Irish Ministry of Justice; and the UK Parliamentary Office of Science and Technology among many others. Ron was founding Executive Editor of the Emerald gerontology journal *Quality in Ageing and Older Adults*. He published *Ethical Decision Making in Social Research: A Practical Guide* (Palgrave Macmillan, 2009 and 2011) and coedited with Martin Tolich *The SAGE Handbook of Qualitative Research Ethics* (Sage, 2018).

ABOUT THE VOLUME EDITOR

Nathan Emmerich is a research fellow in the Institute of Ethics, Dublin City University and a Visiting Research Fellow in the School of History, Anthropology, Politics and Philosophy at Queen's University Belfast. His research falls under the broad rubric of Bioethics. He is mostly interested in using social theory to examine how morality and ethics are produced, reproduced and 'done' in various domains of medicine and healthcare including clinical practice, medical education, governance, management and academia.

SERIES PREFACE

This book series, *Advances in Research Ethics and Integrity*, grew out of foundational work with a group of Fellows of the UK Academy of Social Sciences (AcSS) who were all concerned to ensure that lessons learned from previous work were built upon and improved in the interests of the production of robust research practices of high quality. Duplication or unnecessary repetitions of earlier research and ignorance of existing work were seen as hindrances to research progress. Individual researchers, research professions and society all suffer in having to pay the costs in time, energy and money of delayed progress and superfluous repetitions. There is little excuse for failure to build on existing knowledge and practice given modern search technologies unless selfish 'domain protectionism' leads researchers to ignore existing work and seek credit for innovations already accomplished. Our concern was to aid well-motivated researchers to quickly discover existing progress made in ethical research in terms of topic, method and/or discipline and to move on with their own work more productively and to discover the best, most effective means to disseminate their own findings so that other researchers could, in turn, contribute to research progress.

It is true that there is a plethora of ethics codes and guidelines with researchers left to themselves to judge those more appropriate to their proposed activity. The same questions are repeatedly asked on discussion forums about how to proceed when similar longstanding problems in the field are being confronted afresh by novice researchers. Researchers and members of ethics review boards alike are faced with selecting the most appropriate codes or guidelines for their current purpose, eliding differences and similarities in a labyrinth of uncertainty. It is no wonder that novice researchers can despair in their search for guidance and experienced researchers may be tempted by the 'checklist mentality' that appears to characterise a meeting of formalized ethics 'requirements' and permit their conscience-free pursuit of a cherished programme of research.

If risks of harm to the public and to researchers are to be kept to a minimum and if professional standards in the conduct of scientific research are to be maintained, the more that fundamental understandings of ethical behaviour in research are shared the better. If progress is made in one sphere all gain from it being generally acknowledged and understood. If foundational work is conducted all gain from being able to build on and develop further that work.

Nor can it be assumed that formal ethics review committees are able to resolve the dilemmas or meet the challenges involved. Enough has been written about such review bodies to make their limitations clear. Crucially they cannot follow researchers into the field to monitor their every action, they cannot anticipate all of the emergent ethical dilemmas nor, even, follow through to the publication of findings. There is no adequate penalty for neglect through incompetence, nor worse, for conscious omissions of evidence. We have to rely upon the 'virtues' of the individual researcher alongside the skills of journal and grant reviewers. We need constantly to monitor scientific integrity at the corporate and at the individual level. These are issues of 'quality' as well as morality.

Within the research ethics field new problems, issues and concerns and new ways of collecting data continue to emerge regularly. This should not be surprising as social, economic and technological change necessitate constant re-evaluation of research conduct. Standard approaches to research ethics such as valid informed consent, inclusion/exclusion criteria, vulnerable subjects, and covert studies need to be reconsidered as developing social contexts and methodological innovation, interdisciplinary research and economic pressures pose new challenges to convention. Innovations in technology and method challenge our understanding of 'the public' and 'the private'. Researchers need to think even more clearly about the balance of harm and benefit to their subjects, to themselves and to society. This series proposes to address such new and continuing challenges for both ethics committees and researchers in the field as they emerge. The concerns and interests are global and well recognised by researchers and commissioners alike around the world but with varying commitments at both the 'procedural' and the 'practical' levels. This series is designed to suggest realistic solutions to these challenges – this 'practical' angle is the USP for the series. Each volume will raise and address the key issues in the debates, but also strive to suggest ways forward that maintain the key ethical concerns of respect for human rights and dignity, while sustaining pragmatic guidance for future research developments. A series such as this aims to offer practical help and guidance in actual research engagements as well as meeting the often varied and challenging demands of research ethics review. The approach will not be one of abstract moral philosophy; instead it will seek to help researchers think through the potential harms and benefits of their work in the proposal stage and assist their reflection of the big ethical moments that they face in the field often when there may be no one to advise them in terms of their societal impact and acceptance.

While the research community can be highly imaginative both in the fields of study and methodological innovation, the structures of management and funding, and the pressure to publish to fulfil league table quotas can pressure researchers into errors of judgment that have personal and professional consequences. The series aims to adopt an approach that promotes good practice and sets principles, values and standards that serve as models to aid successful research outcomes. There is clear international appeal as commissioners and researchers alike share a vested interest in the global promotion of professional virtues that lead to the public acceptability of good research. In an increasingly global world in research terms, there is little point in applying too localized a morality, nor one that implies a solely Western hegemony of values. If standards 'matter', it seems evident that they should 'matter' to and for all. Only then can the growth of interdisciplinary and multi-national projects be accomplished effectively and with a shared concern for potential harms and benefits. While a diversity of experience and local interests is acknowledged, there are existing, proven models of good practice which can help research practitioners in emergent nations build their policies and processes to suit their own circumstances. We need to see that consensus positions effectively guide the work of scientists across the globe and secure minimal participant harm and maximum societal benefit – and, additionally, that instances of fraudulence, corruption and dishonesty in science decrease as a consequence.

Perhaps some forms of truly independent formal ethics scrutiny can help maintain the integrity of research professions in an era of enhanced concerns over data security, privacy and human rights legislation. But it is essential to guard against rigid conformity to what can become administrative procedures. The consistency we seek to assist researchers in understanding what constitutes 'proper behaviour' does not imply uniformity. Having principles does not lead inexorably to an adherence to principlism. Indeed, sincerely held principles can be in conflict in differing contexts. No one practice is necessarily the best approach in all circumstances. But if researchers are aware of the range of possible ways in which their work can be accomplished ethically and with integrity, they can be free to apply the approach that works or is necessary in their setting. Guides to 'good' ways of doing things should not be taken as the 'only' way of proceeding. A rigidity in outlook does no favours to methodological innovation, nor to the research subjects or participants that they are supposed to 'protect'. If there were to be any principles that should be rigidly adhered to they should include flexibility, open-mindedness, the recognition of the range of challenging situations to be met in the field – principles that in essence amount to a sense of proportionality. And these principles should apply equally to researchers and ethics reviewers alike. To accomplish that requires ethics reviewers to think afresh about each new research proposal, to detach from pre-formed opinions and prejudices, while still learning from and applying the lessons of the past. Principles such as these must also apply to funding and commissioning agencies, to research institutions, and to professional associations and their learned societies. Our integrity as researchers demands that we recognise that the rights of our funders and research participants and/or 'subjects' are to be valued alongside our cherished research goals and seek to embody such principles in the research process from the outset. This series will strive to seek just how that might be accomplished in the best interests of all.

Ron Iphofen (Series Editor)

INTRODUCTION: VIRTUE AND THE ETHICS OF SOCIAL RESEARCH

Nathan Emmerich

INTRODUCTION

Many of the papers collected in this volume have their origins in an event that took place in London in May 2015. It was organised by the UK Academy of Social Science's Working Group on Research Ethics with the support of the British Sociological Association (BSA). Largely to accommodate the additional papers that were commissioned, and appear in Section 3, the title of the event – Virtue Ethics in the Practice and Review of Social Science Research – slightly differs from the one chosen for this volume. The event followed on from the main activities that the Academy Working Group on Research Ethics had been pursuing for a number of years. This was the creation of set of common principles or shared basis for thinking about the ethics of social science research.[1] The call to further investigate the relevance of virtue for the practice and review of social scientific research had been a consistent feature of discussions that took place at events convened by the working group in the pursuit of its primary activities. As such, the event, and the essays collected here, are an organic development of these prior efforts.

As it had previously proved successful at promoting a relatively focused form of dialogue, the event was designed around the presentation of two

Virtue Ethics in the Conduct and Governance of Social Science Research
Advances in Research Ethics and Integrity, Volume 3, 1–17
Copyright © 2018 by Emerald Publishing Limited
All rights of reproduction in any form reserved
ISSN: 2398-6018/doi:10.1108/S2398-601820180000003001

stimulus papers, with morning and afternoon sessions. The two primary papers were to be accompanied by responses from discussants. In the morning the focus was on virtue and the conduct of social research/social researchers, whilst the afternoon concerned the relevance of virtue for ethical review. Not least due to the concern that ethical review was increasingly perceived as a source of difficulties for social research, this latter topic – the ethics of ethical review – had been a feature of previous discussions. The idea seems to have been that if it was to be properly understood, the ethics of social science ought to be considered in the fullest sense possible. Predicated on a model inherited from the biomedical sciences, the focus tended to be on the empirical data collection or fieldwork phase of social research. Furthermore, criticism of the existing approach to ethical review could in itself be understood as having ethical significance. In this context it is easy to see how the notion of virtue ethics, a moral philosophy that is not currently obviously taken up or influential in existing or mainstream discourses of research ethics, might appeal.

Furthermore, the limitations placed on social research in the name of ethics are arguable having distinctly problematic and unethical consequences (van den Hoonaard, 2011). A particular issue is the way in which research ethics may be compromising our, or society's, collective ability to understand ourselves in a manner that is organised and structured by disciplinary norms. Whilst it may not be the best political climate in which to lay claim to some form of expertise, the 'post-fact era' makes it increasingly vital that we nevertheless do so (Collins, Evans, & Weinel, 2017). The idea that some form of ethical analysis could itself provide some remedy to the situation has a certain appeal. Thus, bringing the alternate perspective of virtue ethics to bear on the question of social science research ethics and the ethics of ethical review provided the starting point for thinking about an event on the topic and, therefore, this volume.

Another facet of the discussions that had been taking place under the aegis of the Academy Working Group on Research Ethics was the idea that social researchers should be understood as professionals.[2] Given the extensive role virtue ethics has played and continues to play in debates about professional ethics across a great variety of domains (cf. Clegg, 2011), this clearly resonates with the view that virtue could be fruitfully explored in relation to the ethics of social research. It also resonates with sociological conceptions of professional practice as, say, something that involves the dispositions of a profession-specific habitus. With this in mind, Professor Sarah Banks – who has published an extensive body of work that examines the idea of virtue in relation to matters of professional ethics – was asked to explore the topic, and responses were sought from those that had been involved in previous events convened by the

Academy Working Group. Whilst the initial organisational focus for the event was on virtue ethics, the matter of integrity – both in relation to research and to researchers – rapidly came to the fore. As many of the essays that follow show that the discourse of virtue ethics clearly resonates with contemporary ideas regarding integrity in relation to both research and researchers.

VIRTUE ETHICS AND ITS APPEAL

The origins of virtue ethics lie with those of (western) philosophy itself. It is the moral philosophy of the Ancient Greeks and, in particular, of Aristotle. Whilst a range of substantive ethical perspectives can be found in Ancient Greek thought, Stoicism being one such example, the notion that virtue lays at the heart of morality was shared by virtually all philosophers of that era. Indeed, the idea that morality was a matter of virtue (and vice) remained central to moral philosophy and theology until after Descartes inaugurated modern philosophical thinking. Subsequently, two, or perhaps three, other 'high level' ethical theories have joined the moral philosophy of virtue ethics. These are the universal rationalism of Immanuel Kant, Jeremy Bentham's and John Stuart Mills' utilitarianism – or, more generally, consequentialist theories – and the social contract theories of Hobbes, Locke and Rousseau.[3] Taken together these form what Anscombe (1958) famously termed 'modern moral philosophy'[4] Unsurprisingly, in the modern era, such thinking is highly influential. Whilst it is certainly the case that historical accounts of research ethics show it developed in a particular context that was largely devoid of direct philosophical influences (Schrag, 2010; Stark, 2011), it is subsequently the case that philosophers and philosophical thinking have been influential in shaping the field of research ethics as it is today. Without wishing to deny that, since its inception, there has always been bioethicists for whom virtue ethics has been central – Edmund Pellegrino is an example – it is nevertheless the case that, coupled with a certain sort of ethical rationality, modern moral philosophy has been seen as underpinning the vast majority of thinking in research ethics. Almost by definition, the questions raised in this field are matters for analysis by applied ethics.

However, recent revisions to Beauchamp and Childress' (2009) *Principles of Biomedical Ethics*, perhaps *the* defining text of the field, have included a chapter on moral character that clearly draws on the perspective of virtue ethics. One reason for this is the fact that, whilst the ethical thought they present is clearly consistent with Anscombe's (1958) notion of modern moral philosophy, their account eschews any formal commitment to an overarching moral philosophy, whether that be Kantian, Consequentialist or Social Contractarian. The four principles – respect for autonomy; beneficence; non-maleficence; and justice – offered by Beauchamp and Childress (2009) can be understood as a mid-range theory. It is a conceptual framework, the value of which lies in it being useful for both analytic reflection (on practice) and practical deliberation (in practice). There are various ways to think about this proposition. One might say that, insofar as analytic reflection can inform practical deliberation (and action), and insofar as practical deliberation can draw on the insights of more analytic forms of reflection, then Beauchamp and Childress' (2009) framework can be considered useful and valuable in both practical and (applied) philosophical domains. One might also say that such a view challenges the distinction between ethical analysis and practical deliberation.

Consistent with the insights of Schön (1984), something that has been vital to current thinking about professional practice, reflection-in-action and reflection-on-action, should not be dichotomised but understood as being on a continuum. As Schön (1990, p. 1) points out, properly understood reflection-on-action is actually reflection-on-reflection-in-action. Thus, there is – or, at least, there *should be* – a continuum between the practical deliberation of professionals (those conducting research) and the more analytic reflections of '(bio)ethicists' or moral philosophers. If this is the case, then there is no room for thinking that there is any sharp distinction between the cognitive processes that attend 'practice' and 'analysis'. In short, the process of analytic thought must be understood as a practice, one that involves intellectual or cognitive dispositions of thought, phenomena that are comparable to the dispositions involved in other practices, including those that demand a high degree of cognitive expertise, such as most professional practices, including medicine as well as biomedical and social research.

A further reason for the advent of virtue theory or moral character in Beauchamp and Childress' (2009) thinking about their four principles of biomedical ethics is that, in the absence of an overarching commitment to a specific moral philosophy, they need some way of adjudicating between the principles in particular cases. In saying this I do not mean to imply that particular cases are a matter of one principle or another; that it is a case of selecting the correct one. Rather, I mean to suggest that when using this, and similar, conceptual frameworks to examine the ethics of particular cases one has to find the correct balance between each principle, the degree to which each is relevant, and the strength of the competing claims that such relevance makes. In this context there is a need to acknowledge that the perspectives of individual decision makers are being relied upon; mid-range theories cannot guarantee an ethically correct outcome. They are not – and cannot be[5] – considered as fully determinative of the correct ethical course of action. Mid-range theory can only take us so far. In the final analysis, some form of personal or individual moral disposition is required if a specific judgement is to be formulated and made.[6] Furthermore, such dispositions underlie the way in which each principle is itself understood and 'applied'. Such thinking can be understood in terms of the (collective) moral structure as well as that of (individual) agency. The moral dispositions of individual professionals (imperfectly[7]) reflect the moral structures of the profession they belong to. And the moral structures of a profession (or any other social field) do not determine the outcome of all the moral questions that arise within it.

Whilst this is a far too brief account of why it might be that Beauchamp and Childress (2009) have, in later editions of their book, found reason to offer a chapter on moral character and virtue ethics, it is, I think, enough to show something of the limitations of modern moral philosophy and applied ethics. The issue is remarkably similar to the one Anscombe (1958) diagnosed; modern moral philosophy is in need of an adequate moral psychology and, we might add, an adequate grasp of the social reality of moral agents. Not only does the rationality of contemporary moral philosophy and applied (bio)ethics fail to grasp the way in which morality and ethics are accomplished in everyday life (by everyday people), the same can be said when it comes to professional practice and professionals. Whether explicitly realised or not, it is against this background that the appeal of virtue ethics for social researchers should be understood.

As suggested, virtue ethics has its roots in Ancient Greek thought and, since that time, has been co-opted by various theological discourses, particularly Christian theology, throughout the middle ages and beyond. Whilst the star of virtue ethics waned as philosophical (and scientific) modernity took hold, the middle of the 20th century saw a number of philosophers (such as the aforementioned Anscombe, but also Phillipa Foot and Iris Murdoch) arguing for a renewed recognition of its relevance and significance. Subsequently, virtue ethics has been taken up in a number of ways and, in some instances, developed in directions that go beyond what can be found in Aristotle. For example, in an innovative and fascinating book, Nancy Snow (2009) considers virtue as social intelligence, and does so by building on a range of insights from contemporary psychological research. Whilst Anscombe (1958) felt that, unlike virtue ethics, modern moral philosophy lacked an adequate moral psychology, it is nevertheless the case that the moral psychology embedded in much of contemporary virtue theory marks a significant development in the tradition. In this light, whilst those who lay claim to virtue ethics can be understood as drawing on the implicit authority of a moral philosophy that has contributed to 2,500 years of human history, one should bear in mind that it has undergone significant development, particularly in recent years.[8]

Aristotelian virtue ethics is, one might say, a moral philosophy that centers on agents rather than actions. The universalism of modern moral philosophy is based on the presumption that human beings are all moral agents. As such, we are all equal, and each of us has the same moral significance as any one else.[9] Furthermore, whether or not something is the morally correct course of action cannot be related to whomsoever that agent might be. If killing is wrong, then it is equally wrong for all moral agents, regardless of who happen to be. Such thinking allows for moral or ethical issues to be objectified in 'cases' and thought experiments in which the individual identity of the participants is considered irrelevant. It also allows for the structure of the case to be foregrounded, and for the concerns they represent to be universalised.[10] In contrast, virtue ethics places the question of who we are or, perhaps better, *who we want to be* at the centre of moral philosophy. This makes ethics a matter of moral character, their virtues, or moral dispositions. The question is, therefore, what the right and wrong moral dispositions might be; or how can we distinguish between the virtues and vices of moral character.

There are two distinct facets of Aristotle's discussion that are important to note. The first is his suggestion that virtues are not independent of vices. Rather, they are related to one another. However, a particular virtue is not simply the antonym or opposite of some vice. Instead, a virtue is to be found at the (golden) mean, at a point that lies between two different vices. Thus, classical notions of virtue include such things as courage, generosity, and humility, each of which lies between the respective extremes of recklessness and cowardice, wastefulness and stinginess, and vanity and servility. For the most part, virtues should be understood in this way as representing a balance between two different vices, one of deficiency and another of excess. However, Aristotle also accepts the existence of complex virtues. The primary example of which is phrónēsis, practical wisdom, or prudence. This is the virtue of good judgement and involves correctly balancing the relevant virtues when acting in a particular situation or set of circumstances. In what follows the notion of integrity can be understood as a complex virtue.

The second aspect of Aristotle's accent of virtue ethics we should note is the view that 'the good' is directly informed by a particular, and teleological, conception of human beings, and what he calls *eudaimonia* or human flourishing. This is used by Aristotle to inform the question of who we (should) want to be and how we (should) want to live, something that is predicated on what, given our nature or teleology, is good for us, or our flourishing. Thus, virtue becomes a matter of human flourishing and acting in accordance with the teleology of our nature or being. Of course, it is not only difficult to determine what human flourishing might consist in but also what this might cannot lead us to think that all human beings ought to pursue some sort singular ideal; being surrounded by people the same as ourselves is, certainly, inimical to human flourishing. Thus, Aristotle distinguishes between three differing levels, kinds, or types of eudaimonia. These are the life of pleasure, the life of political activity and the life of contemplation or philosophical reflection.[11]

Of course, Aristotle's moral and political philosophy reflects certain sociopolitical presumptions and the way in which society was organised in Ancient Greece. In order to properly situate virtue ethics in relation to contemporary social life it is necessary to reconceptualise eudaimonia and human flourishing. Modernity is marked by a high degree of social differentiation and change. In this context a notion of human flourishing that is primarily expressed in terms of human biology is distinctly unhelpful. Rather, what is required is a conception of eudaimonia that is tied to particular social endeavours. Thus, we might ask, what is it to flourish as a doctor, a parent or a social scientist in the contemporary era. Whilst there are ongoing efforts to apply virtue ethics to particular moral problems (cf. Austin, 2013), there is a certain degree of circularity to the theory. This can most clearly be seen in the notion of *phronimos*, an individual who possesses the highest degree of phrónēsis or practical wisdom, particularly in the domain of ethics, or right and wrong. In modern terms we might think of them as individuals who have or embody moral expertise, or as moral experts (Khan, 2005). Such individuals are those who can be relied upon to embody practical wisdom and pursue the ethical course of action. However, consider the problem of how to identify the *phronimos*. On the one hand, these are be identified through their actions. However, on the other, those who can offer such identifications must, themselves, embody a high degree of practical wisdom. How else can it be reliably recognised in others? When it comes to highly stratified societies, such as the one we inhabit, such thinking also indicates that being able to understand what counts as human flourishing in a particular context – for a particular activity or practice – requires one to inhabit that particular social context; to be a member and, in all probability, a practicing member, of a particular group or tradition.

Putting such considerations to one side, at least for the moment, we might acknowledge that whilst the literature on virtue ethics has undergone serious development in recent years, perhaps the single most important late 20th century contribution is Alasdair MacIntyre's *After Virtue* (1981). This is particularly true in the context of understanding the ethics of social science research as MacIntyre's (1981) account is not merely a critical and philosophical enterprise but one that also stands as a rebuke to the more deterministic, behavioural and simplistically causal approaches to research ethics. If, as seems to be the case, part of the concerns social scientists have about a model of research ethics inherited from the biomedical sciences is to do with the way scientific enquiries into the natural world and the social world differ, then MacIntyre's (1981) account would seem to be a good place from which to start rethinking our ethical understanding.

One significant point of difference between Aristotelian virtue ethics and MacIntyre's (1981) account is the latter's conception of a tradition. As Lutz (2012, p. 9, FN. 34) points out, in *After Virtue* the notion of tradition can be understood as having a number of distinct senses. Nevertheless, there is an important sense in which a tradition can be considered as historically durable conceptual schemes that inform the ethical judgements that take place at particular times and places. Whilst something like 'the four principles of biomedical ethics' can be understood as a tradition in this sense, it would be a mistake to compare the MacIntyrian perspective with the notion that the four principles are a conceptual framework, a way of discussing ethical problems that pre-exist in some way. Thus Lutz (2012, p. 7) suggests that rather than thinking of MacIntyre's (1981) traditions as paradigms (in the Kuhnian sense) they can be thought of as research programmes (in Lakatos' sense).[12] Traditions are not, therefore, incommensurable with one another in any strict sense. Rather, different conceptual programmes stand in some historically defined relationship with one another. This can be understood in two ways: First, in the normal sense that one might find in the history of ideas, i.e., the notion that there can be genealogical relationships between different theoretical perspectives. More interesting is, however, the second sense: the notion that histories of particular individuals entail them having their own specific histories and mutually informative encounters with traditions.[13] An individual will, therefore, have their own particular ethical understanding, their own ethical perspectives. Whilst such perspectives may, to greater or lesser degrees, be shared with others – as may be the case for individuals with similar histories (such as those who were educated at a particular set of private boarding schools), or for individuals who now occupy the same social space (such as members of the medical profession) – it is, nevertheless, dependant on their own unique moral history or biography. In relation to ethics, then, one might concur with Lutz (2012, p. 9, FN. 34) who calls traditions 'the inherited circumstances of life that constitute one's moral starting point'.

Of course, consistent with the above, while the circumstances we inherit will vary, our differing starting points do not mean that our ethical outlooks are morally incommensurable with each other. We can and do engage with each other on issues of normative significance. However, we should be aware of the potential for the differing sides of our moral conversations to talk past one another. Furthermore, given that, at differing times and places, we may occupy a variety of social locations, it may be that not only do we have differing moral starting points but we also have a number of different moral starting points, depending on the particular role, location or situation we are in. Thus, the moral perspectives of researchers, research participants, and research ethics committee (REC) members can all be considered as inhabiting differing moral standpoints.

For social scientists this is a compelling picture, one that acknowledges the moral complexities of social world – the object of their study. Furthermore, as Higgins (2010) has it, MacIntryre's vision is one that entails various 'worlds of practice' and presents a direct challenge to applied ethics, at least as it is commonly understood. At least in part, to good of practices (traditions) can only be fully realised from within. As such, practitioners occupy a privileged position in debates about the ethics of whatever it is that they do. Whilst it would be wrong to conclude that any professional ethics ought to be turned over to practitioners alone, such thinking does provide a basis for reconsidering the ethical and procedural formalism of a research ethics developed in the context of biomedical research – a natural rather than social science. Taken further, it suggests a more dialogical approach to the ethical governance of social research. Whether implicitly or explicitly, this is something that many of the following contributions advocate.

SUMMARY OF CHAPTERS

The first section, entitled 'Virtue and Integrity in Social Science Research', opens with an essay that reflects and develops the talk given by Professor Sarah Banks in May 2015. In it she argues that the recent focus on integrity needs to be concerned with the integrity of researchers as well as that of research. In making this point she identifies an ethical space within research that, properly understood, can only be addressed by a moral philosophy such as virtue ethics. As a result her contention is that the way integrity is currently conceptualised is too 'thin' to do the work required. Drawing on virtue ethics, Banks develops a 'thicker' account. However, rather than arguing that we should embrace this thicker account of researcher integrity, she shows how the third way, or happy medium, can be found between thick and thin.

Adopting a self-avowedly polemical stance, Richard Kwiatkowski takes issue with the recent turn to integrity and virtue in social scientific research ethics.

He deploys the hermeneutics of suspicion and casts a critical gaze onto the social sciences and current thinking around the ethics of social research. Perhaps, consistent with his polemical stance, the essay seems to pull us in a number of directions, and no clear conclusion of way forward is on offer. However, at the heart of his essay is, one might suggest, a point that is relatively commonplace, at least in the sociology of professions. His claim is that self-interest may be what underlies many of the ethical claims made by established social groups. He suggests that, collectively, the social sciences are a powerful interest group and, like many professions, whilst it may be true to say that they act in the interests of others, it is also possible for them to act in ways that are less than selfless. Such claims are not easy to make or act upon. As Kwiatkowski points out, doing so involves examining ones own position and presumptions. Nevertheless, one cannot do so from outside of those same positions and presumptions. The same can be said for those reading his essay; we all occupy standpoints of our own. Kwiatkowski offers a timely reminder regarding the rhetorical value and power of ethical claims, particularly when it comes to terms such as 'integrity' and 'virtue'.

The following essay 'Just tell me how to get through the REC' does not respond to Banks directly. However, its first author, Nicole Palmer, was present at the event and responded to an invitation to write a chapter for this volume. The account offered by Palmer and her coauthor, Forrester-Jones, draws on Palmer's experience as a research governance officer at the University of Kent. The chapter also reflects the doctoral research she is currently undertaking. The essay sets out a virtue ethics approach to the training and support given to social researchers, particularly with regard to the development of integrity. As such, it directly complements the chapter written by Banks and shows how ideas about research integrity and virtue ethics can be incorporated into training activities that, all too often, can devolve into little more than familiarising researchers with the administrative procedures that govern ethical review at a particular institution.

The final chapter in this section was also commissioned following the May 2015 event. In it Kath Melia considers the idea of professional integrity for social researchers and the way in which virtue ethics can be used to inform and develop such notions. Melia is evidently not referring to 'the social sciences' in general but only those more specifically involved in health and social care. At the same time researchers in these fields are often at more pains than most to evidence their reflexive, caring – indeed virtuous – concerns for their fields of interest, their 'subjects' – both topic and participants. While in some senses Melia attempts to 'help' the social sciences steer towards a form of integrity based upon virtues, one could question the latent assumption that the social sciences do in fact need some 'assistance' in this regard.

David Carpenter, a protagonist in the previous debates held by the Academy Working Group (see Carpenter, 2017), was invited to consider the question of virtue ethics and the ethics of ethical review in more detail – not least because, during previous events, he had voiced support for the idea that virtue ethics had something to offer social research ethics as well as the notion that ethics review was itself a practice in need of ethical analysis. Drawing on the contacts that the Academy Working Group had made during the course of its activities, suitable interlocutors were again invited to provide commentaries. Building on his contribution to the first volume in this series, Carpenter makes extensive use of Macfarlane's (2008) work to taking forward his analysis of the virtues required for social research and reorientate his thinking towards RECs and their members. Having determined that a particular set of virtues is of specific relevance to the ethical review of social research, he provides some interpretation of their meaning in this context.

This first of Carpenters' interlocutors, Helen Brown Coverdale, argues for the value of introducing the ethics of care and feminist perspectives into the debate. Her suggestion is that, whilst the virtues Carpenter identifies involve some degree of care, the relationality of the ethics of care remains an implicit, and thereby neglected, facet of his account. Building on the ethical importance of the relationship between the researcher and the researched, Coverdale suggests that the relationship between researchers and reviewers has a similar sort of significance. Her account, or so she claims, further 'responsibilises' all those involved in the process of social research. One might add that part of this further responsiblisation might entail a degree of mutual engagement. Arguable, part of the problem with ethical review is a lack of dialogue between researchers and reviewers, leading to misunderstanding and confusion. Modulated by an ethics of care, the virtues Carpenter advocates should lead to a greater degree of interaction on matters of research ethics.

In his focus on participatory action research, the second commentator on Carpenter's paper, John Elliott, also highlights the relationship between researchers and reviewers. He suggests that, collectively, we ought to transcend the boundaries of review as a bureaucratic exercise and aim at a more participatory and democratic exercise. Elliott constructs his argument on his experiences of conducting participatory action research where the principles that guide the project are the subject of mutual agreement, and emerge from a process of engagement between researchers and those they hope to research. This provides a model for a process of ethical review that could better serve the need of researchers and, one might add, ethical research.

The final comment on Carpenter's paper is by Morris and Morris. They were invited to comment as a result of their article 'The importance of virtue ethics in the IRB' (Morris & Morris, 2016) in the journal *Research Ethics*. In that paper they are concerned with the review of biomedical research. They assign virtue ethics a role in balancing between the dual imperatives that motivate their work, namely, the protection of subjects and the facilitation of research. However, they question Carpenter's dismissive treatment of the value and role of principles, codes, and regulations. Indeed, their point can be understood as suggesting that the problems Carpenter perceives to exist with principles can be resolved if one properly understands the relevance of the virtues and, in particular, phrónēsis when applying them to particular cases or in particular contexts and situations.

Phrónēsis is the topic of the third and final section of this collection. In her contribution Anna Traianou explores the notion of phrónēsis and how it might contribute to our understanding of the situated judgements that researchers must make during the course of their work. She argues that the term, which might be translated as 'wise judgement', accords with claims about the nature of social research and the fact that it is inimical to prospective ethical evaluation. In her view, both methodological and ethical dimensions of research not only overlap but are also intertwined. While some degree of planning can be undertaken, the actual conduct of research can take on a life of its own. This means that researchers, and not review board members, are those that are best placed to decide how to proceed. Furthermore, Traianou takes issue with the assumption that it is desirable or legitimate to aim for the highest ethical standards in the conduct of research. She argues that the conduct of research is such that there must be a trade-off between ethical and methodological imperatives. Thus, a more pragmatic approach is required. Provocatively, she draws on Machiavellian notions of virtue and argues for an 'ethic of responsibility'. Whilst both Aristotle and Machiavelli conceive of phrónēsis as the skill required to negotiate the contingencies of social life, the latter more clearly grasped the degree to which 'pragmatic' ethical compromises might have to be made in the pursuit of higher order goals. Thus, the ethic of responsibility is one in which researchers are empowered to decide whether or not the ends justify the means, not least because they are the only individuals in a position to do so.

Hammersley's contribution also adopts a critical perspective on the notion of phrónēsis. He questions whether a moral philosophy generated in the social, cultural and political context of Ancient Greece can be considered of any direct or significant relevance to present day activities such as social science research. Whilst such questions are not absent from the philosophical discourse on virtue ethics, Hammersley poses them as a social scientist, where they take on a more pointed meaning. Philosophically speaking, question regarding a moral theory's social, cultural and political influences are largely concerned with identifying a theory's potential biases or blindspots and, subsequently, their elimination. Whilst such thinking may result in a constant philosophical reworking, there is some implication that the end or purpose being pursued is a correct or universal moral theory. However, if philosophical analysis takes this a possibility, it is far from clear that the same can be said of critical theory or sociology. Even as his theoretical perspective gained (and continues to gain) broad, cross-cultural acceptance, Bourdieu (2000) (and most Bourdieuans) refuse or reject any claim to universality. Nevertheless, it seems Hammersley sees little choice but to embrace the notion of phrónēsis and, one assumes, virtue ethics more generally, concluding that we are in need of the term or, at least, something that is very much like it.

The final essay in the collection is my own. Here I explore the notion of phrónēsis and question if the normativity conveyed by the concept is appropriate for guiding social research or, for that matter, the ethics of any contemporary practice. I argue that much of the work virtue ethics is being asked to do in the context of the ethics of social research can be better accomplished by developing a Bourdieuan account of the practice coupled with the notion of synderesis, the moral sensibility associated with habitus.

FINAL REMARKS

The chapters in this volume can be considered as the beginnings of a conversation about the relationship between virtue ethics and social research. There remains a great deal further to be said. In the first instance, this conversation will continue as the notion of integrity becomes developed further in relation to research. However, there is another strand of thought that, in my view at least, has remained untapped and deserves to be brought into this dialogue. This the studies of ethics and morality that have been a particular feature of contemporary research in both anthropology (Fassin, 2012; Zigon, 2008) and sociology (Hitlin & Vaisey, 2010). Particularly in anthropology, a good deal of attention has been paid to virtue ethics as a theoretical basis for understanding the normative dimension of our sociocultural worlds. Some of those working in this area can be thought of as having an Aristotelian orientation (Laidlaw, 2013), whilst others take a more Foucaultian approach (Faubion, 2011). In both cases, there is an attempt to understand ordinary ethics (Lambek, 2010). If, as a matter of the ethics of research, social research ought to be concerned with the moral and ethical perspectives of those they study, then such work would seem to offer a certain degree of illumination.

Furthermore, if social researchers seek to engage research participants on moral and ethical issues, then an understanding of how morality and ethics form part of everyday life would seem to have an additional contribution to make: such work can also contribute to research ethics in a reflexive mode. Part of the problem that social researchers have with research ethics as it currently exists is the way in which the discourse of applied ethics, coupled with the bureaucracies of research ethics governance, has produced something that feels overly external to the modes of social life of both the researcher and the researched (Emmerich, 2013; Sleeboom-Faulkner, Simpson, Burgos-Martinez, & McMurray, 2017). Adopting an anthropological perspective can offer researchers a greater understanding of their own position vis-à-vis the ethics of research and contribute to the reformation of ethical governance. This is, I think, the hope of many of the chapters presented here.

NOTES

1. For more insight into the activities of the Academy Working Group on Research Ethics, see the first volume of this series (Iphofen, 2017), especially Chapter 10 (Dingwall, Iphofen, Lewis, Oates, & Emmerich, 2017).

2. For a fuller exploration of this point, and an argument to the effect that social research ethics are, simply, the professional ethics of social researchers, see Emmerich (2016).

3. Social contract theory, or something like it, can be traced back to Socrates. Arguably, the manner of his death reflects his commitment to such thinking, or something very close to it.

4. Anscombe's moral philosophy is best understood as entailing a commitment to virtue ethics. However, any consideration of her views should not neglect the influence of Catholicism on the moral perspectives that she advanced. Equally, neither should one neglect the unique influence of Wittgenstein (2009). Both of these factors render her distinct from others, including Phillipa Foot and Iris Murdoch, who engaged with virtue ethics at a similar time.

5. As has been clear since the publication of Wittgenstein's *Philosophical Investigations* (2009), no set of rules contains the complete set of rules required for their own application (Taylor, 1993).

6. The problem is akin to that of Buridian's Ass, where a donkey positioned equidistant from two bales of hay of exactly equal size cannot decide which of the two to eat, as consuming either one represent an equally rational course of action. As a result of being unable to make a choice, the donkey starves to death. In the case of research ethics, the difficulty is with curtailing increasingly detailed rational deliberation in accordance with each of the relevant principles and deciding which principle should take priority in some particular case. At some point, one simply has to decide, and pursue one course of action over another. Beauchamp and Childress (2009) introduce

the notion of moral character to normatively explain and guide how, as a matter of practical necessity, this happens.

7. Of course, the idea that the moral dispositions of individual professionals can or should perfectly reflect the moral structures of the profession as a whole is deeply problematic and, as such, far from perfect. It would imply a deterministic picture, one in which moral agency and, therefore, morality per se would no longer be present. However, it is relatively easy to respond to such criticism. One simply has to point out that the (moral) structure of a particular field results from, is maintained by, the (moral) agency of those within it. In any process of social reproduction, particularly ongoing or continual processes, there are a great variety of indeterminate points, gaps into which (moral) changes can occur.

8. Such development has, at least in part, been prompted by virtue ethics being in receipt of relatively acute criticisms, such as the questions posed by the situationist challenge (Doris, 2002; Harman, 1999). For response to this challenge see Annas, Narvaez, and Snow (2016), Kristjánsson (2015) and Miller (2013, 2017).

9. Of course, what the moral significance might be predicated upon is the source of might debate. For some moral philosophers it is the capacity for rationality and the fact that we are ends in ourselves. For others it is personhood, something that can itself be defined in a variety of ways. For others it is the capacity to experience pleasure or pain and, therefore, to be accounted for within consequentialist and utilitarian calculations.

10. Perhaps the clearest example of this is the thought experiments of trolleyology. But one might also consider Rachels' bathtub case, Judith Jarvis Thompson's violinist, and various lifeboat cases.

11. The fact that all three of these lives depend upon the labour of others, and the particular socio-political conditions that Aristotle saw as natural should be seen as a problematic aspect of his virtue ethics. Furthermore, it is not clear that these problems can easily be surmounted.

12. In his discussion of MacIntyre's response to Winch, Blakely (2013) makes a similar point.

13. A similar point is made by Bourdieu (2000, p. 151), who considers social fields to be 'history objectified in the form of structures', whilst the habitus is 'history incarnated in bodies'. Bourdieu offers a social theory that clearly intersects with Aristotelian thinking, but cannot realistically be positioned as his genealogical heir. See, for example, Crossley (2013) on the history of habitus.

REFERENCES

Annas, J., Narvaez, D., & Snow, N. E. (Eds.). (2016). *Developing the virtues: Integrating perspectives*. Oxford; New York, NY: Oxford University Press.

Anscombe, G. E. M. (1958). Modern moral philosophy. *Philosophy*, *33*(124), 1–19.

Austin, M. W. (2013). *Virtues in action: New essays in applied virtue ethics*. Basingstoke, UK: Palgrave.

Beauchamp, T. L., & Childress, J. F. (2009). *Principles of biomedical ethics* (6th ed.). Oxford: Oxford University Press.

Blakely, J. (2013). The forgotten Alasdair MacIntyre: Beyond value neutrality in the social sciences. *Polity, 45*(3), 445–463. Retrieved from https://doi.org/10.1057/pol.2013.13

Bourdieu, P. (2000). *Pascalian meditations*. Cambridge: Polity Press.

Carpenter, D. (2017). The quest for generic ethics principles in social science research. In R. Iphofen (Ed.), *Finding common ground: Consensus in research ethics across the social sciences* (Vol. 1, pp. 3–17). Bingley: Emerald Publishing Limited. Retrieved from http://www.emeraldinsight.com/doi/full/10.1108/S2398-601820170000001001

Clegg, C. (Ed.). (2011). *Towards professional wisdom*. Farnham; Burlington, VT: Routledge.

Collins, H., Evans, R., & Weinel, M. (2017). STS as science or politics? *Social Studies of Science, 47*(4), 580–586. Retrieved from https://doi.org/10.1177/0306312717710131

Crossley, N. (2013). Pierre Bourdieu's habitus. In T. Sparrow & A. Hutchinson (Eds.), *A history of habit: From Aristotle to Bourdieu* (pp. 291–307). UK, Plymouth: Lexington Books.

Dingwall, R., Iphofen, R., Lewis, J., Oates, J., & Emmerich, N. (2017). Towards common principles for social science research ethics: A discussion document for the Academy of Social Sciences. In R. Iphofen (Ed.), *Finding common ground: Consensus in research ethics across the social sciences* (Vol. 1, pp. 111–123). Bingley: Emerald Publishing Limited. Retrieved from http://www.emeraldinsight.com/doi/full/10.1108/S2398-601820170000001010

Doris, J. M. (2002). *Lack of character: Personality and moral behavior*. Cambridge, UK: Cambridge University Press.

Emmerich, N. (2013). Between the accountable and the auditable: Ethics and ethical governance in the social sciences. *Research Ethics, 9*(4), 175–186.

Emmerich, N. (2016). Reframing research ethics: Towards a professional ethics for the social sciences. *Sociological Research Online, 21*(4), 7.

Fassin, D. (Ed.). (2012). *A companion to moral anthropology*. London: Wiley-Blackwell.

Faubion, J. D. (2011). *An anthropology of ethics*. Cambridge: Cambridge University Press.

Harman, G. (1999). Moral philosophy meets social psychology: Virtue ethics and the fundamental attribution error. *Proceedings of the Aristotelian Society, 99*, 315–331.

Higgins, C. (2010). Worlds of practice: MacIntyre's challenge to applied ethics. *Journal of Philosophy of Education, 44*(2–3), 237–273. Retrieved from https://doi.org/10.1111/j.1467-9752.2010.00755.x.

Hitlin, S., & Vaisey, S. (Eds.). (2010). *Handbook of the sociology of morality*. London: Springer.

Iphofen, R. (2017). *Finding common ground – Consensus in research ethics across the social sciences*. Bingley: Emerald Group Publishing.

Khan, C. A. (2005). Aristotle's moral expert: The phronimos. In Rasmussen, L. (Ed). *Ethics expertise* (pp. 39–53). Dordrecht: The Netherlands. Springer.

Kristjánsson, K. (2015). *Aristotelian character education*. New York, NY: Routledge.

Laidlaw, J. (2013). *The subject of virtue: An anthropology of ethics and freedom*. Cambridge: Cambridge University Press.

Lambek, M. (2010). *Ordinary ethics: Anthropology, language, and action*. New York, NY: Fordham University Press.

Lutz, C. S. (2012). *Reading Alasdair MacIntyre's after virtue*. New York, NY: Continuum.

Macfarlane, B. (2008). *Researching with integrity* (1st ed.). London: Routledge.

MacIntyre, A. (1981). *After virtue: A study in moral theory*. London: Duckworth.

Miller, C. B. (2013). *Moral character: An empirical theory*. Oxford: Oxford University Press.

Miller, C. B. (2017). Character and situationism: New directions. *Ethical Theory and Moral Practice, 20*(3), 459–471. Retrieved from https://doi.org/10.1007/s10677-017-9791-4

Morris, M. C., & Morris, J. Z. (2016). The importance of virtue ethics in the IRB. *Research Ethics, 12*(4), 201–216.

Schön, D. A. (1984). *The reflective practitioner: How professionals think in action*. New York, NY: Basic Books.

Schön, D. A. (1990). *Educating the reflective practitioner: Toward a new design for teaching and learning*. San Francisco, CA: Jossey Bass.

Schrag, Z. M. (2010). *Ethical imperialism: Institutional review boards and the social sciences, 1965–2009*. Baltimore, MD: The Johns Hopkins University Press.

Sleeboom-Faulkner, M., Simpson, B., Burgos-Martinez, E., & McMurray, J. (2017). The formalisation of social-science research ethics: How did we get there? *Journal of Ethnographic Theory*, *7*(1), 71–79.

Snow, N. E. (2009). *Virtue as social intelligence: An empirically grounded theory*. New York, NY: Taylor & Francis. Retrieved from http://books.google.co.uk/books?hl=en&lr=&id=hvtO tUCnhR4C&oi=fnd&pg=PR3&dq=habitual+virtuous+actions+snow&ots=EvjDrD WCrl&sig=UEvJozEMlbIEjQ5veFiCk2FjfsI

Stark, L. (2011). *Behind closed doors: IRBs and the making of ethical research*. Chicago, IL: University of Chicago Press.

Taylor, C. (1993). To follow a rule. In C. Calhoun, E. LiPuma, & M. Postone (Eds.), *Bourdieu: Critical perspectives* (pp. 45–60). Cambridge: Polity Press.

van den Hoonaard, W. C. (2011). *The seduction of ethics: Transforming the social sciences*. Toronto: University of Toronto Press.

Wittgenstein, L. (2009). *Philosophical investigations* (4th ed.). Sussex: Wiley-Blackwell.

Zigon, J. (2008). *Morality: An anthropological perspective*. Oxford: Berg.

SECTION 1

VIRTUE AND INTEGRITY IN SOCIAL SCIENCE RESEARCH

CHAPTER 1

CULTIVATING RESEARCHER INTEGRITY: VIRTUE-BASED APPROACHES TO RESEARCH ETHICS

Sarah Banks

ABSTRACT

This chapter presents a virtue-based approach to research ethics which both complements and challenges dominant principle- and rule-based ethical codes and governance frameworks. Virtues are qualities of character that contribute to human and ecological flourishing, focussing on the dispositions and motivations of moral agents (in this case, researchers) as opposed to simply their actions. The chapter argues for the usefulness of 'researcher integrity', in the context of increasing interest internationally in 'research integrity' frameworks for regulating research practice. 'Researcher integrity' is analysed, including weak and strong versions of the concept (conduct according to current standards, versus reflexive commitment to ideals of what research should be at its best). Researcher integrity in its stronger sense is depicted as an overarching complex virtue, holding together and balancing other virtues such as courage, care, trustworthiness, respectfulness and practical wisdom. Consideration is given to educating researchers

Virtue Ethics in the Conduct and Governance of Social Science Research
Advances in Research Ethics and Integrity, Volume 3, 21–44
ISSN: 2398-6018/doi:10.1108/S2398-601820180000003002

and university students as virtuous researchers, rather than simply ensuring that rules are followed and risks minimised. Several approaches are outlined, including Socratic dialogue, to develop attentiveness and respectfulness and participatory theatre to rehearse different responses to ethical challenges in research. Some limitations of virtue ethics are noted, including dangers of reinforcing a culture of blaming researchers for institutional failings, and its potential to be co-opted by those who wish to indoctrinate rather than cultivate virtues. Nevertheless, it is an important counter-weight to current trends that see research ethics as entailing learning sets of rules and how to implement them (to satisfy institutional research governance requirements), rather than processes of critical and responsible reflection.

Keywords: Research ethics; research integrity; researcher integrity, virtue ethics; Socratic dialogue; participatory theatre

INTRODUCTION

In recent years there has been an increasing concern with ethics in the conduct of social research, resulting in a growth of ethical codes, guidance and policies for good conduct and governance. Furthermore, the discourse of research ethics has developed in such a way that the notion of 'research integrity' has emerged to offer a broader framework for understanding and governing the practice of research. Under this heading we now find principles, policies and procedures covering issues of plagiarism, the fabrication and falsification of data as well as protection of research participants from harm and efforts to ensure that their rights to privacy and informed consent are respected. Most policy and practice guidance takes the form of prescriptions for action and adopts a regulatory approach to ensuring good conduct through requiring researchers to submit applications for review by research ethics committees (RECs). In such applications researchers are expected to evidence their knowledge of, and an intention to follow, what are essentially principle- or rule-based codes of ethical research.

This chapter will discuss the concept of researcher integrity in the context of this rapidly growing concern with research integrity. I will explore the notion of researcher integrity as a complex quality of character or 'virtue', which has a focus on the motivations and commitments of the researcher as a *practitioner* and a member of a research community. This contrasts with the common focus of research integrity, which usually considers the integrity of the research *practice* – although clearly the integrity of the researcher and the research organisation influences the conduct of research. I will discuss the nature of virtue ethics and what it might contribute to the field of research ethics, before exploring what is meant by researcher integrity, including weak and strong versions of the concept (conducted according to extant standards versus reflexive commitment to ideals of what research should be at its best), and how character-based approaches to ethics complement and extend regulatory approaches focussed on the conduct of research.

In the light of this discussion, I will consider what the virtues of a good researcher might be, and how these can be effectively cultivated. This is an area that has been under-explored to date, although the work of Macfarlane (2009) offers a useful starting point on which to build. I will consider how education of researchers and university students might be configured so as to focus on the development of virtuous researchers, rather than simply ensuring that rules are followed and risks minimised. I will outline several approaches to research ethics education, including the use of Socratic dialogue to engage people in practising the virtues of attentiveness and respectfulness while discussing substantive ethical issues in a group; and the use of participatory theatre to act out and rehearse different responses to ethical challenges in research.

VIRTUE ETHICS

Virtue ethics is a philosophical approach that focusses on the excellent qualities of character or moral dispositions (virtues) of moral agents. Examples of virtues might include trustworthiness, courage or compassion. Often linked in Western philosophy with Aristotle, virtue ethics is experiencing a recent revival in moral philosophy (Adams, 2006; Alfano, 2015; Crisp & Slote, 1997; Foot, 1978; Hursthouse, 1999; Swanton, 2003), and a number of different theoretical perspectives have been developed. It is often contrasted with principle-based ethics (including Kantianism and utilitarianism), which focusses on abstract, general principles of action that pertain to right conduct, and questions of how moral agents ought to act and what they ought to do. In contrast, the key ethical questions in virtue ethics are: 'What kind of person should I be?' or 'how should I live?'

A virtue-based approach to ethics can be regarded either as an alternative, or as a supplement, to principle-based ethics. In this chapter I will take virtue ethics as supplementary to a principle-based approach rather than as an alternative. Virtues can then be regarded as either subsidiary or complementary to principles. If virtues are subsidiary, then one approach is to take the principles and ask 'what virtues can we derive from these principles?' For example, taking the principle of respect for autonomy, we might ask what it might mean for someone to be respectful towards the autonomy of others. This is one useful way of starting to think about how to put the principles into practice. On the other hand, if virtues are regarded as complementary to principles, then this entails extending the concept of ethics from a narrow focus on abstract moral principles implemented by a process of deductive reasoning to include a range of different types of elements, including a person's moral character, as well as the principles that should guide their actions in a particular domain. On this view of ethics, virtues and principles are not in direct competition with each other. Rather, they are fundamentally different types of values that are not commensurable with each other. This kind of pluralistic ethics eschews the search for a foundational ethical theory (similar to Kantianism or utilitarianism) and acknowledges that there are several different types of values that cannot be ranked or weighed against each other on a single scale, nor derived from each other (Nagel, 1979). It is interesting that Beauchamp and Childress (Beauchamp, 2003; Beauchamp & Childress, 2009), who have been very influential in the development and sustaining of a principle-based approach to research ethics, nevertheless reject the assumption that one must defend a single type of moral theory that is solely principle-based, virtue-based, and so forth. They express this view in the fifth edition of their text on biomedical ethics as follows:

> In everyday moral reasoning, we effortlessly blend appeals to principles, rules, rights, virtues, passions, analogies, paradigms, narratives and parables.... To assign priority to one of these moral categories as the key ingredient in the moral life is a dubious project of certain writers in ethics who wish to refashion in their own image what is most central in the moral life. (Beauchamp & Childress, 2001, p. 408)

Virtues are also required to specify, interpret, and implement principles. Indeed, in the fourth edition of their book, Beauchamp and Childress (1994) introduced a whole chapter relating to virtues in professional life and acknowledged the following:

> Principles require judgement, which in turn depends on character, moral discernment, and a person's sense of responsibility and accountability ... Often what counts most in the moral life is not consistent adherence to principles and rules, but reliable character, moral good sense, and emotional responsiveness. (p. 462)

Retitled as 'Moral Character' in the fifth and sixth editions of their book, this chapter acts as a precursor to their account of the principles of biomedical ethics (Beauchamp & Childress, 2001, 2009).

Whether we regard the virtues as primary, or as one among many sources of moral values, there is clearly a scope to explore the nature of virtues and the role they play in the ethical life of researchers. The discussion that follows will be illuminated by insights from virtue ethics, although this does not necessarily entail subscribing to virtue ethics as an ethical theory. Indeed, some philosophers distinguish 'virtue theory' (a theory about the nature of virtues) from 'virtue ethics' (a theory or theoretical approach to ethics that places virtues at the heart of ethical life). Therefore, my aim here is not to develop a virtue ethical theory for research, but to explore how a shift of focus from abstract principles and specific rules for research practice to the virtues of the researcher might help in improving ethical practice.

THE NATURE OF VIRTUES

In the philosophical literature, there is considerable debate about what counts as a virtue, including whether a virtue consists in good motives, good ends/ effects or whether both are required (Battaly, 2015; van Zyl, 2015). Given the concern of this chapter – understanding and improving ethical practice in social research – I will use the term 'virtue' to refer to a moral disposition to feel, think and act in such a way as to promote human and ecological flourishing, entailing both a motivation to act well and, typically, the achievement of good ends. Virtues are often described as excellent traits of character, and entail a reliable disposition to act in certain predictable ways across contexts.

One of the recent challenges to virtue ethics, known as the 'situationist critique', draws on empirical (largely psychological) research to argue that the idea that human beings embody robust, enduring character traits may be little more that a folk concept, better thought of as a moral fiction rather than a reflection of reality (Alfano, 2013; Doris, 2002; Harman, 1999; Merritt, Doris, & Harman, 2010). For example, whether people respond in a caring way to a person in need seems to depend on whether or not they are in a hurry. Furthermore, as Milgram's (1974) experiment infamously demonstrated, the majority of people seem to be prepared to torture others if instructed to do so by an authority figure. However, rather than concluding that the concept of a virtue is untenable, we could equally use this 'evidence' as part of an argument that becoming and being virtuous requires considerable work. The fact that people whom we would expect to be caring or honest may act in cruel or dishonest ways in certain contexts can lead to several conclusions, including that virtues are rare, or that character traits (and hence virtues as excellences of character) are not just qualities of the individual, but rather the interaction between person, social milieu and circumstances (Alfano, 2013; Lapsley & Narvaez, 2004; Miller, 2015; Russell, 2015b). Arguably, the most useful responses to the situationist critique for the purposes of this chapter are those that conclude that in order to become virtuous we need to pay particular, conscious attention to situations where virtue may be hard to achieve. The analogy between virtues and skills may be helpful here

(Annas, 2011; Russell, 2015a). As Russell (2015b, p. 105) comments: '[Virtue] is the sort of achievement that takes time, effort, and focused, directed practice. Virtue is like a skill, but it is like the sorts of skills it takes a lifetime to master'.

RESEARCH INTEGRITY AND RESEARCHER INTEGRITY

I will now move on to consider ethics in the practice of research, with a particular focus on research integrity. In recent years the term 'integrity' has moved from relative obscurity to becoming almost commonplace in codes and guidance for conduct in public and professional life (Banks, 2010). With the emergence of well-publicised cases of politicians overclaiming expenses, systematic child abuse and high-profile scientists falsifying research results, integrity is on the socio-political agenda. In several countries agencies have been specifically set up to promote good conduct in research, and have 'research integrity' in their names (e.g., Offices of Research Integrity in the United States,[1] United Kingdom,[2] Austria[3] and Holland[4]). There is even a European Network of Research Integrity Offices.[5]

Nevertheless, it is worth considering what, exactly, is covered by the term 'research integrity?' I will start by considering 'integrity'. Taken literally, 'integrity' means wholeness. It is about parts fitting together, and the whole being complete or in some way unified, as well as being undamaged or uncorrupted. It can be applied to people, objects, practices or institutions. It can also be applied in different domains: for example, aesthetic, intellectual, scientific or moral, where it can have different meanings.

Indeed, as Parry (2013) points out, the term 'research integrity' is used in many different and confusing ways. Sometimes it is used as an overarching concept that includes all aspects of good research – scientific standards, ethical conduct and good governance. On other occasions it may be used just to refer to one aspect of good research – either scientifically good or ethically good research. Clearly, scientific and ethical integrity are inter-related – for example, research based on falsified data lacks both scientific and ethical integrity. And since 'integrity' is about wholeness, there is an argument that separation of scientific from ethical aspects would in itself be damaging to the integrity of research, or to research in general. Certainly, several of the significant codes or guides current in the United Kingdom that have 'research integrity' in the title, or are produced by an organisation with 'research integrity' in its name, embrace both scientific and ethical integrity (e.g., UK Research Integrity Office [UKRIO], 2009; Universities UK, 2012). However, surprisingly few of these documents give a detailed and substantive description of what is meant by 'integrity'. Instead, we have to discover its meaning by looking at the content of such documents – which includes principles and standards of good scientific and ethical practice.

In these kinds of documents (codes and guidelines), 'research integrity' is primarily focussed on *research practice* – what is actually done and how it is achieved. Obviously, it is researchers who actually do the research, hence attention is paid to their conduct. For research practice to have integrity, we would expect the researchers who conduct it to do so with integrity. Hence, any conception of 'research integrity' ought to include some notion of researcher integrity. Similarly, the actual practice of research is influenced by the ethos, policies and procedures of the organisation or discipline within which it takes place, while, in turn, the integrity of the organisation and/or specific academic or professional discipline is related to the practices that go on within its realm, and the researchers who belong to it. Fig. 1 illustrates this

Fig. 1. Elements of Research Integrity.

relationship between these elements of research integrity (practice, research and organisation), offering examples of what each of the elements might mean in practice, and in relation to scientific and ethical integrity.

RESEARCHER INTEGRITY

In this chapter, I will focus on what it means for a researcher to be regarded as a person of integrity. I will identify a 'thin' conduct-focussed version of researcher integrity and a 'thicker' character-focussed version. It is the latter that would be regarded as a virtue. Starting with the thin version, integrity in a work context is often taken to involve the person (practitioner/worker/ professional) being aware of, and acting consistently with, generally accepted norms and standards of their occupation/area of work. In a research context, this is exemplified by one of the following seven principles listed by UKRIO (2009, p. 7) in their code of practice for research:

> INTEGRITY: *Organizations and researchers* must comply with all legal and ethical requirements relevant to their field of study. They should declare any potential or actual conflicts of interest relating to research and where necessary take steps to resolve them. [emphasis in the original]

This description of integrity is at the extreme end of conduct-focussed integrity. The use of the term 'compliance' is particularly noteworthy; use of the term suggests that there is no room for any critical consideration of ethical requirements, nor any non-codified context-related variation or flexibility. Arguably this is a regulatory and managerialist version of integrity. It makes no reference to the researcher as a critical actor. Indeed, it could be viewed as a co-option or even corruption of the concept and practice of integrity for managerialist ends.

What would a thicker, character-focussed version look like? Cox, La Caze, and Levine (2003, p. 41) talk of integrity as involving a capacity to respond to change and a continual remaking of the self. They suggest that it may be instructive to think of integrity as a virtue in Aristotle's (1954) sense, as a mean between two excesses (or vices). In such a case, it may be best described as standing between qualities associated with inflexibility (such as arrogance or dogmatism) and those associated with superficiality (such as weakness of will or hypocrisy). Cox et al. (2003) talk of people of integrity living their lives in a 'fragile balance' between such traits. This characterisation of integrity emphasises the psychological and practical work that people need to undertake if they are to maintain their integrity. Such ideas are particularly pertinent for the consideration of integrity in professional life. This approach also has resonances with Walker's (2007) characterisation of integrity as 'reliable accountability', requiring a kind of moral competence in resolving conflicts and priorities, readjusting ideals and compromising principles (although Walker does not characterise integrity as a virtue). Walker (2007, p. 113) argues that the point of integrity is 'to maintain – or re-establish – our reliability in matters involving important commitments and goods'. It is based on the assumption that human lives are continually changing and are deeply entangled with others. We are often seeking, therefore a local dependability (rather than global wholeness) and a responsiveness to the moral costs of error and change rather than consistency.

What would researcher integrity look like on the basis of this description of integrity? Researcher integrity, in its thick sense, is about researchers being aware of, and critically committed to, the purpose, values, ethical principles and standards of their discipline and/or broader research field; making sense of them as a whole; and putting them into practice in their research work, including upholding them in challenging circumstances. Stated in this way, researcher integrity is an over-arching, complex virtue. It entails not just upholding and acting upon all the values of the profession, but also working to revise, re-evaluate and hold them, and the profession, together as a whole.

This clearly entails some effort on the part of the research practitioner, not only to understand and commit to the purpose and values of the discipline/ research area, but also to negotiate contradictions and conflicts in theory and practice. This requires other virtues, including practical wisdom (*phronesis*) and moral courage. By practical wisdom I mean a capacity to perceive the features of a situation that have ethical salience, and to make discerning judgements about what the right course of action might be, given the context and particular circumstances at hand (Banks & Gallagher, 2009, pp. 72–95; Bondi, Carr, Clark, & Clegg, 2011). This entails a high degree of criticality and reflexivity on the part of researchers. The notion of criticality entails researchers not taking the values, principles and standards found in codes of ethics or current practice for granted, nor taking features of situations as they first appear. Having a critical stance also entails closely examining and questioning a situation and people's perspectives on it, uncovering hidden assumptions and unspoken implications and placing the situation in a bigger political and social context. Similarly, 'reflexivity' means researchers should endeavor to put themselves in the picture – seeing what roles they are playing *qua* researchers and what are the effects of their positionality in terms of ethnicity, gender, sexuality, age and so on. 'Moral courage' involves being willing and able to act on one's moral judgments when facing situations of risk or danger, being neither cowardly nor over-confident (Banks & Gallagher, 2009, pp. 174–94).

Understood as a complex virtue, or excellence of character, 'researcher integrity' is a relatively demanding phenomenon. Critical reflexivity entails that researchers have sophisticated abilities to reflect on how they themselves perceive and think about the principles and rules of their organisations and disciplines – which requires what some organisational theorists call 'triple loop' learning (Yuthas, Dillard, & Rogers, 2004). It also assumes a high degree of ethical expertise, with researchers able to take responsibility for going beyond extant principles and standards and offering alternative visions of good practice (Dreyfus & Dreyfus, 1986; Dreyfus, Dreyfus, & Benner, 2009).

Taking a critical stance towards the principles and standards in extant codes of conduct/ethics/integrity requires a reference point outside current norms and laws. In their brief discussion of professional integrity as a virtue, Cox et al. (2003, p. 103) talk about practitioners committing themselves to a 'semi-independent ideal of what the profession might be at its best'. In the literature on professional ethics, this is sometimes referred to as a 'service ideal' or 'regulative ideal' (Banks, 2004, pp. 53–58; Oakley & Cocking, 2001, pp. 25–31). As an ideal, it can be regarded as providing a vision to work for. It is 'semi-independent' in that while it may be defined and given meaning in the context of current professional practice, it is also aspirational and goes beyond current practice. According to the traditional view of professions, all professions have a service ideal, which encapsulates their roles in contributing to human flourishing. Service ideals are very general and abstract, such as the promotion of health for the profession of medicine, justice for law, and social welfare for social work (Banks & Gallagher, 2009, pp. 20–27). While 'research' is not a unified and distinct profession in the same way as medicine, law or social work, it can take this form within particular disciplines or disciplinary areas. In the AcSS discussion document *Towards Common Principles for Social Science Research Ethics* (Academy of Social Sciences Working Group, 2014, reprinted in Iphofen, 2017, p. 4 of the original document), the elaboration of the first principle (regarding a free social science being fundamental to the United Kingdom as a democratic society) makes reference to 'the core mission of all social science disciplines to better inform public debate and public policy actions'.

The idea of a 'semi-independent ideal of research at its best' might also be linked with another aspect of integrity in professional life – namely, its relationship to practitioners' personal lives, their commitments and their integrity as whole people across all the areas of their lives. This raises many complex issues and debates that cannot be covered here. However, it is worth noting that, in his book on researching with integrity, Macfarlane (2009, p. 45) adopts the idea of integrity as 'the integration of a person's true self and linking their values and identity as a person with their practice as a researcher'. For Macfarlane, it seems that integrity is not a virtue per se (it does not feature in his list of virtues for research), but rather an over-arching concept that frames the discussion in his book and perhaps covers the ways researchers hold together and make sense of the virtues of the good researcher and integrate these into their characters. This is not dissimilar to Aristotle's account of integrity – as an over-arching virtue holding together the other virtues as a whole.

VERSIONS OF RESEARCHER INTEGRITY

Understood as an excellence of character, the virtue-based account of 'researcher integrity' is quite demanding of researchers. It may therefore be useful also to outline a version of researcher integrity as an ordinary quality of character (rather than an excellence). In my view this can be positioned between the 'thin' conduct-focussed version of researcher integrity that is assumed in some of the codes of practice mentioned earlier (e.g., UKRIO, 2009, p. 7), and the notion of integrity as an 'excellence of character' that I have outlined. These are depicted in Table 1 as three possible versions of researcher integrity.

Insofar as RECs or institutional review boards pay any attention to researcher integrity (they usually focus on the integrity of the research practice, as this is the main 'evidence' available to them), then it would tend to be researcher integrity as good or professional conduct (column 1). RECs are concerned that researchers follow the minimum standards that are laid down in relevant codes of practice or are currently accepted practices in research institutions or disciplines. Paradoxically, it is only after there is a complaint or allegation of misconduct (e.g., breach of privacy and use of questionable data) that the investigating agency (such as the employer or professional body) may take account of the ordinary good character of the researcher (column 2). Questions may be asked, such as: Was this an isolated incident of breach of privacy, or is the researcher routinely cavalier in storing data and using names; do their colleagues regard them as generally reliable according to ordinary conceptions of trustworthiness? Finally, researcher integrity as a complex virtue or excellence of character (column 3) tends to be the concern of educators, research supervisors and researchers themselves, and is a quality to be worked on and cultivated, entailing what I have called elsewhere 'ethics work' (Banks, 2016).

Table 1.   Versions of Researcher Integrity.

	Researcher Integrity as Good Conduct	Researcher Integrity as an Ordinary Quality of Character	Researcher Integrity as a Complex Virtue
A researcher exhibits	Professional conduct	Ordinary good character	Excellence of character
by showing	Conformity/compliance	Ordinary commitment	Critical and reflexive commitment
to	Current standards	The mission, values, principles, standards of codes of ethics, etc.	A semi-independent ideal of research at its best
and	A capacity to take action in accordance with standards	A capacity to interpret and act on principles, etc.	A capacity to reason and act in ways that contribute to the flourishing of self- and ecosystem

THE VIRTUES OF A RESEARCHER

The next step for anyone writing about virtue ethics in a professional context is generally to offer a list of relevant virtues and then elaborate upon what they mean in practice. Macfarlane (2009, p. 42) does this, selecting and setting out the relevance of courage, respectfulness, resoluteness, sincerity, humility and reflexivity for social researchers. There are many other virtues that could be identified as relevant and useful for researchers. For example van den Hoonard (2013, p. 27) has compiled a list of 23 virtues that he has inferred directly or indirectly from the text of Canada's Tri-Council policy statement on ethical conduct (Canadian Institutes of Health Research et al. 2010). Top of the list is 'respect', followed by a cluster called 'openness, transparency, honesty', then 'sensitivity', 'trustworthiness', 'responsibility', 'justice' and so on. Interestingly, only one of the top six identified by van den Hoonard ('respect') features in Macfarlane's (2009) list. Furthermore, in neither list is there any mention of virtues such as benevolence, care or compassion – which, arguably, are particularly pertinent in social scientific research, and above all in qualitative research where the relationships between researchers and participants may be sensitive and often generate and draw on emotions. Similarly, in much participatory research (where the people who are usually regarded as subjects of research often play a role as co-researchers), feminist research and other forms of committed action research, care has been identified as a key virtue. Here, care ethics and other situated approaches to ethics are also relevant, as well as virtue ethics (Banks, Armstrong et al., 2013).

Any list of virtues is selective, and many virtue concepts overlap with each other. The fact that different authors select different virtues – most of which would equally apply to ordinary people living their everyday lives, and certainly to many other occupations in addition to research – suggests that simply producing and studying lists of virtues may not be particularly useful in helping us to identify what counts as a good researcher (as opposed to a good nurse or a good human being). Unless they are carefully elaborated upon and contextualised in practice, lists of virtues can be criticised in the same way as lists of principles – as being abstract and unhelpful in guiding practitioners. However, Macfarlane (2009) does elaborate on each of his chosen virtues in depth, and contextualises his discussions in relation to many practice examples.

In my work with Gallagher on virtues for health and social care practitioners (Banks & Gallagher, 2009), we identified seven virtues and discussed each one in detail. Many of these are equally relevant to good research, and I will briefly list them here, adapted to the research context. This gives a feel for what such a list of virtues might look like, may serve as a starting point for discussion of how useful such an exercise might be and what might be included and excluded.

List 1: Some Virtues for Researchers (Adapted from Banks & Gallagher, 2009)

Researcher integrity. In Aristotelian ethics, integrity was not regarded as a virtue per se, but as something that held all the virtues together as a whole. In the context of research, it means the overarching capacity or disposition to hold true to the values of the research discipline or field and to balance other virtues as necessary. It might be regarded as a kind of moral competence or capacity that researchers use to make sense of their ideals and actions as a whole and act accordingly.

Practical wisdom ('phronesis'). This is the excellence by which researchers deliberate well about what to do in their research practice. A person of practical wisdom has a capacity to engage in practical reasoning, which includes the ability to perceive and appreciate ethically salient features of situations; the exercise of ethical imagination; and reflective and deliberative capabilities (to make judgements and act). This process of reasoning is used to make the appropriate practical choices that constitute good research.

Courage. This is, according to Aristotle (1954, p. 1115a6), 'a mean with regard to feelings of fear and confidence'. By this he means that a courageous person, when facing situations of risk and danger, is neither cowardly and lacking in confidence, nor foolhardy and over-confident. We need to know what is the right thing to fear and how much to fear. Courage is a complex virtue – with distinctions often being made between moral, physical and psychological courage, for example. Moral courage may be required as a researcher to face dangerous and risky situations or to communicate unwelcome research findings to research commissioners or funders.

Respectfulness. Respectfulness towards someone or something entails acknowledging the value of the person or thing, preserving and/or not destroying it and engaging with what is valued. Respectful researchers make use of the self in developing relationships and getting to know and understand the perspective of those people with whom they work, respecting their dignity, privacy and choices as far as possible.

Care. This is about how one person relates to others, related to the goal of enhancing the existence of others. A caring person in a research context is one who has a motive of attentiveness towards particular others for whom the researcher enters into relationships of responsibility.

Trustworthiness. This is about not letting others down. A trustworthy researcher is someone who behaves as relied upon; is aware and accepts that they are liable to be held responsible for this behaviour; and is able to give a plausible performance as a reliable and responsible person.

Justice. This is associated with the fair allocation of benefits and burdens and relies upon a capacity to make good judgements in weighing up how people should be treated. A just researcher is someone who has a disposition to act fairly in relation to individuals to whom she or he owes a particular obligation and to act in a way that promotes and reflects just social arrangements.

In a brief chapter 'Learning About the Virtues', Macfarlane (2009, pp. 156–158) considers approaches to teaching postgraduate research students about research ethics. He criticises current education and training as focussing on discourses of compliance, extreme examples of wrongdoing and theoretical approaches drawn from principle-based ethics. He argues for more 'fine-grained' scenarios, including students' own stories and use of narratives, but does not develop these ideas in any detail. I will consider what might be involved in cultivating researchers of integrity and illustrate with examples from university-based education.

CULTIVATING RESEARCHERS OF INTEGRITY

I have described researcher integrity in its strong sense as a complex and overarching virtue. In the context of research, it might be regarded as the reliable disposition of researchers to hold true to the values of the research discipline or field and to balance the specific virtues relevant to research, enabling them to make sense of and critically re-evaluate their ideals and actions as a whole and act accordingly. We might expect a researcher of integrity to have at least the following characteristics:

- *A situated understanding* of the ideals and values of good research and the nature of the virtues relevant to the role of researcher. For example, what is meant by respectfulness, courage, honesty, trustworthiness, justice and care in a research context, and how do they relate to each other?
- *A critical and emotional commitment* to these ideals, values and virtues – sincerely and wholeheartedly believing in the value of respectfulness, honesty, etc., and being motivated to cultivate and enact these virtues.
- *A developed capacity to do 'ethics work'* (Banks, 2016), which entails recognising situations where virtues are relevant; seeing the ethical issues at stake from multiple perspectives; managing and engendering emotions; working on ethical identity (e.g., becoming and being a respectful/honest person); working on relationships with research participants and other stakeholders; undertaking practical reasoning, including working out how to act; taking action; and questioning critically the currently accepted values and standards of research.

If this is what it means to be regarded as a researcher of integrity, how are these qualities cultivated? There are many approaches to virtue cultivation in life in general (see Snow, 2015) and in the context of informal and formal education (e.g., Carr, 1991; Carr & Harrison, 2015; Jubilee Centre for Character and Virtues, 2013). I will briefly offer a few specific examples of approaches in supervision and teaching in universities, with slightly more detailed discussions about neo-Socratic dialogue and forum theatre.

Supervision and critical dialogue with peers in a research team: An important part of educating for the virtues is having role models – teachers in both academic institutions and practice settings. According to Statman (1997, p. 13):

> Becoming a good person is not a matter of learning or 'applying' principles, but of imitating some models. We learn to be virtuous in the same way we learn to dance, to cook, and to play football – by watching people who are competent in these areas and trying to do the same.

This gives an important mentoring role to teachers, research supervisors and research leaders. For research students and inexperienced researchers, the role of a supervisor is crucial in encouraging critical reflection. Even experienced researchers can benefit from dialogue with their peers and exposure to questioning and new ideas. Such people can fulfil the role of moral exemplars or role models, which is often regarded as crucial in developing virtues, although not without its pitfalls (Lockwood, 2009). Above all, it is through being challenged and/or exposed to new perspectives that researchers develop their understanding of themselves and their research practices. It also contributes to the critical reflexivity that is a mark of quality social research. Writing a research journal or diary and then sharing with supervisors or tutors is a particularly effective way of developing such reflexivity. In collaborative and participatory research, this sharing of a range of perspectives from peer/co-researchers is built into the process and is both challenging and productive (Banks, Armstrong et al., 2013).

Working with longer, real life cases: Typical textbook cases tend to be relatively short, abstracted from context and often constructed for teaching purposes to exemplify a dilemma or difficult choice (Banks & Nyboe, 2003; Chambers, 1997). This tends to encourage discussion and interpretation in terms of principles and rational decision-making. Real-life, longer cases can also be used, which give more information about political, social and geographical context about the emotions, motivations and dispositions of the teller and other key actors, and tell a story that might not culminate in an action-focussed question: 'what would you do?' or 'did the researcher do the right thing?' This encourages consideration of the character of the people involved, and their interactions with the situations in which they find themselves (see Banks & Armstrong, 2012, for a collection of longer cases).

Moral case deliberation, dilemmas cafés: These methods involve people working in groups exploring a case presented by a member of the group (Centre for Social Justice and Community Action, 2015; Molewijk et al., 2008; Weidema, Molewijk, Widdershoven, & Abma, 2012). Here the cases are not only 'real life', but the protagonist is present and can benefit from gaining multiple perspectives on the situation described. The participants have a degree of distance from the case and may approach it from the perspective of 'impartial spectator'. However, since the teller of the case is present, more details of context can be given, the character and emotions of the teller are drawn out and consideration given to the response of this person in this context.

Neo-Socratic dialogue: This approach was developed in Germany by philosopher Leonard Nelson and later modified and developed by several of his students (Nelson, 1940; Saran & Neisser, 2004). It involves taking an abstract philosophical question (e.g., 'What is integrity/honesty/respectfulness?' or 'What can we know together?') and starting by asking participants to give specific examples from their own experience relevant to the question (Banks, 2013; Saran & Neisser, 2004; Van Hooft, 1999, 2003). One example is chosen for deeper analysis, with the aim of the group working together slowly and deliberately to answer the question in relation to this example, before moving to the more abstract level. A facilitator guides the process, which encourages members not only to engage collaboratively in analysis and logical philosophical argument, but also requires a great deal of attentiveness to each other, respectfulness to alternative views and careful listening. Group dynamics are very important, and the process involves engaging with emotions as well as cognitions. As with moral case deliberation and dilemmas cafés, the presence of an example-giver (teller) stimulates the empathy of participants. In one version of Socratic dialogue, participants are asked by the facilitator to put themselves in the shoes of the example-giver. After the example-giver has fully elaborated the example, and the facilitator has noted key points on a flipchart (usually dictated by the example-giver), the example starts to belong to the group, taking on a life of its own, partially abstracted from the ownership of the example-giver. This enables the example-giver to distance herself from the example and look at it with fresh eyes as she hears the analyses and evaluations of others about what was at stake.

Forum theatre: This is based on the work of the Brazilian theatre director, Augusto Boal, and is part of his theatre system known as 'Theatre of the Oppressed' (Boal, 1985, 1992). Forum theatre involves a group of people working together to produce a performance of a scenario showing "an instance of 'oppression'": a difficulty or obstruction – a problematic or unjust use of power. The scenario may be generated by participants in the workshop or performed to participants by others. The aim of the work is creatively to resolve, or review and re-frame, issues participants may not have previously analysed or expressed clearly. The structure needs to focus on a protagonist, a baffled but determined hero, 'the oppressed'. The scene is played once through. It is then re-enacted. Members of the 'audience', the group, become 'spect-actors', spectators and actors combined. They call out 'stop' to signal that they would like to try another strategy. Another person then, classically, replaces the hero, or 'oppressed', to explore a new approach. Boal coined the term 'spect-actor' to refer to the fact that members of the audience (so often condemned to passivity in the theatre) can also become actors both in the theatre and back in the 'real' world. They play a role in the performance as a 'rehearsal for change' and also reflect on and learn from the experience. As Babbage (2004, p. 45) comments: 'Empathic identification and distant observation exist alongside each other'.

Forum theatre can be used to work on ethically challenging situations encountered in the research process. I have used this to work with people who are engaged in community-based participatory research, involving university and community researchers working together to undertake a research project (Banks, Rifkin, Davidson, Holmes, & Moore, 2014). Here ethical issues relating to the use and sharing of power, ownership of data and findings, communication, inclusivity and reciprocity can be particularly challenging (Banks, Armstrong et al., 2013) and participatory theatre can be a very useful way of exploring these and developing participants' skills, confidence and, arguably, virtues to tackle ethical difficulties. If an ethically challenging event and the associated relationships are acted out, with participants representing different characters and groupings, then the possibility for empathy and wider understanding is enlarged. Participants can explore the emotions triggered by the situations. The ethical aspects of a situation can be understood as embedded in the broader context while embodied by the people in the scenario. This helps develop ethical awareness, enabling people to reframe and re-enact situations and experience how they might achieve different outcomes and work for social change. People can also see and feel successes, injustices, oppressions and indignities that they may not have noticed or fully appreciated before. In short, working with participatory theatre to explore ethical issues in research offers many possibilities, including the following:

- Developing attentiveness, noticing a key point when something could be done differently; focussing in on a particular feature of the situation.
- Being an external critic – looking at the whole picture from a distance.

- Empathising with the protagonist, feeling what it is like to be that person and getting the chance to take the place of the protagonist.
- Reframing, repositioning characters and configuring the scene differently.
- Repetition, rehearsal, how to challenge the oppressor; often being courageous, motivated by witnessing injustice.
- Dialogue, sharing perspectives regarding what is going on, how to interpret, possibilities for action.

CONCLUDING COMMENTS

This chapter has suggested that there is value in the field of research ethics in shifting focus from the integrity of the research practice to paying at least equal attention to the integrity of the researcher. This is an important counter-weight to current trends that are turning research ethics into a matter of learning a set of rules and how to implement them (so as to satisfy institutional research governance requirements), rather than a process of critical and responsible reflection.

Nevertheless, there are many critiques of virtue-based approaches to ethics and important reasons to be wary about an excessive focus on the character of the person (in this case the researcher) as moral agent. I have already considered the situationist critique (questioning the notion of virtues as enduring character traits), which can be answered partly by adopting a more social constructionist account of the nature of virtues. Another difficulty with a virtue-based approach in a research context is that it can reinforce a culture of responsibilisation, where individual researchers are blamed for bad practice when it is often the case that institutional conditions are significant contributing factors. This suggests that we should exercise some caution in concluding that the promotion of virtues in individual researchers is the solution to bad practice in research; we should not lose sight of institutional constraints and structural contexts that shape the conduct of research and the formation of researchers. There is also a question about how the notion of moral character, and educating for character, can be co-opted and used as a way of moulding people into a desirable form. The idea of character building raises the following question: In whose interests and according to which role model? We need to take care that we are cultivating rather than indoctrinating virtues. That is partly why none of the approaches discussed in the previous section is directly aimed at developing specific character traits per se. Nevertheless, I believe that they offer a relevant mixture of opportunities for exercising and developing practical wisdom and rehearsing the right emotions and responses according to context.

In spite of these limitations, a virtue-based approach is a good corrective to the tendency to adopt a rule-based approach to research ethics. It conceives of researchers as more than simply rule-following automata. Rather they are people who respect confidentiality because they are the kind of people who are trustworthy and respectful in all aspects of life, not just because their employer, disciplinary or professional body has laid down a rule to this effect. Yet, not everyone is virtuous, and it is not as easy to change or develop people's characters as it is for people to be required to follow a rule. Rules are action-oriented and take account of the fact that people in the role of researcher should behave in certain kinds of ways, even if they do this out of duty, rather than because they have a considered commitment to act in such ways. Specific rules are needed precisely because people are not always virtuous and because they may not always have the capacity (or be trusted) to make good judgements. However, the growth of more and more rules should not lure us away from the need to develop researchers of integrity. That is why consideration of virtue ethics is important, because it emphasises the moral education and development of the researcher as opposed to simply training in research methodology, methods, skills and 'ethics compliance'.

ACKNOWLEDGEMENTS

This chapter is based on papers given at the Academy of Social Sciences and British Sociological Association event, 'Virtue Ethics in the Practice and Review of Social Science Research', London, May 2015 and the Jubilee Centre for Character and Virtues Conference 'Cultivating Virtues: Interdisciplinary Approaches', Oxford, January 2016. I am grateful to discussants and participants at both events for helpful comments and to Nathan Emmerich for editorial suggestions. The chapter also draws in parts on adaptations of my previously published work on professional integrity, particularly Banks (2010, 2012) and Banks and Gallagher (2009).

NOTES

1. The Office of Research Integrity, https://ori.hhs.gov/.
2. UK Research Integrity Office, http://ukrio.org/.
3. *Österreichische Agentur für wissenschaftliche Integrität* (Austrian Agency for Research Integrity), http://www.oeawi.at/en/.

4. Landelijk Orgaan Wetenschappelijke Integriteit (National Board for Research Integrity) https://www.knaw.nl/en/topics/ethiek/landelijk-orgaan-wetenschappelijke-integriteit-lowi/overzicht.
5. European Network of Research Integrity Offices, http://www.enrio.eu/home.

REFERENCES

Academy of Social Sciences Working Group. (2014, June). *Towards common principles for social science research ethics: A discussion document for the Academy of Social Sciences, version 2.* London: AcSS. Retrieved from http://acss.org.uk/wp-content/uploads/2014/06/Ethics-Final-Principles_16_06_2014.pdf

Adams, R. (2006). *A theory of virtue: Excellence in being for the good.* Oxford: Oxford University Press.

Alfano, M. (2013). *Character as Moral Fiction.* Cambridge: Cambridge Univesity Press.

Alfano, M. (Ed.). (2015). *Current controversies in virtue theory.* New York, NY; London: Routledge.

Annas, J. (2011). *Intelligent virtue.* Oxford: Oxford University Press.

Aristotle. (1954). *The Nichomachean ethics of Aristotle* (Sir D. Ross, Trans.). London: Oxford University Press.

Babbage, F. (2004). *Augusto Boal.* Abingdon: Routledge.

Banks, S. (2004). *Ethics, accountability and the social professions.* Basingstoke: Palgrave Macmillan.

Banks, S. (2010). Integrity in professional life: Issues of conduct, commitment and capacity. *British Journal of Social Work, 40*(7), 2168–2184.

Banks, S. (2012). *Ethics and values in social work* (4th ed.). Basingstoke: Palgrave Macmillan.

Banks, S. (2013). Socratic dialogue and co-inquiry: Exploring cognitive, affective and embodied ways of knowing. *Ways of Knowing.* Retrieved from https://waysofknowingresearch.wordpress.com/2013/05/19/socratic-dialogue-and-co-inquiry-exploring-cognitive-affective-and-embodied-ways-of-knowing/

Banks, S. (2016). Everyday ethics in professional life: Social work as ethics work. *Ethics and Social Welfare, 10*(1), 35–52.

Banks, S., & Armstrong, A. (Eds.). (2012). *Ethics in community-based participatory research: Case studies, case examples and commentaries.* Bristol: Centre for Social Justice and Community Action and National Coordinating Centre for Public Engagement. Retrieved from https://www.dur.ac.uk/beacon/socialjustice/ethics_consultation/ethicscases/

Banks, S., Armstrong, A., Carter, K., Graham, H., Hayward, P., Henry, A., Holland, T., Holmes, C., Lee, A., McNulty, A., Moore, N., Nayling, N., Stokoe, A. and Strachan, A. (2013). Everyday ethics in community-based participatory research. *Contemporary Social Science, 8*(3), 263–277.

Banks, S., & Gallagher, A. (2009). *Ethics in professional life: Virtues for health and social care.* Basingstoke: Palgrave Macmillan.

Banks, S., & Nyboe, N.-E. (2003). Writing and using cases. In S. Banks & K. Nøhr (Eds.), *Teaching practical ethics for the social professions* (pp. 19–39). Copenhagen, Denmark: FESET.

Banks, S., Rifkin, F., Davidson, H., Holmes, C., & Moore, N. (2014). *Performing ethics: Using participatory theatre to explore ethical issues in community-based participatory research.* Durham: Centre for Social Justice and Community Action, Durham University. Retrieved from https://www.dur.ac.uk/beacon/socialjustice/ethics_consultation/

Battaly, H. (2015). A pluralist theory of virtue. In M. Alfano (Ed.), *Current controversies in virtue theory*. New York, NY; Abingdon: Routledge.

Beauchamp, T. (2003). The origins, goals, and core commitments of the Belmont report and principles of biomedical ethics. In J. Walter & E. Klein (Eds.), *The story of bioethics: From seminal works to contemporary explorations* (pp. 17–46). Washington, DC: Georgetown University Press.

Beauchamp, T., & Childress, J. (1994). *Principles of biomedical ethics* (4th ed.). Oxford; New York, NY: Oxford University Press.

Beauchamp, T., & Childress, J. (2001). *Principles of biomedical ethics* (5th ed.). Oxford; New York, NY: Oxford University Press.

Beauchamp, T., & Childress, J. (2009). *Principles of biomedical ethics* (6th ed.). Oxford; New York, NY: Oxford University Press.

Boal, A. (1985). *Theatre of the oppressed* (A. Charles & M.-O. L. McBride, Trans.). New York, NY: Theatre Communications Group.

Boal, A. (1992). *Games for actors and non-actors* (A. Jackson, Trans.). London: Routledge.

Bondi, L., Carr, D., Clark, C., & Clegg, C. (Eds.). (2011). *Towards professional wisdom: Practical deliberation in the people professions*. Farnham: Ashgate.

Carr, D. (1991). *Educating the virtues: An essay on the philosophical psychology of moral development*. London: Routledge.

Carr, D., & Harrison, T. (2015). *Educating character through stories*. Exeter: Imprint Academic.

Centre for Social Justice and Community Action. (2015). *Dilemmas cafés: A guide for facilitators*. Durham: Centre for Social Justice and Community Action, Durham University. Retrieved from https://www.dur.ac.uk/beacon/socialjustice/ethics_consultation/dilemmas/

Chambers, T. (1997). What to expect from an ethics case (and what it expects from you). In H. Nelson (Ed.), *Stories and their limits: Narrative approaches to bioethics* (pp. 171–184). New York, NY; London: Routledge.

Cox, D., La Caze, M., & Levine, M. (2003). *Integrity and the fragile self*. Aldershot: Ashgate.

Crisp, R., & Slote, M. (Eds.). (1997). *Virtue ethics*. Oxford: Oxford University Press.

Doris, J. (2002). *Lack of character: Personality and moral behaviour*. Cambridge: Cambridge University Press.

Dreyfus, H., & Dreyfus, S. (1986). *Mind over machine: The power of human intuition and expertise in the age of the computer*. Oxford: Blackwell.

Dreyfus, H., Dreyfus, S., & Benner, P. (2009). The implications of the phenomenology of expertise for teaching and learning everyday skillful ethical comportement. In P. Benner, C. Tanner, & C. Chesla (Eds.), *Expertise in nursing practice: Caring, clinical judgement and ethics* (2nd ed.) (pp. 309–334). New York, NY: Springer.

Foot, P. (1978). *Virtues and vices*. Oxford: Oxford University Press.

Harman, G. (1999). Moral philosophy meets social psychology: Virtue ethics and the fundamental attribution error. *Proceedings of the Aristotelian Society, 99*, 315–331.

Hursthouse, R. (1999). *On virtue ethics*. Oxford: Oxford University Press.

Iphofen, R. (Ed.). (2017). *Finding common ground: Consensus in research ethics across the social sciences (Advances in research ethics and integrity*, Vol. 1). Bingley: Emerald.

Jubilee Centre for Character and Virtues. (2013). *Framework for character education in schools*. Birmingham: Jubilee Centre for Character and Virtues.

Lapsley, D., & Narvaez, D. (2004). A social-cognitive approach to the moral personality. In D. Lapsley, & D. Narvaez (Eds.), *Moral development: Self and identity*. Mahwah, NJ: Lawrence Erlbaum.

Lockwood, A. (2009). *The case for character education: A developmental approach.* New York, NY: Teacher College Press.

Macfarlane, B. (2009). *Researching with integrity: The ethics of academic inquiry.* New York, NY; London: Routledge.

Merritt, M., Doris, J., & Harman, G. (2010). Character. In J. Doris & Moral Psychology Research Group (Eds.), *The moral psychology handbook* (pp. 355–401). Oxford: Oxford University Press.

Milgram, S. (1974). *Obedience to authority: An experimental view.* New York, NY: Harper and Row.

Miller, C. (2015). Russell on acquiring virtue. In M. Alfano (Ed.), *Current controversies in virtue theory* (pp. 106–117). New York, NY; London: Routledge.

Molewijk, A., Abma, T., Stolper, M., & Widdershoven, G. (2008). Teaching ethics in the clinic. The theory and practice of moral case deliberation. *Journal of Medical Ethics, 34*(2), 120–124.

Nagel, T. (1979). The fragmentation of value. In T. Nagel (Ed.), *Mortal questions* (pp. 128–141). Cambridge: Cambridge University Press.

Nelson, L. (1940). *Socratic Method and Critical Philosophy.* New Haven, USA: Yale University Press.

Oakley, J., & Cocking, D. (2001). *Virtue ethics and professional roles.* Cambridge: Cambridge University Press.

Parry, J. (2013). *Developing standards for research practice: Some issues for consideration.* Discussion 'Stimulus' paper for symposium 3: Standards. London: Academy of Social Sciences. Retrieved from http://acss.org.uk/publication-category/professional-briefings/

Russell, D. (2015a). Aristotle on cultivating virtue. In N. Snow (Ed.), *Cultivating virtue: Perspectives from philosophy, theology, and psychology* (pp. 17–48). Oxford: Oxford University Press.

Russell, D. (2015b). From personality to character to virtue. In M. Alfano (Ed.), *Current controversies in virtue theory* (pp. 92–106). New York, NY; London: Routledge.

Saran, R., & Neisser, B. (Eds.). (2004). *Enquiring minds: Socratic dialogue in education.* Stoke on Trent: Trentham Books.

Snow, N. (Ed.). (2015). *Cultivating virtue: Perspectives from philosophy, theology, and psychology.* Oxford: Oxford University Press.

Statman, D. (1997). Introduction to virtue ethics. In D. Statman (Ed.), *Virtue ethics: A critical reader* (pp. 3–14). Edinburgh: Edinburgh University Press.

Swanton, C. (2003). *Virtue ethics: A pluralistic view.* Oxford: Oxford University Press.

UK Research Integrity Office. (2009). *Code of practice for research: Promoting good practice and preventing misconduct.* London: UKRIO.

Universities UK. (2012). *The concordat to support research integrity.* London: Universities UK. Retrieved from http://www.universitiesuk.ac.uk/highereducation/Pages/Theconcordattosupportresearchintegrity.aspx#.VTKnaU8g_IU

van Hooft, S. (1999). Socratic dialogue as collegial reasoning. *Practical Philosophy, 2*(2), 22–32.

van Hooft, S. (2003). Socratic dialogue: an example. In V. Tschudin (Ed.), *Approaches to Ethics: Nursing Beyond Boundaries* (pp. 115–123). London: Butterworth-Heineman.

van den Hoonard, W. (2013). *Discussion paper: Are we asked to 'other' ourselves? Social scientists and the research ethics review process.* London: Academy of Social Sciences. Retrieved from http://acss.org.uk/publication-category/professional-briefings/

van Zyl, L. (2015). Against radical pluralism. In M. Alfano (Ed.), *Current controversies in virtue theory* (pp. 22–33). New York, NY; Abingdon: Routledge.

Walker, M. (2007). *Moral understandings: A feminist study in ethics* (2nd ed.). Oxford: Oxford University Press.

Weidema, F., Molewijk, A., Widdershoven, G., & Abma, T. (2012). Enacting ethics: Bottom-up involvement in implementing moral case deliberation. *Health Care Analysis, 20*, 1–19.

Yuthas, K., Dillard, J., & Rogers, R. (2004). Beyond agency and structure: Triple-loop learning. *Journal of Business Ethics, 51*, 229–243.

CHAPTER 2

QUESTIONING THE VIRTUE OF VIRTUE ETHICS: SLOWING THE RUSH TO VIRTUE IN RESEARCH ETHICS

Richard Kwiatkowski

ABSTRACT

In this unashamedly polemical piece it is argued that we should not jump into bed with virtue too quickly. It is suggested that the concept of virtue is dangerously ill defined, so it becomes what those in power hegemonically define it to be; that virtue's rise may serve factional political purposes within social science; that system implications are frequently missed, side-lined or minimised so that virtue niavely becomes a purely individual construct; that aspirational codes, which expect a-contextual demonstration of 'virtue' from practitioners, need to be tempered with a dose of reality; and that the achievable 'good enough' is better than the unrealisable and idealised virtuously 'perfect'. It is suggested that the implied centrality of 'virtue' in research is problematic, that being 'critically virtuous' has limits, and that better education will not necessarily lead to morality and integrity in research – any more than it does in the general population. Finally it is argued that ethics committees should focus on (probable) behaviours, rather than rather than imagined motives or vague character traits.

Virtue Ethics in the Conduct and Governance of Social Science Research
Advances in Research Ethics and Integrity, Volume 3, 45–64
ISSN: 2398-6018/doi:10.1108/S2398-601820180000003003

Locating virtue in an individual is dangerous because it allows the system to blame and punish an individual, rather than acknowledge the collective responsibility of the whole system. It is suggested that we need to move from a purist pursuit of virtue to a more realistic and nuanced appreciation of the real world consequences of its adoption. Whilst the present emphasis on sound research ethics and responsibility is a positive development, we need to slow down.

Keywords: Virtue ethics; ethics of social research; professional autonomy

INTRODUCTION

In this unashamedly polemical chapter it is suggested that, whilst it is superficially seductive, the current enthusiasm for virtue as core to *individual* research integrity is problematic. I will argue the following:

1. The concept of virtue is dangerously ill-defined.
2. Virtue's rise may serve factional political purposes.
3. Virtue ethics fails to seriously engage with systems, context and structure; implications have been missed or minimised.
4. Aspirational codes, especially when expecting demonstration of 'virtue,' need to be tempered with reality.
5. Being 'critically virtuous' is unlikely.
6. We cannot assume that education will lead to moral or virtuous researchers.
7. Research ethics cannot be predicated on a phantastical belief in 'mind reading' and our responsibility cannot be to speculate about motives, but to focus on the conduct of research and behaviour of researchers rather than their imagined or impugned motives.

Having made these points, I conclude that, given the current level of interest, the future for research ethics seems positive. Nevertheless, we need to stay vigilant and not rush into the arms of virtue, for having made our bed we will have to lie in it.

1. THE CONCEPT OF VIRTUE IS DANGEROUSLY ILL-DEFINED

The availability of numerous different lists of virtues (Banks, 2015) points to the fact that the notion is relatively murky and, as such, the relationship between the general concept of virtue and specific virtues is unclear. Thoughtful authors from Aristotle onwards have provided lists of virtues (Martin, 2011; Mintz, 1996; Moore & Beadle, 2006). However, a shared characteristic of these lists is that they are often culturally and temporally bound; they are inevitably based on assumptions related to the time and place of their creation and, furthermore, to a varying extent, reflect their creators.

One could, therefore, argue that one of their primary functions is to allow the creators (and possessors) of these particular characteristics to feel good about themselves.

This last is not a trivial point. It often seems as though virtues are a bit like 'motherhood and apple pie' – in that one is naturally in favour, and one feels good as a result, particularly when a presently popular virtue is something one believes one possesses in a reassuring quantity. Linking to Social Identity Theory, this is even more satisfying when a personally important reference group also believes that this characteristic is valuable. So, one might further argue that the more general and vague the concept the better, since possession, of a socially endorsed characteristic, then, if desired, becomes easier.

However, if it is difficult to clearly discern when one encounters a virtue, it cannot be thought of as a reliable and stable construct, or a concept readily amenable to proper measurement (Barrett, 2003; Borsboom, Mellenbergh, & van Heerden, 2004; Michell, 2008).

This is a key problem; in spite of the fuzziness of some virtues, proponents of virtue may be dangerously close to saying that 'virtue is what we say it is.' Immediately, then, we must concern ourselves with notions of (academic) power and hegemony (Kwiatkowski, Duncan, & Shimmin, 2006), those that define those desirable virtues are, in a Gramscian sense, taking power; they are creating a social reality where their views are dominant, and are therefore serving their own factional interests and disempowering others. Who defines virtues in research links to our next section.

2. VIRTUE'S RISE MAY SERVE FACTIONAL POLITICAL PURPOSES

Integrity in research is a growing area of interest; for example, we are approaching the 20th anniversary of the Committee on Publication Ethics. This organisation was set up amidst concerns that the integrity of scientific publication was being compromised by organisations using the publication system for their own (often highly commercial) ends rather than for extending scientific understanding. It was suggested that unfavourable medical trials were not being reported, ghost writing and reanalysis (for instance, partial use of data, hidden exclusion criteria for outliers, etc.) was taking place – this was particularly worrying in the medical field.

False medical findings can have serious life-threatening consequences; based on what they read, physicians may inappropriately adopt sub-optimal (or ineffective) treatment or incorrectly privilege one intervention over another. Evidence-based practice is considered essential in medicine, and researcher integrity is presently assayed (if not entirely assured) through mechanisms such as strict disclosure rules on declarations of interest. Pre-registration of clinical trials and clinical guidelines are increasingly being required and being based on external bodies' recommendations (e.g., in the United Kingdom, the National Institute for Health and Care Excellenceand in the United States, the Food and Drugs Administration) and meta-analysis (the Cochrane network, library and database). However, the situation is rather different in social sciences.

In the social sciences there has also been a significant rise in concern for the ethics of research. Numerous bodies have produced a large number of different codes of ethics and conduct (Bell & Bryman, 2007; Brutus, Molson, & Duniewicz, 2010; Dench, Iphofen, & Huws, 2004; Deontologie & Psychologues, 2012; EFPA, 2005; Greenwald, 2009; Pettifor, 1998; Preuss & Lutz, 1998; RESPECT, 2004; The British Psychological Society, n.d.; UK Research Integrity Office, 2009), some of which differ only slightly in content and intention, others more substantively (Williams & Drogin, 2010).

In the case of *some* research, one can see that some negative impact almost analogous to that potentially suffered in medicine might conceivably take place; for example, if research were falsified such that one type of phonological reading instruction was thought more effective, and it was subsequently adopted and it was actually worse, then the reading age of thousands of children could, as a consequence, be retarded. This is not an entirely impossible scenario; we know that there is concern about fake studies in the sciences (Fanelli, 2009) and psychology has recently been undergoing a 'replication crisis' (Schooler, 2014). However, such concerns relate to other systemic factors that need proper consideration on their own terms.

On the other hand, many social sciences (through their professional bodies) spend a good deal of time decrying the fact that they have less influence than they believe they should have. Could it perhaps be the case that in the social sciences (and, at times, in the humanities) there is actually an unconscious mechanism present behind this apparently mounting concern for research ethics and integrity? We can accept that there may be genuine concern about the 'bad apples'; but – more than that – could this be a part of an ongoing desire to create some sort of equivalence between the social and natural sciences? An unconscious project, perhaps based on envy through which the former can implicitly lay claim to the importance commonly afforded to the latter. It is easy to spot the difference between the respect offered to a sociologist in a media interview contrasted to that offered to an astronomer. The fact that the social sciences desire to be seen as being on par with the physical sciences is well documented (e.g., in psychology; Richards, 2010, p. 7). Is it fanciful to suggest that the interest in ethics amongst social scientists may, in part, be due to a possibly unconscious desire to be *dangerous*, to have the capacity to cause harm? Naturally, an ethical or virtuous person would not cause harm. However, by being extolled and exhorted to be virtuous, all manners of social science researchers may be able to feel just a little more dangerous, and thereby of slightly higher status – 'stop me before I do some potentially harmful research.' Speculative, perhaps, but this certainly links to ideas of potency suggested by evolutionary psychology, which is certainly gaining currency (Fitzgerald & Pleasant, 2010). Of course, the argument that ethnographers are careful not to disrupt the societies they investigate; that sociologist ensure they are aware of the power dynamics between them and the socially disadvantaged they interview; and that geographers are careful to consider the societal impact their recommendations may have on urbanisation, population density and well-being might be put forward to suggest that social scientists are genuinely respectful and careful. That may be the case; however, here we are looking at unconscious motives such as envy and a desire for status power and potency, is it really likely that social scientists do not (perhaps uniquely amongst human animals) crave these attributes? Who, working in a university is unaware of the envy that a management department has for engineering, where research funding is on a scale orders of magnitude greater, and which frequently involves huge capital expenditure? And is it really the case that the upset caused by asking an inappropriate question to a senior manager as part of an organisational psychology investigation has as negative a consequence as administering a drug as part of a trial that leads to permanent disability? Of course, social harm can be caused by social scientists, but it is a very visible, concrete, and physical harm that the natural sciences are capable of that demonstrates their potential potency for good and ill, and which, perhaps, we envy.

So, apart from reflecting and exemplifying a rise in the contemporary 'audit culture' (Strathern, 2000), and its seeming bureaucratic inevitability, could there be some 'secondary gain' in the rise of virtue – namely, a way of indirectly enhancing social and political standing of the social sciences and its researchers. Could it be that this is actually, then, a part of a larger (unconscious or covert) political project, one that seeks to increase the status of some branches of research. In human terms this is entirely understandable, although if we like to pretend that social science is simply the accretion of objective facts, this is an uncomfortable idea. Thus, the idea of virtue may simply be a mechanism through which some factional political interests can be served. Of course, if this is the case, then not only is this an undiscussable truth, but its undiscussabilty is itself undiscussable – as is the way with any sort of organisational defensive routine (Argyris, 1995).

On a separate but related point, the concept of 'professionalisation' may be emerging – most professions lay claim to unique expertise in an area, and are awarded a social warrant to practice on the basis of those claims to special knowledge; they create ethical codes and accreditation mechanisms, and are eventually recognised by state or legislation. A particular social science I am familiar with, namely psychology, is now regulated by the Health and Care Professions Council in its professional arm, and is firmly identified as a science, with interesting links to neuroscience in recent years; in the United Kingdom and Europe, Science, Technology Engineering and Mathematics subjects are favoured through funding mechanisms.

So, perhaps other social sciences (setting aside their 'critical' 'post-structuralist' and 'reflexive' wings for a moment) may be using this very project to seek to enhance their own status – if that is the case, it may not be surprising that 'ethics' and specifically the more slippery 'virtue' should be used in the service of this wider project, but, we should note, this is both paradoxical and ironic.

3. Virtue Ethics Fails to Seriously Engage with Systems, Context and Structure; Implications have been Missed or Minimised

We do not function in an a-contextual world; nearly all researchers are part of a complex organisational system. As a consequence, it is politically unrealistic (and naïve) to seek to locate integrity solely within the individual. It is accepted that the context will have an impact on behaviour (Gonin, Palazzo, & Hoffrage, 2012; Staw, 2016; Willmott & Contu, 2003). Some thoughtful authors, such as Banks (2018), temper their positions by presenting 'weak' and 'strong' versions of individual virtue, acknowledging that the impact locating virtue in the individual has consequences, but, regrettably, in either case they are already in thrall to the demands of the wider system. Furthermore, the notion of virtue usefully serves the wider system to perpetuate the notion that morality is fundamentally a characteristic or function of the individual.

Unfortunately, as soon as integrity becomes a function of the person, and not a wider system, then the system will protect itself at the cost of the individual when placed under stress. In order to protect itself the system may expel individuals, or else find them wanting in some way. Once they are found wanting, it becomes legitimate to persecute them (Center, 2011; Kesselheim, Studdert, & Mello, 2010; IBE, 2015; Rice, 2015). This may sound like anthropomorphising, or the beginnings of a Kafkaesque fantasy, but it is worth exploring and developing this line of thought.

We know all about situationalist critiques of virtue ethics. Further, we know from Milgram's experiments, and the horrible sight of 'ethnic cleansing' of recent years, that ordinary human beings can behave extraordinarily badly. People who have previously lived together peacefully as neighbours will, given certain conditions, literally hack each other to death. Zimbardo (2008), amongst others, has argued that this is not simply because there are 'bad apples' but rather that the power of context is all-important (Tolich, 2014)

We also know that, particularly in the West (Norenzayan, Choi, & Nisbett, 1999), we are much more inclined to assign an individual's behaviour to supposed or inferred innate characteristics as opposed to other factors such as context or role. However, when that same individual is questioned about their actions, they are much more likely to invoke their profession or job, aspects of their role, the social or cultural context, their obligations or duties and expectations or perceived, or actual, social pressure and so forth. This is sometimes known as the 'fundamental attribution error' (Harman, 2000). One way to understand the situationalist critique is, then, to accept the unpalatable reality that as human beings we are perhaps much more malleable and shallow than we like to imagine.

One consequence of this is that under certain conditions, perhaps in the spur of the moment, perhaps in the privacy of a voting booth, perhaps as part of a crowd or perhaps more frighteningly with full conscious knowledge, each of us has the capacity to behave badly, indeed, to do terrible things. Yet, more than that, the context may limit our freedom and do so in such a way that bad behaviour may be all that we understand, or think is available to us (I simplify the argument).

So to illustrate, let us imagine a research fellow taking 'short cuts' with the preparation of samples, filtering them a little more rapidly than recommended, because the deadline is only days away and more readings are needed. Some error perhaps creeps in, but (joy upon joy) a paper is produced and submitted to a prestigious journal just in time. Has the research fellow displayed a lack of virtue? A lack of integrity? Or have they simply been manoeuvred into particular behaviour by the circumstances? Now imagine that they are 'found out'; the shortcuts and consequent inadequate samples are exposed. The paper is withdrawn in disgrace. Who believes that citing a lack of time, a lack of resources, supposed pressure from a supervisor, the demands of the institution for publications, the organisational culture, the expectations of funding body or perceived differences in power (especially in the case of a student who is from an underrepresented or minority group, and where the power distance perception may be very skewed) will save the research fellow from disciplinary action? Of course, they will be blamed. They, alone, have lacked virtue.

Now let us consider a different case; that of a good person 'blowing the whistle' on poor research practice. A laudable action, one might suppose. However once again, who really believes that this would be welcomed by many research organisations? In fact, many organisations will use whistleblowing charters to protect themselves. If you do not follow the (complex) process to the letter, it will be declared illegitimate and your action will, by definition, be organisationally wrong (Basran, 2012; Institute of Business Ethics, 2015). Indeed, the very fact that we have whistleblower charters points to the way in which such individuals can typically be treated by an organisation, to say nothing of their reception in their discipline. This fact vividly conveys the difficulty of adopting an individual virtue approach. It also points to a further layer of potential injustice insofar that some people are relatively safe whatever (it may seem) they do. In universities many individuals already have power, status and tenure. They have good networks, links and political and social capital. The fact that you are reading this, just like the fact that I am writing this, suggests that we are both on the inside. We know many of the rules. We know the game. Perhaps, we even police the game. When the whistle is around our neck, it is unlikely that someone will point at us and cry foul. That would, naturally, be absurd. We are probably safe. However, are we, in fact, collaborators?

If an organisation 'has to' protect itself because someone has 'done something wrong' (in its eyes), the tendency will be to shift the blame (in the Kleinian paranoid-schizoid sense) onto that 'wrong' individual; a projective process takes place; they are bad and the rest of us are good (Buckingham, 2011). Therefore, it becomes perfectly legitimate to question their integrity, to take disciplinary action against them, to expel them, to show forcibly that they are not like us and it is entirely their responsibility, and not at all ours, that this bit of research has gone wrong, that these people may have been harmed, that this data may have been falsified, that these paragraphs may have been plagiarised.

This is one of the fundamental difficulties with wholeheartedly accepting the notion of virtue ethics in research; organisations find it all too easy to locate either goodness or badness within an individual; this is simple Kleinian splitting. It is also striking that a large proportion of organisations surveyed by the Institute of Business Ethics (IBE) tell the IBE that they use their whistleblowing rules to deal with whistleblowers; woe betide you if you do not obey the exact procedures:

> You didn't fill in form DF 1746 before speaking to your supervisor, which you should have sent to compliance and HR, you spoke to HR before you spoke to your line manager's line manager; you went to the ombudsman before going to the internal council which would have convened for the first time in ten years to hear your complaint, so by definition you went to the Press too soon – now we are going to sack you, and if you want a nice payoff you have to sign a confidentiality clause and go quietly.

To locate 'virtue' or 'integrity' within an individual is dangerous; the organisation, for reasons we understand, will in certain circumstances bite back. Once virtue is located within the individual, the organisation can assume that if you were virtuous you would not have behaved like this ('this' being a set of values or assumptions seen as non-endogenous to the organisation). Of course, a contrary position would be that we may suppose that organisations can actually be benign and enlightened; but in reality they are composed of fallible, anxious human beings – organisational defensive routines abound, and locating ultimate responsibility for goodness (and thus badness) in an individual makes that individual vulnerable. We minimise the system implications (read dangers) of locating virtue in the individual at our peril. People suffer as a consequence. In promoting virtue in research ethics, this organisational dimension is often simply missed or else minimised.

Perhaps, at this point, as a reviewer of this chapter, you may object to this somewhat dark worldview. Perhaps, you question whether organisations necessarily behave 'badly' to protect their own interests; perhaps, you believe that bureaucrats can be 'virtuous', and perhaps you think that you would still act well in spite of the pressures upon you. Well, you may be right – but the evidence is against you; in general, many people distrust organisations and even the organisations that they work for; in particular, they do not have trust in their own senior managers (Edelman Trust, 2017); however, few raise ethical concerns, and fewer still 'blow the whistle'. Even if they do, it is more than likely that junior staff will be ignored whilst those in senior positions risk ill treatment, retribution and, potentially, dismissal (Public Concern at Work, 2013). People are generally obedient and do what those in authority want; sometimes cooperatively, sometimes going beyond what is asked for by becoming good organisational citizens. This is not the place to debate the nature of organisations; and the sort of model we have in our mind will impact how we see them (e.g., as machines, cultures, psychic prisons, or forces of oppression – see Morgan, 1986). Nor is the place to further discuss Weber and Steiner's claim that bureaucratic processes are not necessarily a force for good. It is, however, the place to point out that an a-contextual acceptable of virtue outside the organisational context is deeply problematic, and most notions of virtue do rather sidestep it. We, especially, really should not.

4. Aspirational Codes, Especially When Expecting Demonstration of 'Virtue', Need to be Tempered with Reality

Anyone who has actually helped to put together a real code of ethics with real world consequences is soon confronted by the difference between an aspirational code and a code fit for human beings acting in the real world. Even if we are naïve enough to start with it, the code that only angels could possibly fulfil is, in my experience, rapidly discarded in favour of one that protects those in positions of relative powerlessness in the face of profession-als embedded within complex systems that they understand (a little bit) more than their clients. This extra understanding and power is important as it can, of course, be misused. Such codes help ensure that clients are protected.

It is easy to think about integrity in the abstract. However, acting as a professional means wearing several different hats simultaneously (Gardner, 2007). For example, a clinical psychologist working within the UK Health Service has numerous stakeholders. They probably have to manage a complex workload involving those who have already been through primary care, thera-peutic services (e.g., Increasing Access to Psychological Therapies (IAPT)) and perhaps psychiatric referrals. The public, the manager, the Health and Care Professions Council and the British Psychological Society are all inter-ested in the standards of the work. There are patients, their families and friends, referral agencies, fellow mental health professionals, family doctors, clinics and, sometimes, local councillors and members of parliament taking an interest in treatment and outcome.

The best possible outcome, given this patient, this context and these resources, taking into account the social, political, financial and familial environment (etc.), may involve a treatment plan that, all else being equal, is just about 'good enough'. Interestingly, the Health and Care Professions Council is interested in threshold competence; they, rather reasonably and realistically, expect someone to be competent and to understand the limits of their own competence (Health and Care Professions Council, 2014). They would like the individual to be more than this, but this base level is enough to allow safe practice.

Like it or not, juggling finite resources requires professional judgement and often involves compromise; 'the perfect is the enemy of the good'. In discussing the notion of professional ethics it is easy to go rapidly to an idealised form, and for expectations to become unrealistic. Theoretically and academically this level of human perfection is seductive but practically; in the real world, this is dangerous. We can only hope to be good enough – not perfect. Whilst some models of ethics, particularly those which draw on MacIntyre, suggest that virtue taken too far may become a vice (e.g., Beech, MacIntosh, & MacLean, 2010; Fernando & Moore, 2014; Higgins, 2011; Martin, 2011; Ormerod, 2005) and a middle ground is to be preferred, they do not typically reflect how virtue is seen on a day-to-day basis amongst non-philosophers operating in the field of research ethics. In fact it is hard to find a model of integrity, based around virtue that is content with 'good enough' in research integrity – usually the rhetorical focus and expectation (quite understandably) is on the highest possible standards. Given that acting competently seems a reasonable baseline for professionals in a health service, why should we expect a higher standard to be required of those undertaking research? We do not, surely, imagine that social researchers have to be more virtuous than clinicians – unless we believe that clinicians will uncritically accept researcher's findings without question, and therefore have to be protected. Once again we are confronted with the suspicion that something else is going on, something that is beyond the 'espoused' rationale (Argyris, 1995).

5. Being 'Critically Virtuous' is Unlikely

Given that the concept of virtue is unclear and, indeed, a-contextual at times, there is a lot to be concerned about. However, and this chapter is also so clearly prey to this tendency, the prevalent notion that we can be 'objective' or 'critical', and somehow be outside the system within which we operate is problematic.

We would all like to be consistently bright, independent and critical; the reality is that actually most of us are not. We are unavoidably embedded within our societal context, and that context, as we have seen, is powerful. By way of illustration consider the fact that only 50 years ago homosexuality was illegal in the United Kingdom and many parts of the world (in some it still is); large swathes of educated population, the professions, security and police services, medical, legal, administrative and other people 'colluded' with that accepted societal view. As already noted, whilst we may like to think that we would be the individual who stood up against that prevailing view, the reality is that we probably would not have been.

In terms of our self-identity as good, and dare we say 'virtuous', individuals, this may be tricky (Gu & Neesham, 2014; Van Stekelenburg, 2013; Weaver, 2006). However, this is not a council of despair. For us to be fully critical of the idea of virtue would suggest that we are magically outside the system that has spawned the concept. In fact it may be the case that we find the idea of virtue attractive because we have collectively and over generations been brought up in the context of a socially constructed system that has predisposed us to like it (after Shultz, Nelson, & Dunbar, 2012). Even our critique here, which is, frankly, designed in part to provoke, is weak in comparison to an entity capable of operating outside a tradition that has been influenced by these concepts for thousands of years and many generations of homo sapiens.

6. We Cannot Assume that Education Will Lead to Moral or Virtuous Researchers

There can often be an excessive reliance on a belief in the innate goodness and morality of education; personally I firmly believe in the power of education, as the offspring of refugees fleeing an oppressive regime in WW2 who arrived in the United Kingdom with nothing, education meant a way out of poverty. However, the middle classes are often remarkably fond of the importance of education; by teaching somebody, by making them think (Heijltjes, van Gog, Leppink, & Paas, 2015), by engaging them with logic, through Socratic dialogues, through questioning, through confrontation, through the disruption of constructs and through freezing and refreezing concepts (Burnes, 2009), the hope may be that somehow, when people recognise what 'good' is, and as a consequence of this educative process, good will prevail. However, this is not the case in society as a whole, and it is hard to know what differentiates researchers to the extent that they should be differentially impacted by 'education' into becoming 'virtuous'.

It can be argued that in spite of liberal protestations to the contrary, the 'good' that is sought is often, in reality, that people should think like us, believe what we believe, and broadly agree with the thinking that fits within a liberal intellectual tradition (Colby, Ehrlich, Sullivan, Dolle, & Shulman, 2011). But is it not equally reasonable to believe that people can make decisions in all sorts of other ways? However, it is not for us to 'educate' those people to 'think better'. Perhaps, they do not want to be educated. Perhaps, they are more 'educated' than we are. Perhaps, their thinking is not faulty. Perhaps, a visceral reaction to issues is all that is necessary. Perhaps, 'common sense', rather than ideas produced by 'experts' or being challenged by logic is a useful fast heuristic. Perhaps, decisions we consider important can be easily made, using 'type 1 thinking' (Kahneman, 2011). Perhaps, 'their' way of coming to a decision is equally legitimate, despite not being understandable in 'our' terms. Surely (and here is an interesting trap), we need to be tolerant; such that we can accept that informing and educating people will not necessarily lead to goodness. Or compassion. Or generosity. Or virtue. However, Aristotle believed that education could do just that. The evidence is, however, hard to come by, save, perhaps through socialisation, and that is another entirely different debate.

Yet, for the effective functioning of society (a deontological argument perhaps) virtues can (and perhaps should) be actively developed; further, one might argue, the 'good life' is the only one worth living – perhaps, even for educators (Higgins, 2011). That depends on an unpacking of various notions, such as 'good' that are outside the scope of this document. One is reminded of the 'selfish gene' hypothesis. Perhaps, collective survival and reproduction as sometimes suggested by extreme evolutionary theorists is all that is really required of us, and 'good' is just a convenient label for achieving those collective ends? However, that is an argument for another place.

7. Research Ethics cannot be Predicated on a Phantastical Belief in 'Mind Reading' and our Responsibility cannot be to Speculate about Motives, but to Focus on the Conduct of Research and Behaviour of Researchers Rather than their Imagined Motives

As a psychologist I know you cannot climb into someone's head and know what they are thinking. Even advances in fMRI technology only allow us to see activity, not to accurately discern complex thoughts. And few of us have an fMRI machine available when we meet a new person.

I also know that predicting criminality or reoffending (i.e., in a population that has already self-selected, and so should be easier to measure) is notoriously hard. In fact, you cannot easily discover whether an individual is a good or bad person except through observing their behaviour. We find the premise of the film *Minority Report*, that people can be detained because their potential future crimes have been somehow predicted, profoundly disturbing.

In the field of occupational and work psychology, assessment centres – which rely on careful definition and observation of required work-related behaviour – have been found to be better predictors than other methods, such as interviews, which are often based on people's subjective opinions and impressions (Ballantyne et al., 2000; Kwiatkowski, 2003). It is odd, therefore, that at times ethics committees implicitly assess the 'virtue' of researchers. This seems to be done without the technology of an assessment centre; yet assessing someone's moral character must surely be a more complex task than assessing their competence for a predefined job of work. Empirically, it is therefore surprising that in the field of research ethics we seem to be relatively happy to assign (poorly defined!) motives – which are notoriously hard to assess, using a somewhat inadequate measuring tool.

We could argue that in considering research ethics we need to be especially mindful of actions. This involves planned actions as well as possible consequences (which sometimes are unknown). If I am driving a car and accidently run over a pedestrian that action is a bad action, it is bad regardless of my motives; if I am running a research study and I lie to participants or have falsified data or have exposed the identity of a participant, that action, equally, is bad regardless of my motives. For the person with a broken pelvis (car) or the participant who has lost their job (study) as a result the fact that I did not mean to harm them is of little interest. In the field of research ethics we must surely be primarily concerned that bad behaviour does not happen. And because it is the behaviour that causes the harm, behaviour needs to be our focus.

Some ethics committees implicitly or explicitly seem to consider the 'character' of the individual submitting a case for approval, or else defending themselves when something has gone wrong. But one could argue that this is not really part of their role. This is much more part of a disciplinary process. Their role is to guard against the risk of something bad happening.

Thus, to impute motives or assign character or personality characteristics to individual is both technically and administratively wrong. Note that imputation or deduction or assigning of character (read 'virtue') is very different from suggesting (say on a statistical basis) that it is much more likely that someone who has done 10 bad things will do an eleventh bad thing when given the same opportunity. That is different; it is, in fact, making a probabilistic judgement on the basis of behaviour. Here there seems to be a high probability that a bad thing will happen, and, if we can, we should prevent it. It could be argued, therefore, that it is entirely legitimate for an ethics committee to consider behaviour, and only behaviour (and that includes future behaviour). If it goes further than that and decides how virtuous someone is, then it is simply speculating and giving an opinion. Unfortunately, this speculation or opinion may subsequently and erroneously be accepted as a defining label, and erroneously taken to be a 'fact'.

CONCLUSION

So, to conclude, I have argued that the concept of virtue is dangerously ill-defined, virtue's rise may serve factional political purposes, system implications have been missed or minimised, aspirational codes, especially when expecting abstract demonstration of 'virtue', need to be tempered with reality; the 'good enough' is better than the perfect, the implied centrality of 'virtue' in research is implausible, being 'critically virtuous' is unlikely, that we cannot assume that education will lead to morality and finally, since we cannot 'mind read' possible behaviour rather than imagined motives should be the focus.

Perhaps, for me the most important argument is the real-world practical one, and one that has real world consequences; specifically that locating virtue in an individual is problematic; it is dangerous for an individual because, particularly if there are organisational failings, and an individual can be blamed, then the system may work so as to blame that individual and punish them. In most cases the danger is that 'we are all in this alone' (as comedienne Lily Tomlin ironically suggested); in other words the individual will be held to assume responsibility, whatever the failings of the system overall, including the constraints on their behaviour that the system itself has created and imposed. Therefore, the underlying fantasy would be that having expelled the 'bad', 'unethical' person, virtue will somehow magically be restored to the system. So too, it is dangerous for the organisation, as the organisation or the system may continue to behave 'badly', in perhaps subtle ways, and actually not learn from its collective poor actions (or near misses). As thoughtful ethicists we must move from a pure understanding of virtue to a realistic appreciation of consequences, positive and negative, of its wholehearted adoption.

As has already been argued, the way in which organisational systems impinge on and influence the behaviour of individuals is crucial. It is, for example, from a cybernetic perspective, possible to see aberrant behaviour as 'error' and for this then to point us to the need for the careful examination of the system that has allowed this error to manifest itself through the 'bad' behaviour of an individual or group. It is increasingly recognised that systems act in complex, interdependent, chaotic and sometimes unpredictable ways. Numerous trade-offs are implicit within the functioning of any system; at a simple level speed versus accuracy; agility versus reliability; fidelity versus power. Of course, complex systems are necessarily more multifaceted, interdependent and, well, more complex than this. Our focus, therefore, needs to be systemic rather than individual, and this again leads to a question that is beyond this chapter. In other words, if the system were designed to be virtuous, could it be, since the agency, intentionality and free will of the people within it would necessarily be compromised. But that is an argument for another place.

Recent writings about morality in organisations come to differing conclusions; at times seeing organisations as:

> a neutraliser of moral emotions and a disabler of individuals' moral impulse 'right the way through to' a neutraliser of untamed passions and a guardian against power abuses by individuals or a crowd mentality that can always find good, moral reasons for doing the wrong thing. (Lindebaum, Geddes, & Gabriel, 2017)

The key point here, though, is that we have to consider the nature of the organisation and the context within which we operate before we can properly consider the role of virtue in research.

Is this then a counsel of despair? Should virtue be thrown away? Actually no; as noted at the beginning, this is a polemical account. I believe that many of the activities described by contributors to this volume will, by supporting high quality, ethical and relevant research, ultimately help make the world a better place; I believe that many of the contributors to this book are indeed 'virtuous'; additionally, I believe that many of the people reading this book will conduct their research with care, respect and integrity, and may whistleblow if they see unethical behaviour occurring. However, these are, alas, beliefs I have and not based on empirical findings. We need to be careful before we seek to adopt individual virtue as the central concept in research ethics. It is for those who are presently championing virtue to address some of the practical difficulties raised; some caution is required, we need to slow down. Just as Peter Rickman often described his approach to philosophy as being part of the 'British eclectic tradition', so we need to consider the complex interplay of ethical, contextual and practical considerations in research ethics, and necessarily adopt an eclectic position. We need to remember that this is not an abstract discussion, that it ultimately involves real researchers, real participants, real funding councils, real sponsors, real champions, a real society and a real world with real impact. If our research really has potency, then it has real consequences in the real world, and for this reason we must be cautious about jumping into bed with virtue.

REFERENCES

Argyris, C. (1995). Action science and organizational learning. *Journal of Managerial Psychology*, *10*(6), 20–26. Retrieved from http://doi.org/10.1108/02683949510093849.

Ballantyne, I., Boyle, S., Brooks, A., Bywater, J., Edenborough, R., Parker, A., ... Wilson, P. (2000). Design, implementation and evaluation of assessment and development centres: Best practice guidelines. *The British Psychological Society*, (229642), 1–25.

Banks, S. (2015) From research integrity to researcher integrity: issues of conduct, competence and commitment paper presented at Academy of Social Sciences "Virtue Ethics in the Practice and Review of Social Science Research" Friday 1st May 2015, London, https://www.acss.org.uk/wp-content/uploads/2015/03/Banks-From-research-integrity-to-researcher-integrity-AcSS-BSA-Virtue-ethics-1st-May-2015.pdf Accessed July 2015.

Barrett, P. (2003). Beyond psychometrics. *Journal of Managerial Psychology*, *18*(5), 421–439. Retrieved from http://doi.org/10.1108/02683940310484026

Basran, S. (IBE). (2012). Employee views of ethics at work. *2012 continental Europe survey* (pp. 1–42). Retrieved from http://www.ibe.org.uk/userfiles/euethicsatwork2012.pdf

Beech, N., MacIntosh, R., & MacLean, D. (2010). Dialogues between academics and practitioners: The role of generative dialogic encounters. *Organization Studies*, *31*(9–10), 1341–1367. Retrieved from http://doi.org/10.1177/0170840610374396

Bell, E., & Bryman, A. (2007). The ethics of management research: An exploratory content analysis. *British Journal of Management*, *18*(1), 63–77. Retrieved from http://doi.org/10.1111/j.1467-8551.2006.00487.x

Borsboom, D., Mellenbergh, G. J., & van Heerden, J. (2004). The concept of validity. *Psychological Review*, *111*(4), 1061–1071. Retrieved from http://doi.org/10.1037/0033-295X.111.4.1061

Brutus, S. E., Molson, J., & Duniewicz, K. (2010). State of science in industrial and organizational psychology: A review of self-reported limitations. *Personnel Psychology*, *63*, 907–936. Retrieved from http://doi.org/10.1111/j.1744-6570.2010.01192.x

Buckingham, L. (2011). *Projective identification revisited: A thread in the labyrinth: Returning to Melanie Klein's concept of projective identification*. Retrieved from http://doi.org/10.1111/j.1752-0118.2011.01256.x

Burnes, B. (2009). Reflections: Ethics and organizational change – Time for a return to Lewinian values. *Journal of Change Management*, *9*(4), 359–381. Retrieved from http://doi.org/10.1080/14697010903360558

Center, E. R. (2011). *Retaliation: When whistleblowers become victims*. A supplemental report of the 2011 National Business Ethics Survey, Arlington, VA.

Colby, A., Ehrlich, T., Sullivan, W. M., & Dolle, J. R. (2011). *Rethinking undergraduate business education: Liberal learning for the profession*. San Francisco: Jossey-Bass, Dalley.

Dench, S., Iphofen, R., & Huws, U. (2004). *An EU code of ethics for socio-economic research [interaktyvus]*. Great Britain: Institute for Employment Studies, [žiūrėta 2011-08-10].

Deontologie, C. D. E., & Psychologues, D. E. S. (2012). *Actualisation du Code de déontologie des psychologues*.

Edelman Trust. (2017). *Edelman trust barometer*. Retrieved from https://www.edelman.com/global-results/. Accessed on September 18, 2017.

EFPA. (2005). Metacode of Ethics, European Federation of Psychological Associations, Geneva. Accessed on July 2009. Retrieved from http://ethics.efpa.eu/metaand-model-code/meta-code

Fanelli, D. (2009). How many scientists fabricate and falsify research? A systematic review and meta-analysis of survey data. *PLoS ONE, 4*(5), e5738. Retrieved from http://doi.org/10.1371/journal.pone.0005738.

Federation, T. E., Associations, P., Associations, N., Associations, N., Efpa, T., & Codes, E. (2005). *Meta-Code of Ethics,* (July), 1–6.

Fernando, M., & Moore, G. (2014). MacIntyrean virtue ethics in business: A cross-cultural comparison. *Journal of Business Ethics,* 185–202. Retrieved from http://doi.org/10.1007/s10551-014-2313-6. Acessed on November 2016.

Fitzgerald, C. J., & Pleasant, M. (2010). *Evolutionary Psychology, 8*(2), 284–296.

Gardner, H. (2007). Good work. *Leadership Excellence, 24*(10), 3–4.

Gonin, M., Palazzo, G., & Hoffrage, U. (2012). Neither bad apple nor bad barrel: How the societal context impacts unethical behavior in organizations. *Business Ethics, 21*(1), 31–46. Retrieved from http://doi.org/10.1111/j.1467-8608.2011.01643.x

Greenwald, A. G. (2009). What (and where) is the ethical code concerning researcher conflict of interest? *Perspectives on Psychological Science, 4*(1), 32–35. Retrieved from http://doi.org/10.1111/j.1745-6924.2009.01086.x

Gu, J., & Neesham, C. (2014). Moral identity as leverage point in teaching business ethics. *Journal of Business Ethics, 124*(3), 527–536. Retrieved from http://doi.org/10.1007/s10551-013-2028-0

Harman, G. (2000). The nonexistence of character traits. *Proceedings of the Aristotelian Society, 100,* 223–226. Retrieved from http://doi.org/10.1111/j.0066-7372.2003.00013.x

Health and Care Professions Council. (2014). *Standards of conduct, performance and ethics. Health professions council documents* (pp. 1–18). London: HCPC.

Heijltjes, A., van Gog, T., Leppink, J., & Paas, F. (2015). Unraveling the effects of critical thinking instructions, practice, and self-explanation on students' reasoning performance. *Instructional Science, 43*(4), 487–506. Retrieved from http://doi.org/10.1007/s11251-015-9347-8

Higgins, C. (2011). Worlds of practice: MacIntyre's challenge to applied ethics. *The Good Life of Teaching: An Ethics of Professional Practice, 1981*(2), 47–83.

IBE. (2015). Press Release: Corporate whistleblowing arrangements are not working effectively. IBE survey shows (1084014). Retrieved from https://www.ibe.org.uk/userassets/pressreleases/2015_eatw_pr.pdf. Accessed on November 2016.

Institute of Business Ethics. (2015). *Business Ethics, 44*(1084014), 16–19.

Kahneman, D. (2011). *Thinking, fast and slow.* London: Allen Lane (Penguin).

Kesselheim, A. S., Studdert, D. M., & Mello, M. M. (2010). Whistle-blowers' experiences in fraud litigation against pharmaceutical companies. *The New England Journal of Medicine, 362*(19), 1832–1839. Retrieved from http://doi.org/10.1056/NEJMsr0912039

Kwiatkowski, R. (2003). Trends in organisations and selection: An introduction. *Journal of Managerial Psychology, 18*(5), 382–394. Retrieved from http://doi.org/10.1108/02683940310483991

Kwiatkowski, R., Duncan, D. C., & Shimmin, S. (2006). What have we forgotten – And why? *Journal of Occupational and Organizational Psychology, 79*(2), 183–201. Retrieved from http://doi.org/10.1348/096317905X70832

Lindebaum, D., Geddes, D., & Gabriel, Y. (2017). Moral emotions and ethics in organisations: Introduction to the special issue. *Journal of Business Ethics, 141*(4), 645–656. Retrieved from http://doi.org/10.1007/s10551-016-3201-z

Martin, F. (2011). Human development and the pursuit of the common good: Social psychology or Aristotelian virtue ethics? *Journal of Business Ethics, 100*(Suppl. 1), 89–98. Retrieved from http://doi.org/10.1007/s10551-011-1189-y

Michell, J. (2008). Is psychometrics pathological science? Measurement: Interdisciplinary research & perspective, *6*(1–2), 7–24. Retrieved from http://doi.org/10.1080/15366360802035489

Mintz, S. M. (1996). Aristotelian virtue and business ethics education. *Journal of Business Ethics*, *15*(8), 827–838. Retrieved from http://doi.org/10.1007/BF00381851

Moore, G., & Beadle, R. (2006). In search of organizational virtue in business: Agents, goods, practices, institutions and environments. *Organization Studies*, *27*(3), 369–389. Retrieved from http://doi.org/10.1177/0170840606062427

Morgan, G. (1986). *Images of organization.* London: Sage.

Norenzayan, A., Choi, I., & Nisbett, R. E. (1999). Eastern and western perceptions of causality for social behaviour: Lay theories about personalities and situations. In D. T. Prentice and D. A. Miller (Eds.), *Cultural divides: Understanding and overcoming group conflict* (pp. 239–272). New York, NY: Russell Sage Foundation.

Ormerod, N. (2005). Faith and reason: Perspectives from Macintyre and Lonergan. *Heythrop Journal*, *46*(1), 11–22. Retrieved from http://doi.org/10.1111/j.1468-2265.2005.00247.x.

Pettifor, J. L. (1998). The Canadian code of ethics for psychologists: A moral context for ethical decision-making in emerging areas of practice. *Canadian Psychology/Psychologie Canadienne*, *39*. Retrieved from http://doi.org/10.1037/h0086812

Preuss, L. (1998). On ethical theory in auditing. *Managerial Auditing Journal*, *13*(9), 500–508. Retrieved from http://doi.org/10.1108/02686909810245910

Public Concern at Work. (2013). *Whistleblowing the inside story: A study of 1,000 whistleblowers carried out by University of Greenwich.* London: PCaW. Retrieved from http://www.pcaw.org.uk/content/4-law-policy/4-document-library/Whistleblowing-the-inside-story-FINAL.pdf. Accessed on June 2017.

Release, P. (2015). Corporate whistleblowing arrangements are not working effectively. IBE survey shows (1084014). Retrieved from https://www.ibe.org.uk/userassets/pressreleases/2015_eatw_pr.pdf. Accessed on November 2016.

RESPECT. (2004). RESPECT code of practice for socio-economic research. *Intellectual Property*, 1–4.

Rice, A. J. (2015). Using scholarship on whistleblowing to inform peer. *Ethics Reporting*, *46*(4), 298–305.

Richards, G. (2010). *Putting psychology in its place: Critical historical perspectives* (3rd ed.). Hove, Sussex: Routledge.

Schooler, J. W. 2014. Metascience could rescue the 'replication crisis.' *Nature News*, 515(7525), 9. doi:10.1038/515009a.

Shultz, S., Nelson, E., & Dunbar, R. I. M. (2012). Hominin cognitive evolution: Identifying patterns and processes in the fossil and archaeological record. *Philosophical Transactions of the Royal Society of London. Series B, Biological Sciences*, *367*(1599), 2130–2140. Retrieved from http://doi.org/10.1098/rstb.2012.0115

Staw, B. M. (2016). Stumbling toward a social psychology of organizations: An autobiographical look at the direction of organizational research. *Annual Review of Organizational Psychology and Organizational Behavior*, *3*(1), 1–19. Retrieved from http://doi.org/10.1146/annurev-orgpsych-041015-062524

Strathern, M. (2000). Introduction: the new accountabilities. In M. Strathern (Ed.) *Audit Cultures; Anthropological studies in accountability, ethics and the academy* (pp. 1–18). London: Routledge.

The British Psychological Society. (2009). *Code of ethics and conduct.* Leicester and London: The British Psychological Society.

Tolich, M. (2014). What can Milgram and Zimbardo teach ethics committees and qualitative researchers about minimizing harm? *Research Ethics, 10*(2), 86–96. Retrieved from http://doi.org/10.1177/1747016114523771.

UK Research Integrity Office. (2009). *Code of practice for research: Promoting good practice and preventing misconduct.* Retrieved from http://ukrio.org/publications/code-of-practice-for-research/.

Van Stekelenburg, J. (2013). The political psychology of protest: Sacrificing for a cause. *European Psychologist, 18*(4), 224–234. Retrieved from http://doi.org/10.1027/1016-9040/a000156

Weaver, G. R. (2006). Virtue in organizations: Moral identity as a foundation for moral agency. *Organization Studies, 27*(3), 341–368. Retrieved from http://doi.org/10.1177/0170840606062426

Williams, J., & Drogin, E. (2010). A comparison of North American and British codes of ethics for psychologists. *Cambrian Law Review, 41*, 73–85.

Willmott, H., & Contu, A. (2003). Re-embedding situatedness: The importance of power relations in learning theory. *Organization Science, 14*(3), 283–296. Retrieved from http://doi.org/10.1287/orsc.14.3.283.15167

Zimbardo, P. G. (2008). *The Lucifer effect: How good people turn evil.* New York, NY: Random House.

CHAPTER 3

RESEARCH ETHICS TRAINING: USING A VIRTUE ETHICS APPROACH TO TRAINING TO SUPPORT DEVELOPMENT OF RESEARCHER INTEGRITY

Nicole Palmer and Rachel Forrester-Jones

ABSTRACT

Training in research ethics in higher education institutions tends to be increasingly focussed on operational instruction and how to navigate review processes. This has largely come about as a result of the gradual extension of the 'medical model' of prospective ethics review to all research involving human participants over the last few decades. Often devolved to an administrator, the purpose of instruction in research ethics is sometimes reduced to form-filling techniques. While this may serve to facilitate researchers' compliance with 'auditable' regulatory requirements, and to reassure risk-averse universities that they can demonstrate rigorous oversight, it does nothing to skill researchers in assessing the ethical implications of their own research. Mastering the skills to address and mitigate the moral dilemmas that can

Virtue Ethics in the Conduct and Governance of Social Science Research
Advances in Research Ethics and Integrity, Volume 3, 65–82
ISSN: 2398-6018/doi:10.1108/S2398-601820180000003004

emerge during a research project involves more than having a pre-determined set of options for research practice. Changing their perception means enabling researchers to view themselves as ethical practitioners within a broader community of researchers. In this chapter we discuss the implementation of a university training programme that has been designed to improve both the moral character, and thus the moral competence of researchers. Using a virtue ethics approach, we employed case studies and discussion, backed up by provision of individualised advice, to help researchers to consider the moral implications of research and to improve their moral decision-making skills. Attendees reported greater engagement with the issues and increased confidence in facing ethical dilemmas in their own research.

Keywords: Research ethics training; virtue ethics; research integrity; moral development; research ethics review

INTRODUCTION

Within the social sciences there has been much critical discussion on the transposition of the bioethics model of research ethics onto social science research, and the associated regulation that this has entailed (Hammersley, 2010; Macfarlane, 2009, 2010). Of particular interest has been the bureaucratisation of research ethics review, the over-reliance on principles that has reduced research ethics to a series of largely administrative requirements, and the resultant inflexibility regarding social science research methodology.[1]

Training in research ethics in higher education institutions (HEIs) tends to be increasingly focussed on operational instruction and how to navigate research ethics review processes. Consistent with our opening points, this has largely come about as a result of the gradual extension of the 'medical model' of prospective ethics review to all research involving human participants over the last few decades (see Bosk & De Vries, 2004; Dyer & Demeritt, 2009; Ramcharan & Cutliffe, 2001; Truman, 2003). Often devolved to an administrator, the purpose of instruction in research ethics is sometimes reduced to form-filling techniques. While this may serve to facilitate researchers' compliance with 'auditable' regulatory requirements, and to reassure risk-averse universities that they can demonstrate rigorous review procedures and oversight, it does nothing to skill researchers in assessing the ethical implications of their own research. Nor does it enable them to deal with any emergent ethical issues as they arise in the course of conducting research. Mastering the skills to address and mitigate the moral dilemmas that can emerge during a research project involves more than having a predetermined set of options for research practice. Such a 'compliance culture' does nothing to enhance the quality of research or researcher integrity. Rather, researchers need to understand the ethical reasoning on which the regulatory environment is based (Geller, Boyce, Ford, & Sugarman, 2010). Changing their perception means enabling researchers to view themselves as ethical practitioners within a broader community of researchers (Banks, 2018). Doing so means that researchers fully realise the responsibilities and commitments that this entails, and can help to develop integrity.

Publication of the *Concordat to Support Research Integrity* by Universities UK (2012) emphasised to HEIs the importance of integrity in research. This corresponds to recent wider cultural concerns relating to corruption exemplified by the global financial crisis, the Fédération Internationale de Football Association corruption scandal and the discovery of widespread doping in international sport, all of which have highlighted the significant ill effects that a lack of integrity can have on behaviour. On account of the increasing scrutiny that funding bodies, including research councils, are applying to ethical practices within research, funding for UK universities is becoming contingent on mechanisms for demonstrating sound practice. While organisations utilise rules, disciplinary measures and rewards in an effort to directly influence researcher behaviour, these cannot improve the deeper qualities of character such as integrity. Character-focussed approaches are needed to support and complement what has become a regulatory-based process (Banks, 2018).

In this chapter we discuss the implementation of a university training programme that has been designed to improve both the moral character, and thus the moral competence of researchers. Using a virtue ethics approach, we employed examples of ethical dilemmas from actual research projects, case studies and discussion, backed up by provision of individualised advice, to help researchers to consider the moral implications of research and to improve their moral decision-making skills. Attendees reported greater engagement with the issues and increased confidence in facing ethical dilemmas in their own research.

BACKGROUND

UK university research is governed by a deontological or duty-based approach to research ethics. Research projects must be pre-reviewed and provided with a 'favourable opinion' by a Research Ethics Committee (REC in the United Kingdom) or Institutional Review Board (in the United States) before they can proceed (Department of Health, 2012; Economic & Social Research Council,

2016; Tinker & Coomber, 2004). Ethical scrutiny has been a part of clinical research for some time, and there are also legislative requirements for seeking research ethics review for certain kinds of research.[2] However, in recent years ethical scrutiny has been applied much more widely and to areas of research which have traditionally not been subject to independent ethics review.

This widening of the scope of ethical scrutiny is partly the result of research funders' concerns with the poor quality of ethical discussions in research funding applications (Tinker & Coomber, 2004, p. 5). This has been taken to demonstrate a lack of awareness of research ethics, and the potential consequences of poor ethical practice, on the part of applicants. As Tinker and Coomber (2004, p. 7) note, funders took action on applicants' apparent failure to recognise ethical issues in their proposals, even those planning to involve vulnerable participants, by drawing up codes of practice that make research ethics review a requirement.

As a result, universities have also become increasingly concerned to ensure that they maintain an appropriate degree of oversight of the research activities of their staff and students. The consequences of a research scandal for organisations such as universities can be severe (Allen, 2008); research funders may withdraw funding, for both current and future applications, and reputational damage from adverse publicity can potentially lead to a reduction in student recruitment and, therefore, income. Hedgecoe (2016) suggests that university RECs are increasingly being co-opted 'to serve as mechanisms for institutional reputation management' as a result of the 'adoption of risk management processes from the private sector', which developed following the financial crash (p. 488). Robertson (2014) provides an example of this in operation at her own institution, where reputational risk is considered in relation to every research ethics application.

Universities are also subject to the research integrity requirements set out in policy documents such as the *Concordat to Support Research Integrity* (2012), the UK Research Integrity Office's (2009) *Code of Practice for Research* and Research Councils UK's (2015) *Policy and Guidelines on the Governance of Good Research Conduct*, and so are obliged to maintain and, in the case of the Concordat, *demonstrate* their compliance with research integrity standards.

The expanding reach of ethical scrutiny to incorporate research areas such as social sciences and humanities, and the increasing bureaucratisation of the review process, have been widely criticised (Hedgecoe, 2008, 2016; McCarthy, Hunt, & Milne-Skillman, 2017; McCormack et al., 2012; Rhodes, 2005). Haggerty (2004) and Guta, Nixon, and Wilson (2013) describe this widening remit as 'ethics creep', claiming that notions of 'risk' and 'harm', and the interpretation of these somewhat ambiguous terms, have become disproportionate to the activities to which they are applied (Haggerty, 2004, p. 392). While initially established to ensure the ethical conduct of research and to protect research participants, Hedgecoe (2016, p. 488) complains that RECs have been commandeered by university management to exert a form of control over internal organisational behaviour with a view to manage external reputations. He asserts that this both overreaches their remit and threatens academic freedom. Wilson (2011, p. 391) compares the expansion of research ethics review procedures as akin to Weber's (2005) concept that the 'iron cage' of bureaucratisation is an inevitable result of material progress, which serves to smother individual creativity and autonomy. Referring to the clinical research arena, Warlow (2005, p. 33) complains that the delays caused by over-regulation compromise public health by placing emphasis on 'process and political correctness' rather than ethics. Similar concerns have been expressed by academics and researchers regarding social research (see Bosk & De Vries, 2004; Dyer & Demeritt, 2009; Ramcharan & Cutliffe, 2001; Truman, 2003). In addition to the inevitable frustrations linked with any mandatory bureau-cratic process, many academics agree that the institution of research ethics review has expanded to serve purposes other than ethics assessment alone.

Historically, it was researchers' professionalism and discipline-specific codes of conduct that were relied upon to ensure ethical behaviour in the conduct of research. More recently, it has been argued that the regulatory model of research ethics has served to remove responsibility for the integrity of actions from the researcher to the REC (Wainwright, Williams, Michael, Farsides, & Cribb, 2006). Research ethics review procedures have a tendency to situate the focus of the review on the research study and its design rather than the researcher's behaviour (Carpenter, 2013). Thus, rather than a researcher becoming certified to work ethically, a favourable opinion is granted to a par-ticular project after a satisfactory review of a research proposal (Department of Health, 2012, p. 16). There are therefore concerns that the formalisation of ethical scrutiny has reduced the ethics review process to a 'tick-box' exer-cise, one that is concerned with matters of procedure and protocol (Allen, 2008; Guta et al., 2013; Spike, 2005). Having complied with an institutional research ethics review process and having gained the necessary 'approval[s],'[3] researchers may believe that their engagement with ethics is over and they no longer need to consider research ethics while conducting their project. With little or no ongoing monitoring carried out by RECs, researchers are rarely subject to any oversight of their conduct and no one checks that they are complying with the protocol approved by the REC (Tinker & Coomber, 2004). This failure to close the regulatory circle supports Hedgecoe's asser-tion (2016) that universities view the main purpose of RECs to be to provide evidence of auditable risk management processes rather than to ensure the protection of research participants.

There are also concerns that compliance-based ethical scrutiny can be counterproductive in other ways. Researchers who perceive this review model as being symptomatic of 'institutionalised distrust' may feel alienated. Rather than supporting researchers to make ethical decisions for themselves, a perception of the process as a one-off, tick-box event can have the result of deskilling and disempowering them (Johnsson, Eriksson, Helgesson, & Hansson, 2014). A lack of confidence and expertise in dealing with emergent ethical issues during the conduct of a research project could leave participants in danger of harm and researchers at risk of inadvertent misconduct. It is therefore crucial that researchers are facilitated to develop their knowledge and awareness of research ethics and integrity. This suggests that if universities (and other research institutions) are to be in a position to reassure themselves that the research they support is being carried out to the highest ethical standards, then a different model of research ethics and integrity instruction is required. It should be one that has the potential to enhance the moral development of researchers, one that helps them to think ethically, and does not merely instruct them on the best ways to complete review documentation or to navigate a tick-box review process.

TOWARDS AN IMPROVED MODEL FOR INSTRUCTION IN RESEARCH ETHICS AND INTEGRITY

In spite of the criticisms of the formalisation of ethical scrutiny and the resulting 'ethics creep', it cannot be denied that both universities and those who criticise their research ethics review procedures aspire to conduct and support ethical research. Universities devote resources to the development and administration of research ethics review procedures and staff to provide advice, guidance and instruction to researchers regarding research governance, ethics and integrity.

Certainly, in our own institution, research ethics review procedures have been designed to accomplish more than the provision of a tick-box process. Having been developed in accordance with a reflexivity-based rather than a compliance-based model, the aim is to encourage applicants to identify and engage with the ethical dimension of their research (Jennings, 2010). The wording of the application documentation and associated guidance has been formulated to encourage researchers to consider the full range of ethical issues that their research might encounter. It also draws their attention to potential ethical questions that could arise, and for which mitigation plans should be in place. By asking directed questions under headings such as 'risks and ethical issues', 'recruitment and informed consent' and 'confidentiality', researchers can be led to address the main ethical concerns in their research, even without having in-depth knowledge of research ethics principles.

However, it is the case that researchers should be considering potential ethical issues from the design phase of a project, and not leaving this vital task until the project reaches ethics review stage. Furthermore, they should have the perception and insight to be able to 'do the right thing' when faced with an unexpected ethical problem during their research, especially in the field where ethical issues often arise unexpectedly. In order to be able to do this effectively, they will require a working knowledge of research ethics and integrity. Where university training and instruction have been inadequate, however, researchers may not have developed the requisite skills. Ideally, training in research ethics and integrity should be something that is discussed from the very beginning of a researcher's career, that is, from when they were a student, and universities might provide ongoing training for researchers at all levels.[4] Unfortunately, when time is tight and teaching schedules already full, the nature of this instruction generally takes the form of practical guidance on how to comply with research ethics review processes and procedures.

Training of this kind is often either delivered by an academic in one small unit of teaching (e.g., one hour within a whole module on research methods), or it is delivered by an administrator, with little scope for in-depth, philosophical discussion of wider issues and principles of research ethics and integrity. Some commentators have suggested that such discussions are crucial for the effectiveness of such training programmes (DuBois, Dueker, Anderson, & Campbell, 2008; Rivera, Borasky, Rice, & Carayon, 2005). Particularly when stimulated by consideration of case studies, as opposed to instruction on compliance with regulatory processes, engaging in broader ethical discussions has been demonstrated to foster development of ethical sensitivity and moral judgement (Bebeau, Pimple, Muskavitch, Borden, & Smith, 1995; Rest, Bebeau, & Volker, 1986). It is these qualities that will assist researchers with both designing an ethically sound project and dealing with unanticipated ethical issues that arise during research in the field.

THE VIRTUE ETHICS APPROACH

Virtue ethics has been described as 'an approach to ethics that focusses on the excellent qualities of character or moral dispositions of moral agents (e.g., trustworthiness, courage or compassion)' (Banks, chapter 1 in this volume 2018). A virtue-based approach to research ethics and integrity facilitates a change of focus, from one that is concerned with the conduct of research to one that is concerned with the character of researchers. The latter indicates that we should emphasise the personal qualities of the researcher over an ability to comply with rules and principles. Banks proposes that true researcher integrity can only result from character-focussed virtue, and where researchers are able to achieve criticality and reflexivity in their research activities as well as in the assessment of ethical issues.

Rather than concentrating on 'the integrity of the research *practice*', Banks notes that taking a virtue ethics approach to *researcher* integrity means viewing the researcher 'as *practitioner* in the research community' with a focus on their 'motivations and commitments' (*ibid.*, chapter 1 in this volume, italics in the original, 2018). The current regulatory environment is such that scrutiny of the proposed research is prioritised, while the moral development of researchers as practitioners is neglected. This has led to an approach to training that is founded on a principle-based approach to ethics, which places more importance on rule-based action ('what should I do?') rather than qualities of character ('how should I be?') (*ibid.*).

While rule-based action can serve to reassure researchers and research institutions that legislative requirements will be met, it is the qualities of a researcher's character that can help them to successfully navigate the ambiguities of research ethics. Indeed, as Banks (chapter 1 in this volume, 2018) notes that the originators of the widely adopted and preeminent Four Principles theory of research ethics, Beauchamp and Childress (1994, p. 462) have recently acknowledged that 'character and moral discernment' are crucial to the 'emotional responsiveness' required for the appropriate interpretation and application of the Four Principles. Thus, virtue ethics and principle-based ethics need not be mutually exclusive; they can be thought of as having a complementary relationship.

Parallels have also been drawn between virtue ethics and an ethic of care (see Allmark, 1995; Edwards & Mauthner, 2005; Ferdinand, Pearson, Rowe, & Worthington, 2007; Robertson, 2014; Tong, 1993). Building on Gilligan's (1982) feminist approach to ethics, an ethic of care has been promoted as a '*supplement* [to] the traditional ethics of justice and rights' (emphasis in the original) that underpins biomedical research ethics models to bring 'an ethics of care and responsibilities' (Tong, 1993, p. 25). 'Researchers' understanding of research ethics is often reduced to a focus on avoiding harm when they are required to navigate overly bureaucratic and risk averse review procedures.' However, a virtue ethics approach, informed by an ethic of care, can be used to re-emphasise the importance of affording care, and this has implications not only for participant protection but also researcher safety and safeguarding the university's reputation (Robertson, 2014).

INFLUENCES ON RESEARCHER BEHAVIOUR

There are, of course, many factors that can influence a researcher's integrity, in addition to their character-focussed virtue. Structural pressures such as competition for jobs and research funding, preconceptions about promotion criteria, and mistrust about research assessment policies have all been identified as having the potential to incline researchers towards engaging in questionable research practices (Nuffield Council on Bioethics, 2014). These 'perverse incentives' are implicated in the incitement of bad research practices, such as reporting an unexpected finding as having been predicted from the start, inappropriately assigning authorship credit, or the selective reporting of studies that worked (Fang & Casadevall, 2015).

The Concordat stipulates that it is the responsibility of universities to ensure that a culture of research integrity is fostered, and that best practice is facilitated and misconduct is not tolerated (Universities UK, 2012). Furthermore, universities should promote 'mentoring opportunities to support the development of researchers' (*ibid.*, p. 15). Banks also identifies the importance of role models to new researchers. She advocates for the role of research supervisors, research leaders and university leaders, arguing that they should act as mentors for students and early career staff whilst also setting the tone for research practice within the institution (Banks, 2018). A perceived lack of commitment to ethical research conduct on the part of institutional leadership has been shown to negatively affect the conduct of researchers (Gunsalas, 1993).

However, in spite of an intensified focus on research integrity, there is increasing evidence of both growing incidence of research misconduct (Fanelli, 2009; Martinson, Anderson, & De Vries, 2005) and the under-reporting of research misconduct by researchers who witness it within their institution or among their colleagues (Titus, Wells, & Rhoades, 2008). This suggests that there is more to do to improve researcher integrity.

BAD RESEARCH PRACTICE MODEL

Fig. 1 shows the 'vicious circle' effect of the unethical researcher. Certainly, for a postgraduate researcher, the main motivation for conducting a piece of research is to contribute towards a dissertation, a thesis or a paper for publication. Provision of ineffective training that is rule- and compliance-based and conduct-focussed, combined with the pressures of the 'perverse incentives' described above, can potentially lead to questionable research practices

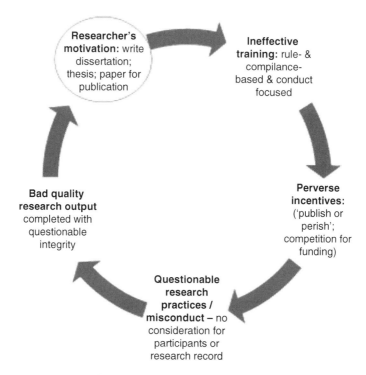

Fig. 1.   The 'Vicious Circle' of the unethical researcher.

and possible misconduct. These can contribute to bad quality research outputs. Where these bad behaviours are not identified and amended, they can
persist to affect the researcher's future work.

TRAINING FOR INTEGRITY

It is clear that administrator-led instruction on compliance with a formalised
research ethics review process will not be sufficient for developing a character-
focussed approach to fostering research ethics and integrity expertise for students
and staff. Universities cannot, therefore, rely on this kind of method to safeguard against researcher misconduct and breaches of the Concordat to Support
Research Integrity (2012). In order to stress the importance of the wider issues,
more emphasis is required on researchers' responsibilities. These include both
the requirement to behave ethically and the duty to foster the personal qualities
necessary to assess the ethical course of action when a researcher encounters an
emergent ethical dilemma during the conduct of a study.

GOOD RESEARCH PRACTICE MODEL

Fig. 2 shows the 'virtuous circle' effect of the ethical researcher. The researcher's motivation is the same as that for the unethical researcher depicted above: to complete a dissertation, a thesis or a paper for publication. However, provision of training that follows a virtue ethics model, with a focus on qualities of character and reflexivity, can encourage researchers to employ consideration and care in their practice. This can contribute to good research conduct and lead to good quality research outputs. The ethical researcher is more likely to perpetuate these behaviours in their future research practice.

Fig. 2. The 'Vicious Circle' of the ethical researcher.

It is with the aim of promoting virtue, rather than simply providing practical instruction on approval processes, that we have developed our postgraduate research ethics and integrity training programme at the University of Kent. Research ethics and integrity workshops are provided as part of the researcher development programme, and separate sessions are designed for social science, science and humanities students in order to allow discussion of issues specific to those research areas. The workshops are run by the authors: Professor Rachel Forrester-Jones, an experienced academic researcher who is also the chair of the University's Research Ethics and Governance Committee, and Nicole Palmer, the University's Research Ethics and Governance Officer, who has responsibility for provision of guidance and advice on research ethics and governance, as well as oversight of the University's research ethics review processes. Numbers of attendees at the workshops are limited so as to facilitate interaction. Students are encouraged to raise issues specific to their own research during the sessions to engage in wider discussions regarding the ethics of research. At the beginning of the session attendees are asked to briefly describe their area of research and planned research project. In addition to positioning their own concerns at the forefront of the researchers' minds at the outset, this enables the facilitators of the sessions to tailor the time (each session lasts for three hours) to the particular needs of attendees, and to make it as relevant and useful to them as possible.

As part of these sessions, a background to the contemporary research ethics and integrity landscape is provided. This includes discussion of notorious historical examples of bad research practice, and their subsequent effect on the regulatory environment. This is followed by brief explanations of research-related legislation and the regulatory and review requirements for different types of research. Beauchamp and Childress's (2009) Four Principles theory of research ethics is presented and demonstrated as an effective tool to apply principles of research ethics to a specific research project. To emphasise their practical applications, each of the Four Principles is expounded by discussion in relation to informed consent procedures, the development of confidentiality and disclosure policies and to justice and the fair distribution of the benefits and burdens of research. There is also a focus on the character virtues that are required if, for example, the researcher is to respect the autonomy of a research participant.

The session includes a discussion of real ethical dilemmas that have been faced by actual researchers in the field. Attendees are encouraged to consider how they may have acted had they found themselves in a similar position, and what qualities of character they believe would influence their decision-making. Following this virtue-oriented discussion, the facilitators relate issues back to the principles of research ethics so as to provide a rationale for appropriate options for action within the boundaries of ethical research. Students and early-career researchers can often be apprehensive about research ethics, as it can be rather nebulous with very few right or wrong answers. We often find that they attend our training seeking clarity and a set of instructions to follow.

We have found that discussion of actual dilemmas, and consideration of the qualities of character that can help in their resolution, are valuable in this regard. Set against a background of relevant principles and examples of good practice, this can assist individuals in situating the ethics of their research projects, and in addressing any ethical concerns they may have, within a framework of research and researcher integrity.

During our sessions we also work through some case studies. These have been developed from previous real-life fieldwork situations combined with knowledge of the literature on ethics. This enables individuals to assess their reactions to the ethical dilemmas contained in the case studies, both from a character-focussed viewpoint and by utilising a principle-based approach. Feedback has shown that attendees value the opportunity to test out their intuitions and their understanding of the application of the Four Principles in the presence of instructors, as this helps them to gain confidence in their abilities. For example, in the last three years 94% of attendees have rated the sessions as good or excellent.

To capitalise on the workshop atmosphere of the sessions, and to provide students with real practical and personalised assistance, time and space is also provided for attendees to discuss ethical aspects of their own projects, either with the group or individually with one of the facilitators. Individual researchers are thus able to raise existing concerns, or query issues that may have arisen as a result of the workshop. Individuals report that this practical element is instrumental in encouraging them to attend the workshop as it provides a tangible benefit in terms of their own research projects, as exemplified by the following feedback from attendees:

> Great workshop. The time available to discuss specific points of contention regarding ethics in our own research projects was really useful. It was also useful to be able to hear other people's ethical issues from other disciplines... (Social sciences student, 2014)

> This was an excellent workshop. I would highly recommend it for all students. I found it helpful to discuss my project with the trainers and fellow students. (Social sciences student, 2015)

> The facilitators brought lots of experience and examples as well as practical tips to the session. The responses to our specific research projects were extremely helpful. (Social sciences student, 2016)

> Good, clear and practical advice. (Humanities student, 2016)

THE VIRTUE ETHICS TRAINING MODEL

Fig. 3 depicts the training model we have developed to inform our postgraduate training sessions, based on our assessment of the literature in the field and reflection on our respective experiences teaching, supervising and advising postgraduate researchers. Encouraging trainees to examine their practice 'reflectively and reflexively' (Bolton, 2010, p. xix) with discussion of their own research experiences alongside case studies based on their research areas, helps

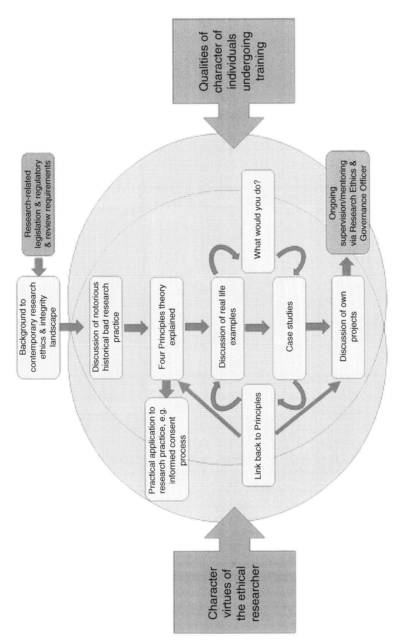

Fig. 3   The Virtue Ethics Training Model.

to situate the training within a framework of virtue ethics. The aim is that students are supported to more fully realise which of their personal qualities of character are relevant to the character virtues of the ethical researcher, and thus align their behaviour accordingly. In this way it is hoped that they will be better equipped to exercise integrity when undertaking their own projects.

CONCLUSION

Institutional research ethics procedures should, 'as a minimum, enhance the ethical awareness of the applicants concerning the research and its consequences rather than promote mere rule-following' (CEN, European Committee for Standardisation, 2017, p. 21). Using a virtue ethics approach in research integrity instruction can help to achieve this by enabling researchers to reflect on the contribution that qualities of character make to ethical research practice, alongside an understanding of research ethics principles and the legislative environment.

While an emphasis on the regulatory aspects of research integrity can devalue virtues such as responsibility, reflection and regard for human relationships, a moral discourse can seem 'vague, impractical, ideologically suspect, and discretionary' to risk-averse research institutions mindful of the potential of a research scandal to damage reputations (Ashcroft, 2003, p. 41). However, we have found that by combining a virtue ethics approach with a foundation of practice-based knowledge, we can help researchers to incorporate virtue ethics into their research activities and thus become reflective and ethical researchers rather than simply competent rule-followers.

Eisen and Berry (2002, p. 38) remark that in order to become an integral part of research integrity, formal ethics education should begin in high school, and that this would greatly 'reduce the challenges to those who teach ethics to graduate students.' However, our virtue ethics approach to researcher training for postgraduate students is proving successful in making attendees aware of the ethical dimension of research, in addition to providing them with the necessary skills to successfully navigate a research ethics review process.

NOTES

1. For discussion of these issues see the first volume in this series (Iphofen, 2016).
2. For example, Human Tissue Act (2004), Mental Capacity Act (2005), Medicines for Human Use (Clinical Trials) Regulations (2004), and Animals (Scientific Procedures) Act (1986).

3. In the United Kingdom, RECs of the National Research Ethics Service will provide a "favourable opinion" rather than "approval" as it is acknowledged that they are providing an "ethical opinion" only (see Health Research Authority, 2017).

4. We are, of course, not alone in making such suggestions. See Iphofen (2011, pp. 34–35, 49, and passim) and Iphofen, Krayer, and Robinson (2009).

REFERENCES

Allen, G. (2008). Getting beyond form filling: The role of institutional governance in human research ethics. *Journal of Academic Ethics*, 6(2), 105–116.

Allmark, P. (1995). Can there be an ethics of care? *Journal of Medical Ethics, 21*(1), 19–24.

Ashcroft, R. E. (2003). The ethics and governance of medical research: What does regulation have to do with it? *New Review of Bioethics*, 1(1), 41–58.

Banks, S. (2018). Cultivating researcher integrity: Virtue-based approaches to research ethics. In Emmerich, N. (Ed.), *Advances in Research Ethics and Integrity vol. 3: Virtue Ethics in the Conduct and Governance of Social Science Research.* Bingley: Emerald Publishing Limited.

Beauchamp, T. L., & Childress, J. F. (1994). *Principles of biomedical ethics* (4th ed.). Oxford & New York: Oxford University Press.

Beauchamp, T. L., & Childress, J. F. (2009). *Principles of biomedical ethics* (6th ed.). New York, NY: Oxford University Press.

Bebeau, M. J., Pimple, K. D., Muskavitch, K. M. T., Borden, S. L., & Smith, D. H. (1995). *Moral reasoning in scientific research: Cases for teaching and assessment.* Bloomington, IN: Indiana University.

Bolton, G. (2010). *Reflective practice: Writing and professional development* (3rd ed.). London: Sage Publications.

Bosk, C. L., & De Vries, R. G. (2004). Bureaucracies of mass deception: Institutional review boards and the ethics of ethnographic research. *Annals of American Academy*, 595, 249–263.

Carpenter, D. (2013). *Generic ethics principles in social science research.* Discussion "Stimulus" paper, AcSS symposium, March 5, 2013. Retrieved from https://www.acss.org.uk/wp-content/uploads/2014/01/Carpenter-AcSS-Discussion-Paper-5-March-2013-Principles-for-Generic-Ethics-Principles-in-Social-Science-Research.pdf. Accessed on January 14, 2017.

CEN, European Committee for Standardisation. (2017). *Ethics assessment of research & innovation CEN – Part 1 Ethics committee.* Brussels: CEN.

Department of Health. (2012). *Governance arrangements for research ethics committees: A harmonised edition.* London: Department of Health.

DuBois, J. M., Dueker, J. M., Anderson, E. E., & Campbell, J. (2008). The development and assessment of an NIH-funded research ethics training programme. *Academic Medicine*, 83(6), 596–603.

Dyer, S., & Demeritt, D. (2009). Un-ethical review? Why it is wrong to apply the medical model of research governance to human geography. *Progress in Human Geography*, 33(1), 46–64.

Economic & Social Research Council. (2015). *Framework for research ethics.* Swindon: ESRC.

Edwards, R., & Mauthner, M. (2002). Ethics and feminist research: Theory and practice. In M. Mauthner, M. Birch, J. Jessop, & T. Miller (Eds.), *Ethics in qualitative research* (pp. 14–28). London: Sage Publications.

Eisen, A., & Berry, R. M. (2002). The absent professor: Why we don't teach research ethics and what to do about it. *The American Journal of Bioethics, 2*(4), 38–49.

Fanelli, D. (2009). How many scientists fabricate and falsify research? A systematic review and meta-analysis of survey data. *PLoS ONE, 4*(5), 1–11.

Fang, F. C., & Casadevall, A. (2015). Competitive science: Is competition ruining science? *Infection and Immunity, 83*(4), 1229–1233.

Ferdinand, J., Pearson, G., Rowe, M., & Worthington, F. (2007). A different kind of ethics. *Ethnography, 8*(4), 519–543.

Geller, G., Boyce, A., Ford, D., & Sugarman, J. (2010). Beyond "compliance": The role of institutional culture in promoting research integrity. *Academic Medicine, 85*(8), 1296–1302.

Gilligan, C. (1982). *In a different voice: Psychological theory and women's development.* Cambridge, MA: Harvard University Press.

Gunsalas, C. K. (1993). Institutional structure to ensure research integrity. *Academic Medicine, 68*(9, September Supplement), S33–S38.

Guta, A., Nixon, S. A., & Wilson, M. G. (2013). Resisting the seduction of "ethics creep": Using Foucault to surface complexity and contradiction in research ethics review. *Social Science and Medicine, 98*(1), 301–310.

Haggerty, K. D. (2004). Ethics creep: Governing social science research in the name of ethics. *Qualitative Sociology, 27*(4), 391–414.

Hammersley, M. (2010). Creeping ethical regulation and the strangling of research. *Sociological Research Online, 15*(4), online.

Health Research Authority. (2017). *Standard operating procedures for research ethics committees, version 7.2* (p. 30). London: HRA. Accessed on December 1, 2017. https://www.hra.nhs.uk/about-us/committees-and-services/res-and-recs/research-ethics-committee-standard-operating-procedures/.

Hedgecoe, A. (2008). Research ethics review and the sociological research relationship. *Sociology, 42*(5), 873–886.

Hedgecoe, A. (2016). Reputational risk, academic freedom and research ethics review. *Sociology, 50*(3), 486–501.

Iphofen, R. (2011). *Ethical decision making in social research: A practical guide.* London: Palgrave Macmillan.

Iphofen, R. (Ed.). (2017). *Finding common ground: Consensus in research ethics across the social sciences (Advances in research ethics and integrity*, Vol. 1). Bingley: Emerald Publishing Limited.

Iphofen, R., Krayer, A., & Robinson, C. (Eds.). (2009). *Reviewing and reading social care research: From ideas to findings (A training manual with support materials).* Bangor: Bangor University.

Jennings, S. L. M. (2010). Two models of social science research ethics review. *Research Ethics Review, 6*(3), 86–90.

Johnsson, L., Eriksson, S., Helgesson, G., Hansson, M. G. (2014). Making researchers moral: Why trustworthiness requires more than ethics guidelines and review. *Research Ethics, 10*(1), 29–46.

Macfarlane, B. (2009). *Researching with integrity: The ethics of academic inquiry.* New York, NY: Routledge.

Macfarlane, B. (2010). Values and virtues in qualitative research. In M. Savin-Baden & C. H. Major (Eds.), *New approaches to qualitative research: Wisdom and uncertainty* (pp. 19–27). New York, NY: Routledge.

Martinson, B. C., Anderson, M. S., & De Vries, R. (2005). Scientists behaving badly. *Nature, 435*(7043), 737–738.

McCarthy, M., Hunt, S., & Milne-Skillman, K. (2017). "I know it was every week, but I can't be sure if it was every day": Domestic violence and women with learning disabilities. *Journal of Applied Research in Intellectual Disabilities, 30*(2), 269–282.

McCormack, D., Carr, T., McCloskey, R., Keeping-Burke, L., Furlong, K. E., & Doucet, S. (2012). Getting through ethics: The fit between research ethics board assessments and qualitative research. *Journal of Empirical Research on Human Research Ethics: An International Journal, 7*(5), 30–36.

Nuffield Council on Bioethics. (2014). *The culture of scientific research in the UK.* London: Nuffield.

Ramcharan, P., & Cutliffe, J. R. (2001). Judging the ethics of qualitative research: Considering the "ethics as process" model. *Health and Social Care in the Community, 9*(6), 358–366.

Research Councils UK. (2015). *Policy and guidelines on governance of good research conduct.* Swindon: RCUK.

Rest, J. R., Bebeau, M. J., & Volker, J. (1986). An overview of the psychology of morality. In J. R. Rest (Ed.), *Moral development: Advances in research and theory* (pp. 1–28). Boston: Prager Publishers.

Rhodes, R. (2005). Rethinking research ethics. *The American Journal of Bioethics, 5*(1), 7–28.

Rivera, R., Borasky, D., Rice, R., & Carayon, F. (2005). Many worlds, one ethic: Design and development of a global research ethics training curriculum. *Developing World Bioethics, 5*(2), 169–175.

Robertson, M. (2014). The case for ethics review in the social sciences: Drawing from practice at Queen Mary University of London. *Research Ethics, 10*(2), 69–76.

Spike, J. (2005). Putting the "ethics" into "research ethics." *The American Journal of Bioethics, 5*, 51–53.

Tinker, A., & Coomber, V. (2004). *University research ethics committees: Their role, remit and conduct.* London: King's College London.

Titus, S. L., Wells. J. A., & Rhoades, L. J. (2008). Repairing research integrity. *Nature, 453*(7198), 980–982.

Tong, R. (1993). *Feminine and feminist ethics.* Belmont, CA: Wadsworth Publishing Company.

Truman, C. (2003). Ethics and the ruling relations of research production. *Sociological Research Online, 8*(1), online.

UK Research Integrity Office. (2009). *Code of practice for research.* London: UKRIO.

Universities UK. (2012). *Concordat to support research integrity.* London: UUK.

Wainwright, S. P., Williams, C., Michael, M., Farsides, B., Cribb, A. (2006). Ethical boundary-work in the embryonic stem cell laboratory. *Sociology of Health & Illness, 28*(6), 732–748.

Warlow, C. (2005). Over-regulation of clinical research: A threat to public health. *Clinical Medicine, 5*(1), 33–38.

Weber, M. (2005). *The protestant ethic and the spirit of capitalism* (T. Parsons, Trans.). London: Routledge.

Wilson, A. (2011). Research ethics and the "iron cage" of bureaucratic rationality. *Addiction Research and Theory, 19*(5), 391–393.

CHAPTER 4

THE PROFESSIONAL INTEGRITY OF SOCIAL SCIENCE RESEARCHERS – CAN VIRTUE ETHICS HELP?

Kath Melia

ABSTRACT

This chapter is concerned with the professional integrity of researchers in social science. Social science researchers who undertake data collection and fieldwork, which involves spending time with those who have volunteered to be part of the research, have ethical responsibilities towards those who participate in their research. Particularly when research is publicly funded, they also have duties towards the social groups they study, and to wider society in which the findings of the research are of relevance. The position taken here is that social science researchers should be regarded as professionals who share common concerns and practices similar to the professionals working in health care.

Keywords: Integrity; virtue ethics; research ethics; social science

Virtue Ethics in the Conduct and Governance of Social Science Research
Advances in Research Ethics and Integrity, Volume 3, 83–101
Copyright © 2018 by Emerald Publishing Limited
All rights of reproduction in any form reserved
ISSN: 2398-6018/doi:10.1108/S2398-601820180000003005

INTRODUCTION

This chapter is concerned with the professional integrity of researchers in social science. Social science researchers who undertake data collection and fieldwork, which involves spending time with those who have volunteered to be part of the research, have ethical responsibilities towards those who participate in their research. Particularly when research is publicly funded, they also have duties towards the social groups they study, and to wider society in which the findings of the research are of relevance. The position taken here is that social science researchers should be regarded as professionals who share common concerns and practices similar to those professionals working in healthcare.

Health and social care practitioners are expected to conduct themselves in ways that respect the needs of their patients and clients towards whom they have a duty of care. Whether taken collectively or individually, this duty goes beyond that generally expected of 'ordinary' citizens with respect to each other. This is because the patients and clients are in an unequal power relationship with the professionals they encounter. Professions, as the sociological literature has it (Freidson, 1970), are afforded a particular social status or standing, and are allowed to act in ways that, in other circumstances, would not be acceptable. This is particularly true with regard to maintaining the privacy and confidentiality of their clients or patients. All this is a function of specialist knowledge and skills offered by the professions. The price the professionals pay for this privileged position in the hierarchy of occupations is that they behave ethically and do not exploit their positions. Patients and clients on their part can expect to be treated fairly when they may be in no position to be in control of their life. This approach to care is usually assured by professionals practising according to an ethical code.

Rather than discussing social science research in general, I am focussing on researchers in health and social care who are involved in fieldwork, participant observation, qualitative interviews and other means of data collection, all of which involve contact with people who have agreed to be research participants. The similarities between the ethical duties of clinical and research professionals stem from the fact that they have contact with people whilst they are in a sensitive position or situation. Furthermore, ethical approval is required for research to take place in these contexts, and the informed consent of the research participant can be considered similar to that required from patients for nonemergency medical treatment.

Writings on the ethics of professional practice in healthcare invariably feature the principles of non-maleficence and respect for persons. It may be argued that these principles would work equally well for social science researchers. There are, certainly, parallels between clinical practitioners and researchers, particularly in terms of acting as a professional and taking an ethical approach towards patients/research participants. It therefore makes sense to consider the relevance of the ethical principles that underlie the codes of ethics in healthcare.

Hume ([1777] 1978, p. 415), philosopher and friend of Adam Smith, claimed that: '[R]eason is, and ought only to be, the slave of the passions, and can never pretend to any other office than to serve and obey them'.

Today 'passions' might be expressed in terms of emotions or sentiments, the terms that Smith preferred. Nevertheless, even if the notion is unfamiliar to the 21st century mind, Hume's statement suggests that at the very least we need to take account of emotions in our efforts to behave ethically in clinical practice and social science research. A more contemporary position might be to say that action must be based on evidence. We demand good reasons for actions. This being the case we would have to ask if we can rely on the instincts and emotions of our healthcare practitioners and social science researchers. When we are dependent upon others, we need to be assured of their motivations and trustworthiness. In the clinical situation this need is clear. Perhaps it is less obvious in social science research, but if we think about privacy and confidentiality – and the uses to which social science data can be put – then the need for trust is evident. In addition, offering to be a participant in social science research can be an uncertain business, particularly if the area of research is sensitive, as, for example, is the case when the research concerns abuse or violence.

Since at least the 1960s and the advent of 'bioethics', the health care professions have drawn on ethics, the branch of philosophy that is concerned with moral questions, in order to address more general moral questions as well as those that arise in practice. Morality has to do with our sense of the right and wrong. For the very practical business of healthcare, moral philosophy and applied ethics offer a language in which the moral dimension of practice can be discussed. More than this, it provides a means by which individual practitioners can examine their own (and each other's) values and moral positions against a wider intellectual context. Increasingly, clinicians have found that a relatively neglected area of moral philosophy, virtue ethics, has appeal when considering the ethical dimension of practice. Virtue ethics focusses on individual practitioners and their virtues – integrity, wisdom, kindness and so on. We will return to this. However, as the other essays in this collection demonstrate, this ethical approach is as useful to the social science researcher engaged in fieldwork as it is for the practitioner caring for patients.

Suffice to say that individual practitioners or social science researchers who want to take a closer look at integrity, and to consider the ethics of their practice, could do worse than consider the moral philosophy of virtue ethics.

ETHICAL APPROVAL AND ACCESS TO PARTICIPANTS FOR RESEARCH WORK

Ethical approval for research and access to participants can all too easily be regarded as a one-off bureaucratic exercise insofar as once access to the research participants has been secured, the degree to which the researcher must directly attend to the ethical concerns of the work for formal bureaucratic reasons lessens. This is unsurprising. Securing ethical approval is a critical part of the research proposal and, for the purposes of grant-seeking and university administration, it is necessarily bureaucratic. Whilst needing to hold to promises they have made – such as maintaining confidentiality and the like – once the work is underway, researchers may be more preoccupied with actually conducting the research in a sustainable manner, and maintaining the cooperation of their participants. Outside any particular prompt to do so, revisiting the ethical dimension of the research is not something that receives priority. Once a research project has secured ethical approval and the researchers have gained access, once 'we are in', as it were, it is understandable that the focus might shift to practical matters; to a concern for the research itself, such as ensuring continuity of access and completing the research. Of course, participants have the option of withdrawing at any point. However, a researcher who is preoccupied with completing the fieldwork and data collection is, perhaps, unlikely to check with any frequency that their participants are content to continue their involvement with the research. And 'why should they?' we might ask.

Whilst there are parallels to be drawn between health professionals and researchers in social science, when it comes to consent and ethical approval, there are differences to note. For example, if the research participant withdraws, then the researcher's work will be affected. Depending upon the nature of the research, the methods employed and the number of participants involved, this will be of greater or lesser importance. Whereas if a patient decides on the basis of information received about their treatment or surgery not to proceed – the effects on the professional are of a different nature.

Both research participants and patients should be given the right to withdraw at any time. To be blunt about it, the loss to the researcher is arguably greater when a participant withdraws from a project than the loss a clinician

experiences when a patient refuses treatment. The loss of a research participant can have significant consequences for both researcher and the particular
project they are conducting. If we take patient autonomy seriously then we
must respect the attendant right to refuse treatment, regardless of the likely
outcome in so doing. It follows that the patient who opts out of treatment cuts
the professional tie, ends the therapeutic relationship, and the responsibilities
that go with it. This does not compromise what has previously transpired.
However, in the case of the researcher, the loss of a participant usually means
the data previously collected from this participant are also lost. Therefore, the
time and effort expended by the researcher has, at worst, been wasted and, at
best, could have been better spent with other research participants.

In terms of the ethical principles to be followed, the researcher should
certainly aim to do no harm. In parallel with the situation for healthcare professionals, the principle of autonomy suggests that social scientists must also
treat the participants in the research with respect. However, when it comes to
autonomy in relation to continuing consent, we might argue less robustly. If
we adhere to the principle of respect for autonomy in a manner that is overly
strict, then we risk patronising participants. If the participants' autonomy
and their right to leave the project are stressed unduly, then it might prompt
them to withdraw. This is both problematic and self-defeating. Plainly, there
is a right to leave, but the researcher is also seeking to complete a project that
has been funded, often with public money. The matter of ongoing consent
and its management is not, then, entirely clear-cut and the integrity of the
researcher plays a part in the outcome.

Aside from the question of an over-zealous approach to consent, its ongoing nature is not straightforward. As the research progresses some participants may feel differently about it as compared to the time when they first
decided to participate. Unexpected topics and situations may be encountered,
which cause them to reconsider their involvement in the research. This poses
practical and ethical questions as to how best to proceed. Depending on the
research, participation may not be a binary choice. There may be room for
negotiation, which would lead to a mutually satisfactory solution, one that
meets the needs of the project and the participant. In other words, after ethical approval has been obtained for a research project it is important to regard
carrying out the research in an ethical way as an ongoing process. If a fair,
which is to say ethical, balance between the rights of the research participants
and the successful completion of the research project is to be achieved, then
the integrity of the researcher is vital.

Researchers therefore need to attend to ethical concerns beyond those
envisaged and answered when approval and access was gained. Once a research

project has been approved and access to the research participants gained, the main means of ensuring that the research proceeds with due regard for ethics lies with the researcher. Thus, if we are concerned with the integrity of social science research, then we also should be concerned with the integrity of social science researchers. The researcher who has integrity may have a further question to consider: namely, how to balance the need to obtain good data whilst acting in the best interests of the participants.

There is, then, a tension between the interests of the participants and the research endeavour. It prompts the questions of how to achieve a balance between these interests without compromising the aims of the research. In health and social care, professional integrity – or professionalism – is often taken to be self-explanatory. The same is true in other areas of work – civil engineers and architects are presumed to be acting with professionalism and in such a way that their work meets the relevant safety standards and, ideally, serves the best interests of the society or community that will make use of their designs.

Beyond the formulaic approach to ethics as part of the research grant approval and access process, the existence of various professional codes of practice and ethics and university research governance rules, there remain questions about how we can ensure the proper conduct of research and researchers. We are reliant upon individuals behaving well. Put in ethical terms, we are reliant on their values, their integrity and their good judgement. Presuming that researchers are not wilfully unethical, we are reliant on what it is that they consider constitutes ethically sound practice.

If we are going to take a virtue ethics approach to the professional conduct of the social science researcher, we might ask 'should ethical approval for research be regarded as a one-off exercise?' A virtuous practitioner might regard ethical approval and the consent of participants to be an ongoing business, and a continuing part of the research endeavour. In order to achieve this ethically alert approach to research, the researcher might find it useful to adopt the approach and strategies that virtue ethics offers to the professions in healthcare.

There are, of course, wider concerns related to social science research. It is not just a matter of gaining access and ethical approval at the outset of the project. A researcher who has integrity will exhibit loyalty to, or a sense of responsibly for, the project; they will want to see it through to completion. This can be difficult for contract researchers, especially for early career researchers, where the need to secure funding for their next post may compete with their existing obligations. The contract researcher needs to balance their relatively short-term responsibilities, i.e., those that they have towards their current research, with their need for job security and to maintain their employment in the medium term. This raises a number of other, wider and institutional, ethical questions. Established academics should recognise that they have responsibilities towards and for both early career researchers and longer standing contract researchers. The way in which these responsibilities are discharged is not, of course, entirely within the control of established academics. Nevertheless, the way in which they discharge these responsibilities is a matter that is closely related to their integrity, and that of the institution.

The ethical issues[1] that arise for the social science researcher have much in common with those faced by healthcare professionals. Clinicians and researchers undertaking fieldwork have duties towards the patients and participants that they encounter. Social science researchers who wish to consider the ethical dimension of practice can take inspiration from the same literature and moral theory that clinicians use in the course of their practice and their encounters with patients.

FOUR PRINCIPLES

A popular approach to healthcare ethics is via what have come to be known as the four principles, these are beneficence, non-maleficence, respect for persons (autonomy) and justice (Beauchamp & Childress, 2001). If we think of the social science researcher as a professional who undertakes work which has similarities to health or social care practice, then we have prima facie reason to think that these four basic principles might be useful. Beauchamp and Childress' four principles can serve as a useful framework to shape, or at least bring some order to, the ethical debate and help to steer a course through the complex terrain of practical ethics, enabling them to discuss the ethically problematic aspects of their work.[2]

The attraction of the four principles is that they provide a basis for practical ethical debate. Also, the approach provides an account of the various justifications for moral decisions and actions that is unrestricted by any explicit commitment to a particular moral philosophy. The four principles approach recognises that ethics is not about adopting this or that theory and disregarding others in the process of moral reasoning. It is above all a practical approach to theory.

As Beauchamp and Childress (2001, p. 397) put it:

> 'The top' (principles and theories) and 'the bottom' (cases, individual judgements) are not solely sufficient for biomedical ethics. Neither general principles nor paradigm cases have sufficient power to generate conclusions.

In other words, we need to move and work between the ethical theories and principles and the substantive details of cases if we are to arrive at a practical course of action which takes account of the moral dimension of the situation.

Gillon (1994, p. 334) makes this clear when he says that the four principles approach provides a practical way into ethics and offers:

> Elements of a common language for such ethical analysis ... Because it is not itself a theory, but instead draws on elements common to most if not all moral theories, it can function peaceably as a tool of practical ethics that may be shared by those whose theories are totally incompatible and antithetical.

MacCormick (2008) considers the issue of practical reason and the law, and does so in a context where there is a need for action to be based on good reasoning, including moral reasoning. MacCormick's central question is: 'Can reason be practical?' In a discussion of Hume's position on 'the passions', MacCormick (2008, p. 1) notes that:

> Human conduct engages both reason and emotion. Acting well and wisely means acting for good reasons, and these must fully allow for our affective as well as our intellectual nature.

Practical reasoning is as important for decisions in health and social care as it is in making legal judgements – both have moral aspects. Indeed, decisions taken on behalf of patients concerning their health and daily living needs frequently have legal dimensions. Practical reasoning has, or so the argument of this chapter goes, something to offer social science researchers when ethical questions arise in the course of their research. Practical reason is, precisely, what is required when we encounter practical problems.

VIRTUE ETHICS

Virtue ethics is a philosophical approach to morality that, in the discourse of health care ethics, has grown in popularity over the past decade or so. This could be due to the fact that, with its focus on the person as practitioner and its concerns with the virtues of individual practitioners, it is consistent with notions of professionalism that also have been a feature of contemporary debate. Virtue ethics has a rather arcane ring to it and, at first glance, it may seem to be no more than a semantic trick. Except for the focus upon what the professional ought to be like, it may seem that there is little difference between it and any other ethical code that professionals might adhere to. However, when we consider that the virtues include the integrity, competence, wisdom and kindness of the practitioner – the attributes that the virtuous practitioner is considered to have – it is hard to find fault with virtue ethics as a good starting point for a consideration of ethical concerns. With its tilt towards the nature of individual practitioner, as opposed to a focus on the role, virtue ethics concentrates the mind on the person and draws attention to the fact that it is the integrity of each individual professional upon which professional ethics depends for its success.

The focus on the professional brings us to a position where we can see that integrity has an important part to play in professional ethics, and provides a basis on which good professional judgement can be predicated. Viewed in this light, it is easy to see why virtue ethics has an appeal for healthcare professionals, and why social science researchers might also be well served by its insights. As a theory, virtue ethics lies somewhere in the middle ground between the overly subjective individual conscience theories and the more objective, abstract and less obviously practical moral theories such as utilitarianism and rights-based theories. This goes some way to explaining the popularity of virtue ethics in the field of health and may be of equal appeal for social science researchers when they are faced with similar issues in the course of their fieldwork.

It is worth pointing out that whilst in ancient Greek 'virtue' referred to an excellence or disposition character, we might now consider it to refer to a skill or a competence, or the dispositions that underlie them (Annas, 1995; Stichter, 2008). In the *Nicomachean Ethics* (Thomson, 1976), Aristotle talks of two kinds of virtues which complement each other. These are the 'intellectual' and the 'moral' virtues. Aristotle's view was that both kinds of virtues are necessary for an individual to be able to decide how to act in morally acceptable ways. The intellectual or theoretical virtues include relevant scientific knowledge, technical skill, intelligence, insight, resourcefulness, discriminatory judgement, practical wisdom and knowledge and competence for decision-making. In a healthcare context, this indicates that we should be concerned with the biomedical and psychosocial bases of the various academic and practice disciplines involved. In contrast, the relevant moral virtues have to do with the character that Aristotle thought to be necessary for reliable and effective action. The moral virtues relate to character and include honesty, courage, integrity, loyalty, justice, generosity and magnanimity. Taken in the round, Aristotle's virtues are essentially about decent behaviour wisdom and justice.[3] The only way to acquire these virtues, Aristotle thought, is through practice. As he said, 'Moral virtues, like crafts are acquired by practice and habituation'. (*Nicomachean Ethics* Book II, 1103a, p. 14-b1)

MacCormick's (2008) work on practical reason is relevant to this discussion of the professional integrity of the social science researcher. MacCormick demonstrates the links between 'feeling, judgement, decision and action'. Whilst he is discussing legal practice, his arguments can be applied to the practice of healthcare and social science research. A central question for MacCormick is, how can we judge what is best for others. He asks, 'How do we know what is right?' If respect for autonomy as a principle holds for each person, it would involve an extreme version of relativism and still remain rather too subjective to be of use in the public enterprise of social science research. Even with respect for autonomy in place, it leaves us with questions concerning trust when it comes to participation in research. We cannot know what is right for others. Yet, as we need to act and act ethically, there must be some means of discussing and arriving at judgements for action. Healthcare practitioners and social science researchers in the course of their work are in this position, namely, having to decide how to act in the best interests of others.

Kant's ([1785] 1953) work is often drawn upon in healthcare ethics. His work is wide-ranging, but it is the duty-based theory, the idea of 'respect for persons', and the 'categorical imperative' that have particular appeal for those concerned with the ethics for practice in healthcare. The same relevance of Kant's work can be seen for the social science researcher undertaking research with volunteer participants. Kant argued that people have an inherent moral worth, and for that reason alone are entitled to respect and have autonomy to get on with their lives within the norms and laws of society.

Kant's basic idea is that human beings are autonomous rational agents and should be treated as such and not, in his famous phrase, as a mere 'means to an end'. Kant's duty-based theory has it that good will come from a focus on the intention of doing one's duty. Kant's idea being that it is the intention rather than the consequences of one's actions that is important. Duty-based theory has it that doing good is the thing that settles the rightness or wrongness of an action and that this counts above the actual consequences of the action. As consequences cannot be predicted, this is not an unreasonable stance. Although one might argue that in the case of healthcare practice, and for that matter social science research, it is good outcomes not merely good intentions that are required. However, this is to miss Kant's point that doing one's duty means doing the right thing according to reasoned principles. And overall good would come from following this course of action even though we know that on occasion this may not be the case.

Virtue ethics focusses on the competence and integrity of the practitioner. MacCormick's (2008) work on practical reasoning in law and morality includes the notion of what he calls the 'Smithian categorical imperative'.

In proposing this MacCormick is seeking to produce a synthesis of Kantian and Smithian thought to, in his words, 'solve the riddle of practical reason'. Drawing on Smith's idea of the 'impartial spectator', and Kant's more objective and universal approach to the process of practical reason when faced with taking decisions in situations which have a moral dimension, MacCormick suggests a synthesis of the two. MacCormick proposes bringing the more objective ideas of Kant's categorical imperative together with Smith's emotional approach to morality. MacCormick's 'Smithian categorical imperative' is a means of reconstructing Kant's 'categorical imperative' so as to give due weight to human sentiment and emotion.

Before getting ahead of ourselves we need to take a closer look at what it is that MacCormick is seeking to achieve with his 'Smithian categorical imperative'. To do this we go back to the idea of individual conscience.

INDIVIDUAL CONSCIENCE APPROACH TO ETHICS

The behaviours of individual professionals, even though they subscribe to a professional code of ethics, will always to some extent depend upon the values and capacity for trustworthy action that each professional possesses. This is going to be true of social science researchers as well as practitioners in healthcare. Codes of ethics and professional conduct serve to ensure some consistency of behaviour by individual professionals in terms of ethics and values, and their existence provides reassurance to the public. Yet, because we must rely on the integrity of individual professionals, we are to some extent thrown back on the rather old-fashioned notion of conscience. Most people if asked about their actions in a particular situation where there is a moral choice to be made are likely to make some reference, explicitly or implicitly, to the idea of a conscience. Those with a religious belief are likely to link conscience to some divine teaching – even those with no particular religious belief may still invest their conscience with some importance in terms of the right way to behave according to a generalised view of morality and human decency when it comes to behaviour towards one another.

The linkage of conscience to a deity or some kind of natural law has its attractions when it comes to working out how to act. The idea of human beings finding their place in the natural order of the world and living accordingly goes all the way back to Aristotle. The idea is that there was a natural order, a natural law and that man, being part of it, should therefore find a place in it. It remains the case, however, that conclusions as to what constitutes good and the right thing to do will differ from professional to professional.

The individual conscience approach to ethics, aside from being a very subjective business, assumes that people have some inbuilt means of knowing what is right and wrong. The voice inside us is, of course, set within a wider social context and works according to societal ideas of what is acceptable or not. Beyond individual conscience as a means of ensuring that people behave in an acceptable way, there are accepted practices and unwritten rules which make up the normative order in society, and beyond that the rule of law and the legal system and its judgements and remedies. The inner voice that we recognise as conscience has to operate in the wider societal idea of right and wrong, so there is an understandable desire to move to a more objective approach. Kantian ethics is often looked to in health care ethics for this objectivity.

Professional integrity has much to do with conscience. Individual conscience is essentially a private matter, but the idea of conscience is public and an idea that is referred to in everyday life. Everyone knows what is meant by conscience, but what is less knowable is how it operates and how we justify what our conscience comes up with. When professionals in healthcare act, they often have to make a judgement as to what is the best course of action in a particular circumstance on behalf of a patient. Professionals have to make decisions, which they deem to be in the patient's best interests. It is not stretching the parallel with social science research too far to suggest that similar issues arise in terms of balance of good and harm – the participants' feelings and the best interests have to be taken into account in deciding how far to press for views in social research when the subject matter is sensitive or requires probing and bringing back difficult memories. Examples for healthcare practice are perhaps more readily understood, but this does not mean that the concerns are not present in social science research.

The longevity of the idea of there being a natural order and human beings having a place in it, thus producing a concept of a natural law, gives us some feel for its appeal. However, relying on conscience is a tricky matter. There is circularity in linking natural law, some higher deity, and individual conscience. If we are looking to include those who do not believe in a god, then this circularity between divine law and natural law is a problem. In a heterogeneous secular society to say this or that particular action is right because it follows the natural law, or because 'God says so' will not do for an answer. However all that may be, we arrive back at the question: 'How do we know?'

Kant's approach to ethics has clearly more objectivity about it than do the subjective individual conscience theories. Writers of texts on ethics for healthcare practice turn to his law-like approach to morality – as represented by the categorical imperative – when they are looking to move from individual conscience theory to something more objective. The 'universal categorical imperative' has about it a strong element of objectivity and justice but is not without difficulties. The basis of the universality, 'if it is right for one it has to be right for all', leaves out of the equation the question of individual circumstances, circumstances that might make one seek to modify the reasoning or indeed the conclusion during the discussion of actual cases. Nevertheless, it takes us on from the individual nature of conscience.

So, how do we know what is good for someone else? This is a difficult question to which the answer is probably 'we don't'. However, in the professional ethics of the healthcare professionals and the social science researchers this is not a useful answer. If we are interested in practical reasoning in order to work out the best action in response to a situation which requires a judgement upon which we can act, MacCormick puts it well when he says, 'But how do you know?' (2008, p. 168), 'how can you say what is good for me?'

OBJECTIVITY AND ADAM SMITH'S IDEA OF 'IMPARTIAL SPECTATOR'

Amartya Sen, in the Introduction to an edition of *The Theory of Moral Sentiments* (Smith, [1790] 2009) notes that it was Smith who was 'the pioneering analyst of the need for impartiality and universality in ethics'. Nevertheless, he points out that it is Kant who is recognised as the most influential philosopher with respect to universality through his 'categorical imperative'. Ironically, it was after reading Smith's work, with which he was much taken, that Kant modified his own objective approach. This led Kant to the view that there were two kinds of reason. The first, 'pure reason', was theoretical and concerned with knowledge and establishing of truths and facts, and was the territory of mathematics and logic. The second, 'practical reason', was about working out how to act and was relevant for morality, law, and politics. It is Kant's work on practical reason that is of interest here.

Smith's idea of the 'impartial spectator' stems from his very practical approach to understand the interaction of human beings. MacCormick (2008) explains how the 'impartial spectator' works by describing the difference in feelings of the affected and those of the more impartial spectator. He says:

> An incident that has annoyed you, who were the target of the malevolence, arouses sympathetic anger in me, not blind rage. This is a fact of which all human beings become to be aware. (MacCormick, 2008, pp. 57–58)

Smith ([1790] 2009, p. 133), in developing this theme of empathy and the workings of the 'impartial spectator', says:

> We endeavour to examine our own conduct as we imagine any other fair and impartial spectator would examine it. If, upon placing ourselves in his situation, we thoroughly enter into all the passions and motives which influenced it, we approve of it, by sympathy with the approbation of this supposed equitable judge. If otherwise, we enter into his disapprobation, and condemn it.

The following is an example from clinical practice where the individual practitioner's conscience and professional integrity are called into play; it demonstrates how the idea of 'impartial spectator' might work in practice:

> In clinical practice, deciding whether or not to report an error or omission in care is a matter of individual moral judgement. If no one other than the person concerned is aware of the omission, it is already a matter of moral judgement. For example, if a nurse fails to administer a treatment or to give medications at the correct time provided that no harm is done it might go unreported if the nurse concerned sees no wrong-doing in the situation. In plain language, less fuss would ensue if no reporting takes place.
>
> This 'least said, soonest mended' approach might appear to be a common-sense response, but the wider ramifications of such behaviour in an organisation carry consequences, moral and practical. (Melia, 2014, p. 49)

Smith's idea of an 'impartial spectator' is a practical way of trying to work out how a right-minded person would think and act. The idea of 'impartial spectator' is a way of standing back, as it were, from the situation and thinking more widely, including the consequences for other parties involved. In this example, use of the 'impartial spectator' might have led to the incident being reported.

It is to Smith's device of the 'impartial spectator' that MacCormick turns to offer some objective slant on the essentially subjective individual conscience. Following Hume, Smith sought to write philosophy without reference to or dependence on divine law and religious faith. Smith's ideas offer a means of moving away from the subjective approach to ethical debate. His work, *The Theory of Moral Sentiments* was concerned with emotions and empathy and offering a very human account of how we behave towards one another.

MacCormick (2008, p. 57) in his work *Practical Reason in Law and Morality* points to Smith's *Moral Sentiments* as a work which takes a very practical approach to the study of interaction between human beings. Smith's thesis is that as humans we are capable of reacting to the experience of others. If we see another person trip and fall, our instinct is to wince or react in some empathic way, this for Smith is evidence for, or at least demonstrates that we as humans have the capacity to feel for others. Since Smith's time research has shown that we are not the only species capable of this empathy; however, this is not the place for a discussion on the behaviour of higher mammals but it does give us pause for thought before singling out human beings for special treatment.

The point about Smith's and Hume's ideas on the capacity that humans have to feel for others, in both their fortunes and misfortunes, is that they offer it as the basis of our capacity for moral judgement. This capacity for judgement extends to our own behaviour and that of others. This involves us observing our own behaviour and that of others. Smith describes what he calls an 'impartial spectator' in his explanation of how we observe our own behaviour and judge it in much the same way as we would observe and judge that of another. In short, the idea is that we can think of an imaginary person with whom we can test our ideas out so as to check whether we are thinking along similar lines as other right-minded people might think. Smith's idea of the 'impartial spectator' is that we can stand aside from ourselves and try to see our actions, and plans for action from the perspective of another, a more objective or impartial other.

Practitioners in health and social care have published codes of conduct and ethics. These whilst offering some guidance for action serve to reassure the public that members of these professional groups – doctors, nurses, social workers, etc. will act in a fair and just manner, respecting the rights and autonomy of those for whom they care. Ethical codes can only take us so far, there is the important question of how the principles and values embodied in the code translate into practice. We are dependent upon the individual practitioner and the context in which they work. We need to remember that statements about ideals, values and how things ought to work do not make it so. We can turn to the ancient Greeks for discourse on how to lead a good life and behave well to one another, but we are reliant upon the here and now and the practice of individual professionals when it comes to the quality and integrity of practice.

SMITHIAN CATEGORICAL IMPERATIVE

MacCormick imagines Smith rethinking the impartial spectator theory to give a revised account of Kant's categorical imperative, one which would involve the way ordinary people arrive at moral judgements in the context of their interaction with others and their mutual relations. MacCormick (2008, p. 64) says that we need 'to distil a "categorical imperative" out of the materials found in Smith's argument'. MacCormick (2008, p. 64) goes on to produce what he calls a 'possible version of such a categorical imperative':

> Enter as fully as you can into the feelings of everyone directly involved in or affected by an incident or relationship, and impartially form a maxim of judgement about what is right that all could accept if they were committed to maintaining mutual beliefs setting a common standard of approval and disapproval among themselves.

MacCormick emphasises the point that we need to take account of both rational and emotional sides of human nature if we are to produce any kind of universal law of human nature. His idea is:

> to see what happens if one reconstructs a version of Kant's basic organising principle of moral thought, the 'categorical imperative' in terms that mesh with the need to give full weight to human sentiment and emotion in any judgement about how to act in human predicaments. (MacCormick, 2008, p. 2)

The 'Smithian categorical imperative' is the term coined by MacCormick for what, had they ever met, could have resulted from Kant's work influencing Smith's Theory of Moral Sentiments. MacCormick envisages the coming together of their ideas of 'categorical imperative' and 'impartial spectator thinking' in very practical terms. MacCormick (2008, p. 64) says that the 'Smithian categorical imperative'[4] 'creates a comprehensible linkage between feeling, judgement, decision and action. We start with bare feelings, we reflect, we judge, we decide, we act'.

The quality of the practice is dependent in large part on the calibre and the nature of the practitioner.

When our politicians talk of doing the right thing, it is presumed that the right thing is self-evident. If pressed for justification it becomes clear that we have a problem as a society if we are to rely on individuals doing the right thing in our best interests without knowing how the right thing is ascertained. MacCormick (2008, p. 168) brings this difficulty into sharp focus when he provides a possible answer to his own question about doing the right thing, namely, 'but how do you know?' MacCormick's suggested reply is rather waspish but carries a serious point, he says: 'How can you say what is good for me? This is just your subjective idea dressed up as objective advice.' Again it illustrates the point that we need to get beyond the individual conscience.

MacCormick's interest in linking Smith's work with the more objective Kantian categorical imperative was to understand practical reason – to make the link between feeling and action via judgement and decision. The idea being that we can bring a measure of objectivity to our individual subjective conscience. This capacity to judge our actions is an important part of professional judgement when there are moral aspects to the question. The professional with this capacity is, we can argue, demonstrating integrity. MacCormick (2008) stresses the practical nature of moral reasoning when coming to decisions to settle the matters of what constitutes lawful behaviour. The practicality transfers to healthcare practitioners and to social science researchers when they take a virtue ethics approach to being professionals with integrity.

There are times and situations when principles and guidelines only take us so far, the law in fact can only take us so far – a judgement is called for. It is in the grey areas where there are no rules, written or unwritten, on how to act, that we rely on integrity of a professional – their good nature, good sense (common sense, even) as well as their technical competence. The individual practitioner is as important as the standing of their profession here, and this is why virtue ethics might assist the practical reasoning which MacCormick (2008) describes.

MacCormick (2008, p. 57) says that if we are looking for a way into morality that is less abstract than that offered by Kant, then Smith's theory of Moral Sentiment is a good starting point. We can add to this virtue ethics and the idea of virtuous practitioner. This term does not have a particularly contemporary ring to it in the sound bite world of 21st-century social science research, but that may be no bad thing.

CONCLUSION

In conclusion, it is worth remembering that the virtuous practitioner needs to make judgements and choices about courses of action, and that this involves practical reasoning. To do this, practitioners must have integrity and be able to demonstrate their integrity. Trustworthiness is an important matter here. The virtuous practitioner who has integrity will be concerned not only to gain the trust of others but also to be trustworthy. O'Neill (2002, p. 4) says:

> Each of us and every profession and every institution needs trust. We need it because we have to be able to rely on others acting as they say they will, and because we need others to accept that we will act as we say we will.

Amid all the organisational safeguards and commitment to governance and ethical codes when it comes to behaving with integrity, we are ultimately reliant upon decent behaviour, virtue if you like, of the professionals involved. Smith's and Hume's talk of the passions may sound rather exotic to our 21st-century ears, but they both had a point. In any human endeavour we are what we are and it is important to take account of both the ordered rational sides of our nature and the emotions which make human interaction what it is.

So, can virtue ethics help? Well, up to a point. It is useful to have the focus on the individual practitioner and to highlight integrity as one of the important virtues for practice. If it is taken too literally, and adopted formu-laically, the virtue ethics approach can be no better than a tick box approach to the complex matter of acting in the best interests of others. Remembering that the whole business of virtue ethics is seriously practical, with decisions for action being the goal, it is the focus on virtues and competencies that is as important as anything else. Participants in social science research and the public recipients of the findings need to be able to rely on the professional integrity of the researcher.

As research and clinical practice become ever closer in a joint venture to improve patient care, it is important that we keep up with these changes in terms of research ethics and governance. It may well be that virtue ethics has a role to play in this enterprise.

NOTES

1. "Issue" in this paper carries the long-standing meaning of a topic for discussion and does not equate to "problem." An issue is a neutral term used to describe matters worthy of discussion, which may or may not be problematic. At times I use "matters" or "concerns" instead of "issues" to avoid confusion for those who equate "issue" with "problem."

2. For further discussion of this point see Melia (2014, Chap. 2) and Beauchamp and Childress (2001). And for many challenges to this point, see Volume 1 in the pre-sent "Advances" series.

3. I discuss these points in more detail in my *Ethics for nursing and healthcare prac-tice* (Melia, 2014, Chap. 9).

4. Kant was impressed by Smith's work; however, Smith was unaware of Kant's work.

REFERENCES

Annas, J. (1995). Virtue as a skill. *International Journal of Philosophical Studies*, 3(2), 227–243.

Beauchamp, T. M., & Childress, J. C. (2001). *Principles of biomedical ethics* (5th ed.). Oxford: Oxford University Press.

Freidson, E. (1970). *Profession of medicine a study of the sociology of applied knowledge.* New York, NY: Dodd Mead and Co.

Gillon, R. (1994). The four principles revisited: A reappraisal. In R. Gillon & A. Lloyd (Eds.), *Principles of health care ethics* (p. 334). Chichester: Wiley.

Hume, D. ([1777] 1978). In L. A. Selby-Bigge & P. H. Nidditch (Eds.), *A treatise of human nature* (2nd ed.). Oxford: Clarendon Press.

Kant, I. ([1785] 1953). *Groundwork of the metaphysic of morals* (H. Paton, Trans.). London: Hutchinson.

MacCormick, N. (2008). *Practical reason in law and morality.* Oxford: Oxford University Press.

Melia, K. (2014). *Ethics for nursing and healthcare practice.* London: Sage.

O'Neill, O. (2002). *A question of trust: The BBC Reith Lectures 2002.* Cambridge: Cambridge University Press.

Smith, A. ([1790] 2009). In R. P. Hanley (Ed.). *The theory of moral sentiments* (6th ed. with notes). London: Penguin.

Stichter, M. (2008). The skill of virtue. *Philosophy in the Contemporary World, 14*(2), 39–49.

Thomson, J. A. K. (1976). *The ethics of Aristotle – The Nicomachean ethics.* Harmondsworth: Penguin.

SECTION 2

VIRTUE AND THE REVIEW/ GOVERNANCE OF SOCIAL SCIENCE RESEARCH

CHAPTER 5

VIRTUE ETHICS IN THE PRACTICE AND REVIEW OF SOCIAL SCIENCE RESEARCH: THE VIRTUOUS ETHICS COMMITTEE

David Carpenter

ABSTRACT

In this chapter I build upon the case I argued in Volume 1 of this series (Carpenter, D. (2016). The quest for generic ethical principles in social science research. In R. Iphofen (Ed.), Advances in research ethics and integrity *(Vol. 1, pp. 3–18). Bingley: Emerald). There I established arguments for eschewing principlism and other well-established theories of practical ethics, such as deontology and consequentialism, in favour of virtue ethics. I drew on the work of Macfarlane (2009, 2010) in making a case for virtuous researcher and virtuous research. In this chapter, I draw attention to the role and conduct of ethics committees in reviewing research. If we are to consider the ethics of research and researchers, then we might also consider the ethics of reviewing and reviewers. Whilst there is an abundance of codes and similar documents aimed at guiding research conduct, there is relatively little to guide ethics committees and their members. Given the argument that a virtue ethics approach might help committees evaluate the ethics of*

Virtue Ethics in the Conduct and Governance of Social Science Research
Advances in Research Ethics and Integrity, Volume 3, 105–125
ISSN: 2398-6018/doi:10.1108/S2398-601820180000003006

proposed research and researchers, it could equally be the case that virtue ethics could be useful when thinking about the work of committees and ethics review. In this chapter I attempt to relocate and develop Macfarlane's work by examining its application to the work of ethics committees and the virtues of their members. In particular, I will consider the virtues that reviewers should exhibit or demonstrate when reviewing research, and what we might take as the telos of ethics committees.

Keywords: Virtue ethics; research ethics; social sciences; ethical review; research ethics committees

INTRODUCTION

The main aim of this chapter is to argue a case for practical ethical guidance for the members of research ethics committees. Ethics committees aim to review the ethics of proposed research and, perhaps to a lesser extent, ethical practice(s) of researchers, including their ethical dispositions and motives. Given the concerns some have raised about the consequences of institutionalised ethical review one key question we might consider is whether ethics committee members conduct their reviews ethically and whether they demonstrate necessary ethical dispositions and motives. Doing so situates the conduct of ethics committees and the nature of review within the field of research ethics alongside the ethical design and conduct of research. In simple terms, the review of research must be ethical.

CRITICISMS OF ETHICS COMMITTEES

It is fair to observe that research ethics committees receive a fair amount of criticism, in particular they are often seen as obstructive, as a barrier to research or a block to academic freedom (van den Hoonaard, 2011). It is also entirely possible that ethics review might serve to block research that is not only ethically defensible but also ethically desirable. Problematic examples include dogmatic adherence to ideas, such as concluding that all non-consensual research is unethical, being paternalistic and tending towards a position which prioritises respect for autonomy above most other considerations, including the common good. This position is evidenced by preoccupation with individual consent and confidentiality. The common good is subordinated to the interests of individuals and grounds, for breach of confidence is typically limited to the prevention of harm rather than gaining some wider social benefit. A general aversion to risk is also commonly observed (Hedgecoe, 2016). Other frequent criticisms include inappropriately focusing on matters of science, methodology and research design whilst, paradoxically, rarely understanding the key scientific and methodological issues. One of the biggest challenges to research ethics committees is lack of consistency both within and between committees; decisions are sometimes seen as arbitrary and idiosyncratic. Many committees are accused of hiding behind matters of law and policy rather than fully engaging with ethical review; in this regard their task inevitably shifts from ethics to regulation, with compliance becoming their overriding concern. It is certainly not unusual for ethics committees to spend inordinate lengths of time identifying errors of spelling, grammar and syntax, matters which rarely have any direct ethical significance, yet these are reported back to researchers as quasi-ethical issues (Stark, 2012).

Attempts to tackle these problems have included encouragement of the use of more systematic approaches to ethical review, enabling committees to provide more defensible opinions. These attempts include the following:

- Reference to various codes, declarations and similar documents setting out the ethical boundaries of research; although variable, these documents tend to focus on specific examples of misconduct or, at least, allude to them. They rarely set out positive moral imperatives. Perhaps with the exception of the Declaration of Helsinki (World Medical Authority, 2013), which has very limited application in social research, ethics committees rarely refer to these documents in their deliberations. The focus of many of these documents tends to be 'protection' of research participants rather than the promotion of research, which might benefit individuals as well as broader society.
- The adoption of a particular normative theoretical position – most commonly principlism but consequentialism and deontology have had some application. It is fair to observe that, in practice, most ethics committees do not overtly review research from any particular theoretical position.
- The use of standardised reviewer forms referring their users to key ethical domains and encouraging responses accordingly. For example, the UK Health Research Authority (HRA) provides ethics committees with documents identifying ethical domains to consider in the course of review. These domains are derived from the UK Health Departments' (2011) governance arrangements for research ethics committees. These domains comprise scientific design and conduct of the study; recruitment of research participants; care and protection of research participants; protection of research

participants' confidentiality; informed consent process; and community considerations. It is fair to observe that there is a tendency for these to be used in the assurance of legal and policy compliance rather than ethics evaluation.

The application of these approaches focuses the reviewers' attentions on the proposal under consideration and, sometimes, the likely conduct of the researcher. There is little consideration of the ethical conduct of the review, approaches to it and what might be used to ethically guide the review process itself.

Key questions relate to the roles of ethics committees; the following are all defensible and not necessarily mutually exclusive:

1. Should ethics committees undertake a skilful analysis of a research protocol by considering its conformity to an agreed code, declaration, treaty or similar document?
2. Should ethics committees analyse research protocols by adopting an agreed normative ethical position or theory?
3. Should ethics committees be guided by checklists or algorithms in systematically reviewing a research proposal?
4. Should ethics committees endeavour to reflect upon members' emotional reactions to proposed research, in pursuit of a 'middle ground', being mindful of the disposition of the committee and the underlying virtues revealed in that pursuit? Essentially, should members of ethics committees be reflecting on their own moral conduct as evidenced in their review of a proposal?

ADDRESSING THE KEY QUESTIONS

The first question – whether members of ethics committees should undertake a skilful analysis of a research protocol by considering its conformity to an agreed code, declaration, treaty or similar document – was alluded to, although probably not explicitly addressed, in the Academy of Social Sciences' (AcSS) symposium which took place in 2013. At this event the primary endeavour was to explore the idea of there being some common principles, which might be shared by the learned societies in the AcSS. Whilst this was partly successful, there was, unsurprisingly, no obvious prospect of all the individual codes being replaced with a single document. Furthermore, the question regarding the usefulness of codes as guides to ethics review was not really addressed. In many years of experience as a member and chair of several ethics committees, I have never witnessed the systematic application of a code in the course of review. Reasons for this are numerous and include the simple observation that most codes are written from the perspective of the researcher or the specific discipline with which they identify. It might also be argued that conformity to a code is a matter for the researcher and in itself is no guarantee that the proposed research is, indeed, ethical. Members of ethics committees might agree that a particular proposal, whilst not in breach of a code, raises significant ethical concerns; those concerns cannot always be articulated by reference to the code. If one takes the view that the primary function of a code is to protect the good standing of the profession or academic discipline responsible for its promulgation, then it is a moot point whether members of ethics committees should have expertise in the relevant discipline and knowledge of its internal ethical standards. Furthermore, that there is broad agreement on the value of lay members – presumably because they are seen as able to make independent judgements, free from any sort of professional code and the discipline it reflects – then it would seem that the idea of internal ethical standards is itself ethically questionable. An ethics committee might be able test conformity or compliance by juxtaposing a relevant code and the proposal under review, but this would not be sufficient to ensure its morality – more significantly, the ethics committee can hardly be said to have undertaken an *ethical review* or, indeed, have undertaken a *review ethically.* Rather than considering ethical issues arising from an application, the committee will have primarily considered its conformity with particular code(s). Testing conformity is an empirical exercise; it will not lead to any consideration of the moral conduct of members of the ethics committee, either collectively or individually. Briefly, the use of codes as reviewing tools is neither necessary nor sufficient as an aid to ethical review.

Turning to the second question – whether members should analyse research protocols by adopting an agreed normative ethical position – it is useful to briefly summarise and offer a critique of the main theories which might be used to guide ethical review; starting with principlism.

Principlism is based on the idea that there are foundational ethical principles, which, in themselves, do not stand in need of any further ethical defence or analysis. There is some sort of implicit understanding that they are universal and can be known a priori, rather like the rights which result from rationalist enquiry. Rights can be derived by reason alone, typically reflecting on what it is to be human and reasons why people are deserving of some sort of moral respect; rights of this nature can be contrasted with those granted by institutions such as the state; for example, rights granted by law. A simple illustration makes this contrast clear. Reason would suggest that people have a prima facie right not to be killed; this might be seen as a universal, inalienable, human right. A right of this nature reflects the intrinsic value of human life. A state might grant a right not to be killed in the form of homicide law, but, arguably, this would be secondary to the universal inalienable right. Perhaps, the biggest contrast is that inalienable rights are just that, they cannot be taken away, whereas rights granted by institutions provide no such security. Principles might be seen in similar light; goods-in-themselves, knowable a priori, by reason alone and whilst inalienability might not be an apt description, they are seen, perhaps as a matter of logical necessity, as incontrovertible. Ethical principles have been adopted by professional institutions, academic disciplines and learned societies as though they sit outside of them, when, in reality, they might well have been constructed by them.

Principles are broadly used as 'headings' which collectively comprise a framework for ethical analysis; the focus of analysis can extend from the design of research to its methodology. In the context of ethics, review principles may be used as benchmarks in the course of a front-loaded review. Less consideration is given to their application in the execution of research or to the ethical conduct of researchers in the course of research. A common approach finds researchers defending their plans by reference to principles and ethics committees adopting similar principles in evaluating research; a tempting, but somewhat cynical conclusion, is that researchers write material using the language ethics committees' wish to read and ethics committees interpret this positively as attention to ethical detail. Research is judged as good or ethically sound insofar as it embraces the relevant principles. This leaves little room for consideration of the role of principles in researcher conduct and, more importantly, their place in the research, which has a *prima facie* objective of achieving some social good as an end point. Of course, not all social 'research' has such an objective; some is theoretical and might have no immediate social impact – in which case principles are redundant. Other examples of research, where the conduct of the researcher is the focus of ethical consideration, rather than some sort of predetermined design, based on principles, aim to achieve significant social impact; here, again, principles are at least partly redundant. There are numerous examples of participatory action research which sets out to achieve some social good as its primary objective; that objective might be self-evident, requiring no reference to any principles.

Principlism as a theory and a tool for ethical analysis was developed by Beauchamp and Childress and used to structure their text *Principles of Biomedical Ethics,* now in its sixth edition (2009). The four principles are beneficence, non-maleficence, respect for autonomy and justice (distributive). Reference to the four principles is relatively commonplace, particularly in biomedical contexts. However, their application is more widespread, particularly the emphasis on respect for autonomy. This emphasis reflects underlying individualism, upon which the principles rest. Given this underlying individualism, their widespread application in social science is questionable. Nevertheless, researchers often frame their proposals accordingly and ethics committees might check compliance (perhaps, in contrast with ethical evaluation) by using the same four headings. The use of the principles as a guide to ethical review is, perhaps, even more questionable, although the UK Association for Research Ethics (AfRE, 2013) has made some advances in this endeavour – discussed in more detail below. It should be noted, however, that ethical principles designed to be applied in the context of professional relationships are unlikely to be pertinent to the ethical review of social research.

Beauchamp and Childress have many critics. Among the most outspoken is Gert (1997) and, more recently, Hanson (2009, p. 77), who highlights the limitations of the principles in a secular, pluralistic society. The main objections are summarised by Gert (1997):

> The dominant view in question we have labelled 'principlism'. It is characterized by its citing of four principles which constitute the core of its account of biomedical ethics: beneficence, autonomy, nonmaleficence, and justice. So entrenched is this 'theory' that clinical moral problems are often grouped (for conferences, papers, and books) according to which principle is deemed most relevant and necessary for solving them. It has become fashionable and customary to cite one or another of these principles as the key for resolving a particular biomedical ethical problem. Throughout much of the biomedical ethical literature, authors seem to believe that they have brought theory to bear on the problem before them insofar as they have mentioned one or more of the principles. Thus, not only do the principles presumably lead to acceptable solutions but they are also treated by many as the ultimate grounds of appeal.

Whilst reference to these principles in the course of ethical review is relatively commonplace, in my experience of UK research ethics committees, I have never witnessed any systematic application of them in structuring an ethics review and providing clear feedback to applicants. Neither has Stark (2012) in writing about the US experience. Arguably, they are often applied in justifying the intuitions of members of a committee rather than being used to identify specific ethical concerns. A committee might, for example, conclude that deception used in the course of research is a violation of autonomy. The label is simply applied post ante – adding nothing of substance to the original intuitions of the committee. In brief, members of the committee might see deception as wrong for a range of fundamental moral reasons but feel obliged to use a label raising the matter of autonomy.

Clearly, the application of principles as regulatory constraints raises at least a possibility of, paradoxically, lost opportunities to conduct research ethically and to be ethically responsive in particular situations. A cursory reflection on the nature of ethnography provides a useful illustration of this point. Just as the research itself is necessarily emergent and iterative, so too will be matters of ethics; the ethics of research of this nature cannot and should not be regulated by reference to an a priori framework of principles, although continuous reflection upon and application of a set of principles might well ensure the overall ethical optimisation of a project.

Arguably, principles relating to the conduct of a research ethics committee might have some place in an endeavour to ensure that it conducts ethics' reviews ethically. There is one clear example of such a set of principles serving this purpose. AfRE (2013) has produced a set of principles which might be viewed as underpinning ethical research. These principles are clearly derived from those identified by Beauchamp and Childress and they have much in common with other sets of principles promulgated by learned societies and research councils. The principles of autonomy, beneficence, non-maleficence, confidentiality and integrity are, perhaps confusingly, described as 'underpinning the ethics review of research' (AfRE, 2013). Whilst they might be used in such a context, I think it no more likely that ethics committees will refer to these in the course of ethical review than any other set of principles. AfRE (2013) has, however, listed principles of governance arrangements: independence, competence, facilitation and openness. These principles might well be useful in the context of ethics review; members of ethics committees should be mindful of them when conducting ethical reviews. Processes for ethical review of research should be part of research governance frameworks; a governance framework adopting the principles stated above should include a requirement that members of ethics committees subscribe to them. Whilst the independence and competence of an ethics committee might be seen as a matter of governance – reflected in its constitution – being open and facilitative refers to the manner in which ethics review is conducted. The adoption of these two principles is a step towards reviewing not only just the ethics of a research protocol, but also doing so ethically.

The application of theories, including consequentialism and deontology, in the context of the ethical review of research, raises further problems. In the case of the former, morality is measured by the outcomes of actions; contemporary accounts of utilitarianism (a form of consequentialism) posit preference satisfactions (Singer (2011) is probably the best known exponent) as an objective measure of morality. An action (we could substitute 'study') is moral insofar as it brings about the greatest net balance of number of preference satisfactions (or the least number of expressions of dissatisfaction) from those affected by it. Again, I have never witnessed any systematic application of this form of consequentialism in the course of ethics review, although there is evidence of it coming into play when considering matters such as risk, which involves the assessment of potential harms and benefits, or the consideration of cost-benefit ratios. This application is, however, often simplistic; ethics committees are often content with a positive balance as opposed to adopting a wider application of the theory. Consequentialism requires the adoption of *the* action that maximises utility across society as a whole. Ethics committees typically focus review of research in terms of its impact on individuals; they do not normally consider implications for wider society. Nevertheless, it would be very unusual for an ethics committee to readily accept any situation resulting in significant disadvantage to the few, no matter how great the benefit to the many. Indeed, one might think that part of the *raison d'être* of ethics committees is to protect research participants from harm caused by scientists who believe they are acting for the greater good or the greater benefit of humankind as whole – in effect having already conducted their own cost-benefit analyses.

Consequentialism can be a useful guide to practical moral conduct in everyday life; its application in the context of research and the ethical review of research is far more problematic. In everyday life, harm to others is often avoidable and even if not so, it can readily be minimised. In research, harm is often unavoidable and can only be justified on the ground of some greater benefit to the research participant, or, more contentiously, the group they might be seen to represent. Participation in research might confer no benefit; the best that might be anticipated is the avoidance of unanticipated harms – harms (intended and anticipated as well as unanticipated) might be accrued and there might be no compensatory benefit. It might also be argued that actions subjected to consequentialist analysis in everyday life are not normally compromised by competing imperatives; *the* moral action determined by consequentialist reasoning might be challenged as a result of competing desires and self-interest but it remains clear even if uncomfortable. The researcher has a potentially competing agenda; determined by the research objectives, this will inevitably compromise his/her everyday consequentialist imperative to maximise utility.

Consequentialism might have a place in ethical review of research, albeit tacitly, and taking account of the caveats identified in the foregoing discussion. However, there is no evidence of its application to the ethical conduct of ethics committees. To what extent do ethics committees reflect on their opinions, considering their consequences to all who might be affected by them? There is certainly some evidence that, to a limited extent, they do. Most ethics committees are mindful of precedent and the need for consistency in their decision-taking. If all ethics committees (and I appreciate that this is unlikely) were to adopt a strict consequentialist position in undertaking their reviews, it would follow that opinions, regardless of the locality of the ethics committees, would be consistent. There may, however, be a tendency to follow local precedents (Stark, 2012), either in terms of limiting analyses to the effects of research on a local population or merely following precedent set as a result of previous ethical opinions.

Deontology is frequently contrasted with consequentialism in that it relates the morality of an action to the duties of the moral agent rather than the consequences of the act. Consequentialism is easily often criticised on the ground that it could be used to support significant degrees of harm to minorities as long as an action results in the maximisation of benefit for a majority. This would obviously be problematic in the case of research and it would run counter to the foundations of research ethics established following the atrocities of Nazi Germany. Deontology is equally criticised on the ground that unwavering adherence to duty could nevertheless lead to significant harm to many as a result; for example, it is not difficult to envisage circumstances when a refusal to lie could have devastating consequences. Notwithstanding the differences in the approach that each take, there is no necessary conflict in the outcomes of moral analyses drawing on the respective theories. For example, in most situations telling lies leads to harmful consequences, so should be avoided; similarly, a duty to not lie generally results in the best consequences. Kantianism in the form of categorical imperative is probably the best example of deontology. The categorical imperative demands that we *act only on that maxim that we can, at the same time, will to be a universal law.*

In simple terms, it is the golden rule – do as you would be done by. An underlying imperative of universalisability strictly implies that an action is right insofar as the moral agent would be content with others behaving similarly in relevantly similar circumstances. The demands of universalisability and the derived duty to treat people as ends in themselves rather than means to ends result in a shift from a focus on the moral agent to the social context in which he acts. At first glance it might be suggested that a strict application of Kantianism would rule out research in several disciplines, basically those where research participants (perhaps 'subjects' would be a more apt term here) take part in research where the primary aim is knowledge that would benefit others; they would be being used as a means to an end. This is reflected in the well-accepted position that the interests of science and wider society should never take precedence over the fundamental rights of any individual. On further analysis, however, this, quite rightly, only rules out involuntary or non-voluntary (lacking the capacity to consent) engagement of research subjects. Voluntary, altruistic participation in research where there is unlikely to be any personal benefit would meet the demands of the categorical imperative; arguably, any participating person would not be being used as a means to an end. Perhaps more importantly, such a participant would be satisfying the categorical imperative in that he or she would wish others to behave similarly.

Whilst there is no evidence of systematic application of deontology as a guide to ethical review, it is reflected in some typical preoccupations of ethics committees, for example, duties to respect privacy and an overriding respect for persons. Furthermore, there is some evidence of concerns for treating others as one would wish to be treated; members of ethics committees often attempt to empathise with potential research participants. It is not unusual for committee members to ask the question: 'would I participate in this study?' Drawing on admittedly anecdotal evidence, the most common response is 'No', even though a favourable ethical opinion might be given. At first glance this seems duplicitous; however, this is to misunderstand deontology. The issue is not concerned with participation itself, it is concerned with the opportunity to make a choice. The fact that members would not choose to participate themselves, should drive an imperative to ensure that potential participants are given a free choice – that is to treat others as one would wish to be treated. Underlying this analysis is the Kantian notion of rational autonomy; respect for persons lies in recognising the capacity they have to make moral decisions. Ethics committees should ensure that free choice is never obstructed.

Ethics committees are often exercised by the issue of autonomy but it is frequently misunderstood. Respect for autonomy does not necessarily require all participants to be granted unrestricted choices nor does it require that explicit consent is sought in all circumstances. Sometimes inclusion criteria will exclude some participants who would like to join a study but the choice to do so has been denied; this does not compromise autonomy. Here the simple issue is that no choice is available; respect for autonomy requires acceptance of available choices. Autonomy is compromised when an individual's freedom of thought, will, or action is obstructed. It is not surprising that ethics committees show concern about studies involving deception, given that the aforementioned freedoms will be obstructed. In practice ethics committees will look for appropriate debriefing which will result in those freedoms being restored if an opportunity to withdraw data is provided. It can also be reasoned that there may be some circumstances where it is defensible not to seek consent if freedoms are not obstructed if it is not sought. It might also be the case that provision of information, in the course of seeking consent, could result in such significant distress that freedoms are obstructed. Deliberately withholding information might be argued as paternalistic, but paternalism typically entails denial of choice when it might be assumed that it could be exercised. Somewhat paradoxically, there might be situations where information could compromise the capacity to make a choice. The foregoing discussion and examples suggest that ethics committees do use, or at least make reference to deontological reasoning in their deliberations – albeit often unwittingly.

Turning to the matter of checklists and algorithms: Checklists in various forms have been developed largely in the pursuit of consistency in ethical review. I gave an example of the one provided by the UK HRA earlier. Checklists are useful in identifying key aspects (sometimes referred to as 'domains') of research which might give rise to ethical concerns; there are, however, limitations to their use. Checklist items often inspire discussion but they rarely help in guiding ethically defensible decisions.

My final question was: Should ethics committees endeavour to reflect upon members' emotional reactions to proposed research in pursuit of a 'middle ground', being mindful of the disposition of the committee and the underlying virtues revealed in that pursuit? Essentially, should members of ethics committees be reflecting on their own moral conduct as evidenced in their review of a proposal?

The question invites an answer drawing upon Aristotelian virtue ethics. Virtue ethics raises the importance of the development of wisdom and, relatedly, virtue. Virtues are dispositions; reflecting the character of a possessor, they are deeply entrenched within the individual, part of their being. According to Aristotle (1955), virtues are acquired through a process of habituation or socialisation, but they can be further developed through the exercise of our faculty for practical reason or *phronesis*. Living a life of virtue requires continual striving, recognising our perfectibility and aiming for moral excellence. Aristotle's starting question related to what might comprise the 'good life'; the answer was derived from the identification of the purpose of life – its *telos,* which he concluded to be *eudaimonia*. Eudaimonia is not easily translated, but it reflects the contentment associated with a life of contemplation, growing wisdom and the development of virtue. In general terms it can be seen as flourishing as a human being; the fulfilment of our *telos* means that we will flourish as human beings. The pursuit of virtue moves through stages. Initially, it is not much more than the copying of others' acts but gradually an understanding of why those acts are virtuous emerges, as a result of continuous reflection and contemplation. Modern understandings of 'virtuous' suggest comparisons with others, typically being 'better than'. The Aristotelian concept of virtuousness is rather different; being virtuous is to adopt a way of understanding, hence its association with wisdom.

The virtues are identified through a mechanism known as the doctrine of the mean. Spheres of action or feelings are established and then the vices of excess and deficiency described; the requisite virtue is seen as a midpoint between the vices. A fairly typical example is reproduced on the following page.

ARISTOTLE'S ETHICS

Table of Virtues and Vices.

Sphere of Action or Feeling	Excess	Mean	Deficiency
Fear and confidence	Rashness	Courage	Cowardice
Pleasure and pain	Licentiousness/ self-indulgence	Temperance	Insensibility
Getting and spending (minor)	Prodigality	Liberality	Illiberality/meanness
Getting and spending (major)	Vulgarity/ tastelessness	Magnificence	Pettiness/stinginess
Honour and dishonour (major)	Vanity	Magnanimity	Pusillanimity
Honour and dishonour (minor)	Ambition/empty vanity	Proper ambition/pride	Unambitiousness/ undue humility
Anger	Irascibility	Patience/good temper	Lack of spirit/ unirascibility
Self-expression	Boastfulness	Truthfulness	Understatement/mock modesty
Conversation	Buffoonery	Wittiness	Boorishness
Social conduct	Obsequiousness	Friendliness	Cantankerousness
Shame	Shyness	Modesty	Shamelessness
Indignation	Envy	Righteous indignation	Malicious enjoyment/ spitefulness

Virtues might be understood as certain dispositions or characteristics. It is not difficult to consider the dispositions of ethics committee members and how they collectively contribute to the general disposition of the committee as a whole. The idea of the virtuous committee, insofar as virtue is evidenced by its reactions to researchers and their research, is relatively straightforward; clearly, some committees more readily display the virtues, identified above, than others. It is equally straightforward to consider the possibility of these virtues being acquired over time, through processes of contemplation and wise reflection – assuming reasonable continuity of membership. Ethics committees certainly have reputations – good and bad – and this is apparent when considering national networks such as that provided by the UK HRA. It might be posited that reputation is at least partly established with some reference to virtues and vices – although this is rarely explicit.

The matter of actual review is quite distinct from that of the general disposition of a committee, as outlined above. Practical guidance encompassing the essential elements of a virtuous review might be adapted from Macfarlane's (2009) work, which focuses on researchers and the nature of research. He constructs a framework identifying phases of research enquiry and associated activity:

Research Phase.

Phase	Meaning
Framing	Questions, problems, hypotheses, issues, projects and proposals
Negotiating	Access, consent, permission, time and support
Generating	Data, materials, ideas and inspiration
Creating	Results, interpretations, models, concepts, theories, critiques, designs and artefacts
Disseminating	Through publication, exhibition and performance
Reflecting	On epistemological and personal learning

An ethics committee could adopt a similar approach, identifying practical steps, in considering research in terms of its prospective phases and the meanings of each of those phases. It is noteworthy that Macfarlane's 'meanings' resonate with the domains identified in typical checklists and reviewing tools, such as the one provided by the UK HRA as discussed earlier. In this respect it might be argued that the above table is little more than a checklist framework. Alternatively, an ethics committee might consider phases of ethics review, seeking associated meanings, thus structuring its review; I posit a very tentative explication as follows:

Reviewing Phases.

Phase	Meaning
Understanding	Research rationale, primary and secondary objectives, methods and design
Empathising	With researcher, participants, sponsors, funders, peers and supervisors
Focussing	On worthwhileness, benefits and burdens, risks, researcher consideration of participants and impact/wider benefits
Clarifying	Key ethical issues, researcher intentions, researcher skills, abilities and experience
Deliberating	To find committee consensus and identify significant ethical issues
Concluding	By arriving at an opinion and establishing clear reasons to support opinion
Reflecting	On the decision and process, consistency with other decisions

Each phase can be viewed as a sphere of action, in an Aristotelian sense. Furthermore, a well-chaired review could be explicitly structured following the phases posited above. What are the virtues associated with each phase? Again, Macfarlane's work can be adapted; he undertakes an Aristotelian analysis to determine the virtues demanded in each phase of the research:

The Virtues and Vices of Research (Macfarlane, 2009).

Phase	Vice (deficit)	Virtue	Vice (excess)
Framing	Cowardice	*Courage*	Recklessness
Negotiating	Manipulativeness	*Respectfulness*	Partiality
Generating	Laziness	*Resoluteness*	Inflexibility
Creating	Concealment	*Sincerity*	Exaggeration
Disseminating	Boastfulness	*Humility*	Timidity
Reflecting	Dogmatism	*Reflexivity*	Indecisiveness

This further analysis adds an important dimension to what would otherwise be a checklist based on typical phases of research, from conception to dissemination. It is not unusual for ethics committees to use the language of virtues in their deliberations and conclusions, but I have never witnessed any formally structured review, starting from the perspective of the researcher's virtues or vices. It would be interesting to consider an ethics committee starting a discussion from the perspective of, for example, the respectfulness of the researcher; this might be more fruitful than the common practice of focusing on content of documents themselves rather than what it reflects in terms of the disposition of the researcher. Alternatively, or perhaps additionally, an ethics committee might identify virtues in relation to the phases of review, again this is a very tentative suggestion:

The Virtues and Vices of Ethical Review.

Phase	Vice (deficit)	Virtue	Vice (excess)
Understanding	Ignorance	*Intelligence*	Ostentatiousness
Empathising	Inconsiderateness	*Sensitivity*	Emotionality
Focusing	Distractibility	*Discernment*	Narrow-mindedness
Clarifying	Vagueness	*Perspicacity*	Punctiliousness
Deliberating	Self-absorption	*Cooperation*	Collusion
Concluding	Aberrance	*Reasonableness*	Pedantry
Reflecting	Inconsistency	*Reflexivity*	Rigidness

Having identified the virtues required for the ethical review of research, the practical question of how they might be acquired and developed needs to be addressed. As noted earlier, virtues are not simply acquired, they have to be lived out through processes of continual striving, recognising perfectibility and aiming for moral excellence. Again, Macfarlane's work can be adapted. He takes each of the virtues sought in researchers and elaborates further in describing how they might be lived out:

Living Out Research Virtues (Macfarlane, 2010).

Courage
• Seeking to challenge one's own presuppositions or conventional wisdom.
• Developing a project that might not necessarily attract funding or represent a 'fashionable' topic.
• Pursuing a line of research without undue regard to career and other financial imperatives.
• Freely admitting when research does not go to plan or when you feel your previous research was factually or conceptually mistaken.

Respectfulness
• Being respectful to others, including vulnerable individuals and communities.
• Being aware of the temptation to take advantage of organisational, social, or intellectual power over others.
• Taking care not to cede too much power to others who may wish to distort the research process for their own ends.

Resoluteness
• Being transparent about circumstances when the extent of data collection or creative endeavour has been compromised from original intentions.
• Being aware of the temptation to start analysing data or other results before a representative sample or case study has been completed.

Sincerity
• Ensuring that the results of research are based on an accurate representation of all the relevant information collected.
• Resisting overt or covert pressure from a powerful sponsor or stakeholder to skew results to meet their needs or expectations.
• Being aware of the temptation to conceal or exaggerate results in order to gain some advantage, either materially and/or to reputation.

Humility
• Fully acknowledging one's intellectual debt to others.
• Ensuring all research partners are fairly represented in being accorded publication credit corresponding with their relative contribution.
• Inviting others to challenge your own thinking and/or results.

Reflexivity
• Being self-critical about one's own research findings or personal performance as a researcher.

In similar vein, the virtues required of ethics committees can be elaborated upon in demonstrating how they might be evidenced in its reviewing activities:

Living Out Research Ethical Review Virtues.

Intelligence
- Trying to understand chosen research designs and methodologies.
- Seeking advice from/within the committee and beyond in endeavouring to improve understanding.
- Cultivating wisdom through experience.
- Admitting limitations of knowledge.

Sensitivity
- Being respectful to researchers, their peers, mentors, supervisors, and supporters.
- Trying to understand the researcher's motivations and goals.
- Endeavouring to share the researcher's enthusiasm.
- Being aware of personal prejudice.
- Trying to empathise with research participants.

Discernment
- Careful analysis of the impact of the research – its general worthwhileness.
- Balancing of risks against benefits.
- Putting research into perspective by focusing on key aspects of context.
- Focusing on key ethical issues.
- Avoidance of paternalism.
- Endeavouring to not be distracted by trivial issues.

Perspicacity
- Seeking clarity.
- Keeping a sharp focus on key issues.
- Staying sharp-witted.
- Avoiding being 'bogged down' by detail.
- Staying flexible and open to new ideas.

Cooperation
- Constant listening.
- Searching for common ground.
- Being willing to challenge.

Reasonableness
- Avoiding dogmatism.
- Endeavouring to give consistent reasons for decisions of a similar nature.

Reflexivity
- Being self-critical about the process and outcomes of ethical review.

The main aim of this chapter was to argue a case for practical ethical guidance for members of research ethics committees. There is clearly a case for adopting a virtue ethics approach by members of ethics committees, both individually and collectively. This approach would be reflected in the committee's disposition to researchers and could also ethically shape ethics review. What might be the practical implications of adopting such an approach? This question is best addressed by considering an example. Imagine a researcher intending to undertake a study of online sexual exploitation of children; the study will be conducted using covert observation of material on the dark web. He is aware that he might identify both victims and perpetrators but he has made it clear that he has no intention of exposing perpetrators or taking steps to protect children. Rather his research aims to understand this complex phenomenon with a view to producing policy guidance intended to minimise its incidence, and, ideally, eventually eradicate it. Ethical issues abound. It would be difficult to argue that this research would not be valuable, but it could readily be ruled out by an ethics committee referring to well-established principles, checklists and typical applications of some aspects of ethical theory. This is not the place to enter in a wide discussion of the ethics of this research in detail, but it is possible to demonstrate the application of a virtue ethics approach.

The ethics committee might start by recognising the virtues of this researcher. Following Macfarlane's proposed virtues, the committee might note the researcher's courage and resoluteness. It might look for ways in which the researcher shows respect, perhaps to the at-risk population of children. The researcher might make the case that children should not be seen as easily influenced or gullible or, more controversially, as in some way complicit; rather it might have been argued that they, like many adults, can be victims of complex psychosocial pressures. The application might also demonstrate sincerity, as shown by the research aim and, perhaps, commitment to achieve some social good rather than conduct the research with less altruistic motives in mind. The application might include elements of humility insofar as it could identify limitations, including those suggesting that the research might not produce any results which might meet the stated aim. Finally, the committee could evaluate the chosen methodology seeking evidence of reflection upon its controversial nature. The committee's response to the researcher might be as follows:

> Thank you for this application. You have shown considerable courage in your plans to undertake this project. It is clear that you have reflected on those plans carefully and considered the implications of the research for all involved. The Committee noted the respectful disposition you showed towards at risk children, generally, and your resolute attempt to conduct research aimed at improving their safety. You are clearly committed to this research; your sincerity is clear and you have wisely pointed out the risk of it having limited impact.

It would obviously be easier for an ethics committee to come to a conclusion, such as that above, if members had the opportunity to meet the researcher in person; this would facilitate a direct appreciation of the virtues of the researcher. Whilst face-to-face contact would be preferable, it is nevertheless possible to come to a similar conclusion by reviewing documents alone.

How might the ethics committee have reached a decision such as that above? It is clear that the decision is not the product of the use of a checklist or a reviewing tool. These have their place and they might be used in establishing some matters of ethical detail requiring attention but, as argued throughout this chapter, their use will not ensure that ethics committees undertake reviews ethically; this could be addressed by the committee following my suggested phases of ethical review whilst striving to develop the associated virtues. A review, based on virtue ethics, could be conducted by starting with an attempt to understand the research, and endeavouring to empathise with all those involved in it, most significantly the researcher and participants. The committee would focus on key ethical issues such as risks, burdens and benefits, and it would have sought assurance that the researcher had the necessary skills or support required to undertake the work. In coming to a consensus, the committee will have deliberated on key ethical issues before coming to a conclusion. Finally, the committee should have reflected on its decision with an aim to maintain consistency.

The virtues required of committees and their members have been proposed in the table above. These should have prominence in the final phase of the review. A disciplined reflection make take the form of, for example, have I/we been aberrant or pedantic rather than reasonable?

CONCLUSIONS

Ethics committees have a range of resources at their disposal aimed at guiding ethical review of research. Many of these resources have limitations and are rarely drawn upon explicitly in the course of ethics review. Reference to codes, checklists and algorithms tends to result in audit-like activity with a focus on compliance, rather than ethical review and evaluation. Normative theories are rarely focused upon explicitly, although there are examples of some limited application. Whilst neither being clearly consequentialist nor deontological, many committees evaluate research in terms of its consequences and the duties of researchers towards participants. Examples of ethics committees overtly (judgements about the moral dispositions and motives of researchers are often made but not formally articulated) considering the virtues of researchers, both directly and as reflected in their proposed research, are extremely rare; however, there is much to commend such an approach.

This chapter has considered research ethics at a meta level by considering the ethical conduct of research ethics committees: how ethical are ethics committees? Processes of ethical review can be evaluated by drawing on normative theories; however, these have limitations in their application in considering how ethics committees ought to conduct themselves ethically. The idea of a virtuous ethics committee has much to commend it. Ethics committees vary in their dispositions towards researchers and research. Arguably, much could be gained by striving to develop virtues, resulting in committees being, for example, sensitive, reasonable and perspicacious.

Using Macfarlane's idea of phases of research, I have proposed phases with tentative 'meanings' which might be used to characterise the process of ethical ethics review. I have focused on the phases in an endeavour to capture key virtues and vices. Whilst the proposed virtues are tentative, the analytical process leading to their identity is less contentious – its roots lying in well-established Aristotelian ethics. In an endeavour to illustrate the virtues and vices I have used Macfarlane's idea of 'living them out'. The examples are not intended to be exhaustive; indeed, they should be expanded and further explicated following Aristotle's emphasis on *phronesis*.

ACKNOWLEDGEMENT

A version of this chapter was originally delivered as a paper at an event organised by the Academy of Social Sciences in conjunction with the British Sociological Association (Carpenter, 2015).

REFERENCES

Academy of Social Sciences. (2013). *Professional briefings (October 2013, Issue 3): Generic ethics principles in social research*. London: Academy of Social Sciences. Retrieved from http://acss.org.uk/publication-category/professional-briefings/

Aristotle. (1955). *The ethics of Aristotle: The Nichomachaen ethics*. (Rev. ed.; J. K. Thomson, Trans., 104 pp.). New York, NY: Viking. Retrieved from http://www.cwu.edu/~warren/Unit1/aristotles_virtues_and_vices.htm

Association for Research Ethics. (2013). *Framework for research ethics*. Retrieved from http://arec.org.uk/framework/

Beauchamp, T., & Childress, J. (2009). *Principles of biomedical ethics* (6th ed.). Oxford: Oxford University Press.

Bettenson, H., & Maunder, C. (2011). *Documents of the Christian church*. Retrieved from https://global.oup.com/academic/product/documents-of-the-christian-church-9780199568987?cc=gb&lang=en&

Callahan, D. (2003). Principlism and communitariansm. *Journal of Medical Ethics, 29*, 287–291.

Carpenter, D. (2013). Generic ethics principles in social science research discussion – Stimulus paper (symposium 1, March 5, 2013). *Professional briefing: Developing generic ethics principles for social science (Vol. 3)*. London: Academy of Social Sciences. Retrieved from http://acss.org.uk/publication-category/professional-briefings/

Carpenter, D. (2015, May). *Virtue ethics in the practice and review of social science research*. Retrieved from https://www.acss.org.uk/wp-content/uploads/2015/03/Carpenter-Virtuous-Ethics-Committee-AcSS-BSA-Virtue-Ethics-1st-May-2015.pdf

ESRC. (2016). *Our core principles.* Retrieved from http://www.esrc.ac.uk/funding/guidance-for-applicants/research-ethics/our-core-principles/

Gert, B. (1997). *Bioethics: A return to fundamentals.* Cary, NC: Oxford University Press.

Giddens, A. (1998). *The third way: The renewal of social democracy.* Cambridge: Polity.

Gillon, R. (1994). Medical ethics: Four principles plus attention to scope. *British Medical Journal.* Retrieved from http://www.bmj.com/content/309/6948/184

Hanson, S. (2009). *Moral acquaintances and moral decisions: Resolving moral conflicts in medical ethics.* New York, NY: Springer.

Hedgecoe, A. (2016). Reputational risk, academic freedom and research ethics review. *Sociology, 50*(3), 486–501. doi: 10.1177/0038038515590756

Israel, M., & Hay, I. (2006). *Research ethics for social scientists.* London: Sage.

Macfarlane, B. (2009). *Researching with integrity: The ethics of academic enquiry.* New York, NY: Routledge.

Macfarlane, B. (2010). Values and virtues in qualitative research. In M. Savin-Baden & C. H. Major (Eds.), *New approaches to qualitative research: Wisdom and uncertainty.* New York, NY: Routledge.

O'Neil, O. (2011). *Broadening bioethics: Clinical ethics, public health and global health.* NCoB Lecture, Royal Society of Arts. Retrieved from http://www.nuffieldbioethics.org/sites/default/files/Broadening_bioethics_clinical_ethics_public_health_&global_health.pdf

Rousseau, J. J. ([1762] 2008). *The social contract.* New York, NY: Cosimo. Retrieved from https://books.google.co.uk/books?id=CyiOSafbzUYC&printsec=frontcover&source=gbs_ge_summary_r&cad=0#v=onepage&q&f=false

Singer, P. (2011). *Practical ethics* (3rd ed.). Cambridge: Cambridge University Press.

Stark, L. (2012). *Behind closed doors: IRBs and the making of ethical research.* Chicago, IL: University of Chicago Press.

UK Health Departments. (2011, updated 2012). *Governance arrangement for research ethics committees.* Retrieved from https://www.gov.uk/government/publications/health-research-ethics-committees-governance-arrangements

Van Den Hoonaard, W. C. (2011). *The seduction of ethics: Transforming the social sciences.* Toronto: University of Toronto Press.

World Medical Authority. (2013). *Declaration of Helsinki – Ethical principles for medical research involving human subjects.* Retrieved from http://www.wma.net/en/30publications/10policies/b3/

CHAPTER 6

RELATING TO CARPENTER'S VIRTUOUS RESEARCH ETHICS COMMITTEE

Helen Brown Coverdale

ABSTRACT

The chapter reflects on the strengths and limitations of David Carpenter's proposal to support the work of research ethics committees through consideration of the virtues required by their members. Carpenter's approach has many strengths, responsibilising researchers and ethics committees, and increasing the scope for robust and active theoretical engagement with ethical issues. I bring two alternative perspectives on research ethics to bear on this discussion. First, I discuss work in care ethics and relational ethics, approaches to ethics that have some similarities with virtue ethics but also distinct differences. Bruce Macfarlane's text, on which Carpenter draws, notes care ethics briefly. I offer a more detailed consideration of what this perspective can offer, both for research ethics and for the virtuous research ethics committee. This helps to identify the relationships that are missing from a virtue ethics focus. Further, a context sensitive relational approach suggests ways in which we can strengthen Carpenter's proposals to help research ethics committees select between competing principles or virtues. Second, my research ethics expertise is in undergraduate teaching for a

Virtue Ethics in the Conduct and Governance of Social Science Research
Advances in Research Ethics and Integrity, Volume 3, 127–140
Copyright © 2018 by Emerald Publishing Limited
All rights of reproduction in any form reserved
ISSN: 2398-6018/doi:10.1108/S2398-601820180000003007

multidisciplinary course, and an enquiry-based learning programme, which allows students in mixed discipline groups to plan, conduct, report and present their own original social research. The research skills training provided includes an interactive introduction to research ethics, what they are for and why they matter. Since we aim to offer practical guidance to research ethics committees when they consider what they should do and how this should be done, such a first principles approach may be useful.

Keywords: Virtue; ethical review; research ethics; ethics committees

INTRODUCTION

David Carpenter argues that while much practical guidance about research ethics is provided to researchers, little practical advice is available for research ethics committees and their members. The guidance that is available exists largely in the form of codes of practice and ethics checklists; however, these tools are intended for, and prepared from the perspective of, researchers. Tools specifically designed to support research ethics committees are vanishingly hard to find.

Checklists and codes are intended to facilitate ethical decision-making in practice. Yet, for the researchers whom these research ethics tools are intended to provide support, it seems that these tools are too often experienced as hurdles to be overcome and put aside; rather than deployed as a continuous support, facilitating good, strong, valid and valuable and above all ethical research. As Iphofen (2011a, p. 147) argues, when ethical approval is necessary for research funding, this becomes a de facto barrier to research. These tools for researchers may be well intentioned, aiming to provide clarity around what researchers in a given field need to demonstrate in order to evidence that they are thinking ethically about their research practice. Anecdotally, at least some professional researchers appear to be made uneasy by checklists, seeing them more as a set of hypersensitive, risk-driven barriers to research. Any tool is of limited use if it cannot be easily employed by its intended users in the environment in which it is most often required. Particularly for those complex, sensitive issues where social research is most needed, overly generalised checklists and codes intended for broad applicability may be insufficiently nuanced, and require careful different operationalisation (Iphofen, 2011a, p. 159). Finally, while checklists and codes designed to support researchers can be useful for research ethics committees, these tools are not crafted with the purpose of directly supporting the work of research ethics committees in their ethical assessment of proposed research.

THE TROUBLE WITH RESEARCH ETHICS COMMITTEES

Carpenter raises further concerns about the codes and checklists which aim to provide practical guidance to researchers to support ethical research. First, the plurality of guidance aimed at researchers is easily confusing. Researchers must often satisfy the separate ethical requirements of their research institutions, professional bodies, funding providers, research partners and key stakeholders. The diversity of requirements may help researchers to ensure the risks affecting their particular research are sufficiently covered from a variety of perspectives. However, this diversity may be confusing for researchers and research ethics committee members alike. Just because one party's set of ethical requirements does not explicitly cover a particular issue pertinent to the proposed research project does not necessarily mean that the committee should not consider these issues, or ask the researchers to do so. However, doing so may cause confusion. This potentially produces a duplication of effort for committees, or conflicting requirements for researchers, or both. How should ethics committees' oversight be guided? Carpenter considers the following resolutions: by conformity to an agreed code, by adherence to an agreed normative ethical position, by following systematic checklists or by reflecting on the committee members' individual emotional reactions and personal moral code.

Carpenter first notes that adherence to codes does not guarantee that ethical issues arising in a research plan are sufficiently acknowledged and addressed. This resonates with another criticism, first raised by Gert, Culver, and Clouser (1997) in relation to Beauchamp and Childress (2013), and which Carpenter picks up in his chapter (2018): it is erroneously and dangerously assumed that, by simply linking a concern with a principle, a research ethics committee has successfully theoretically and critically engaged with the potential ethical problem. When research ethics committees use guidance framed for researchers in their critical ethical oversight work, this provides a shared lexicon. Potentially, linking ethical concerns with tools designed to help researchers may facilitate the communication of problems to researchers by identifying and categorising ethical difficulties. Yet, Carpenter argues that nothing of substance is helpfully added to the original intuitions of the research ethics committee members. He raises further concerns that checklists and codes of practice are in fact used by ethics committees to explain and justify concerns retroactively and to give expression to committee members' intuitions.

REFLEXIVE ETHICAL ENGAGEMENT AND
TEACHING RESEARCH ETHICS

Research ethics tools, such as codes of practice and checklists, can be useful pedagogical devices. Students, at least, like codes of practice, checklists and structured sets of principles. Lists and conceptually related ideas are easier to remember, they can provide a necessary first step in beginning to understand the underlying ethical concerns which might apply to research practice. Understanding is, in turn, a necessary precursor for applying ethical thought to research practice. Checklists are then helpful for introducing new ideas to novice researchers and, when they work well, they help students to begin to understand the ethical issues surrounding research. However, precisely because codes and checklists are easy to remember, there is a danger that these approaches can be uncritically learned by rote.

For the more experienced researcher, practical tools and theories, such as Principlism, allow us to group intuitions and concerns under headings for closer examination. In the case of Principlism, these are autonomy, beneficence, non-maleficence and justice. To be clear, as Macfarlane (2009, p. 27–32) notes that these principles can and do conflict; and as Gert et al. (1997) notes and Carpenter (2018) echoes, simply linking an intuition of concern with a principle is not sufficient for critical engagement. Yet, organising our ideas through the conceptual lenses offered by codes, checklists and theories such as Principlism may be a helpful first step. This approach can facilitate researchers' critical analysis of our research practice to identify where and how the ethical issues around research fit together, come apart and where and how they *conflict*. This critical practice allows researchers to engage reflexively with the ethical issues generated by research at all stages of the research process. Such an approach could be a useful investigatory tool for research ethics committees and could facilitate communication. Yet, Principlism alone may overly emphasise the labelling and grouping of concerns, as identified by Gert et al. (1997) and Carpenter. The ethical oversight provided by research ethics committees further requires critical engagement with these intuitions.

Students and, one might add, more experienced researchers, can sometimes struggle to see the relevance of *all* of the points on a standardised checklist for their particular research projects. This is certainly true of student research projects, which are small-scale, low-budget, and short duration projects. Carpenter notes that it is not easy to identify generalisable principles, particularly those that could be usefully shared in common across the learned societies in the Academy of Social Sciences.[1] While some level of universal ethical code could be desirable for high level shared discussions, they are more difficult to handle in practice. A universal code would have had to be prepared in very abstract terms to command overlapping agreement. However, as an abstract overlapping agreement necessarily has several ways of fleshing out the details, then, by definition, such an overlapping approach could not provide clear, practical and actionable guidance to help us to pin down *how* we should decide *what* we should do in any particular case. The shorthand of codes and checklists might be a good starting point to facilitate communication about general ethical concerns, but each project will raise unique ethical issues.

Complex abstract positions on potential ethical problems can be made accessible and clear to nonspecialists (either lay ethics committee members or researchers who are not ethics specialists themselves) through the use of concrete illustrative examples. Carpenter worries that this may draw the attention of both ethics committee members and researchers to focus on the case study guidance examples, rather than the ethical problems underlying the sample cases, which we then seek to negotiate. So how should research ethics committee members make a decision in any particular case? Which interpretation of which abstract principles should we choose? Which is the relevant exemplar case? How should we make these choices? Potentially, abstract principles that may conflict, such as those of Beauchamp and Childress, could obscure as much as they are intended to elucidate about the core ethical issue of concern.

MACFARLANE'S VIRTUOUS RESEARCHER

In *Researching with Integrity*, Macfarlane (2009) draws on virtue ethics to consider the virtues which researchers need to employ and, ideally, to inhabit and embody, if they are to plan, conduct, analyse, store and report their research and finding ethically. This approach shifts the focus from *what must be shown to others* – in order to evidence that the researcher has undertaken appropriate ethical reflection and action (the focus of checklists) – to *how researchers ought to conduct themselves*. The virtues an ethical researcher ought to embody inform both *what* they should do and *how* this should be done. While research ethics committees are increasingly seeking insight into how ethical oversight will be maintained by researchers during the project, the existence of guidance structures such as codes and checklists and the practical necessity of external approval, may encourage researchers to outsource final decision-making responsibility – on the ethical appropriateness of their proposals and research decisions in practice – to the research ethics committee. Researchers who are pressed for time by funding constraints, or practical needs to begin recruiting participants and gathering data, may understandably become focussed on producing a proposal that achieves research ethics committee's approval, rather than critically and continuously engaging with ethical issues. In short, researchers may rely on achieving external validation, rather than taking full responsibility for making their own critical ethical evaluation. As Iphofen (2011b, pp. 444–445) argues, codes and checklists are most valuable when they are used as a springboard into actively thinking through ethical issues. Macfarlane's notion of the virtuous researcher, who acts with ethical integrity, who will take responsibility for the ethical impacts of her research on individual participants, interested parties and stakeholders, and who is cognisant of her responsibilities towards wider communities, cannot avoid the ethical engagement essential for virtue.

THE VIRTUOUS RESEARCH ETHICS COMMITTEE

Carpenter proposes that we can support research ethics committees in facilitating ethically sound research by identifying the virtues the research ethics committee and its individual members ought to display. We should expect to see these virtues in the consideration of and response to research proposals, and in the individual and collective actions of good research ethics committees and their members. In his chapter, Carpenter (2018) lays solid foundations for such an approach, beginning the work by cataloguing the virtues of research ethics committees and their members: *intelligence* in understanding, *sensitivity* in empathising, *discernment* in focus, *perspicacity* in clarification, *cooperation* in deliberation, *reasonableness* in concluding and *reflexivity* in broader reflections.

Carpenter's virtue ethics approach is broadly successful in remedying the problems he identifies with Principlism. Considering the virtues that are practically important for research ethics committee members helps to address some of Carpenter's core concerns. First, Carpenter's approach makes available research ethics tools designed specifically for research ethics committees, allowing committees to set aside reliance on the confusingly diverse range of research ethics tools primarily designed for researchers. Second, virtue ethics guidance aimed specifically at research ethics committee members has potential to address Carpenter's further concerns about the lack of theoretical ethical critical engagement. This offers scope to both replace and reduce the retroactive use of research ethics guidance as ex post rationalisations as well as providing more ex-ante action guidance for appropriate engagement practices. However, there remains a difficulty with this approach. How can we identify which principle, or more correctly in this mode of thinking, which *virtue* we should apply or prioritise in which case. Furthermore, how can we defend our selection if and when the underlying principles conflict? If we can resolve this problem, then Carpenter's virtue ethics approach has much to recommend it. Drawing on some underdeveloped points from Macfarlane's earlier work, I aim to strengthen the case for thinking about research ethics committee virtues as practicable action guidance. I illustrate what Carpenter's approach might achieve and consider some of its limits.

VIRTUE ETHICS, RESEARCH ETHICS AND CARE ETHICS

Macfarlane (2009) briefly notes the ethics of care in his *Researching with Integrity*. Parallels have been drawn by some between virtue ethics and care ethics; so, while Macfarlane's work focusses on virtue ethics, his gesture towards care ethics remains relevant. Furthermore, Macfarlane's analysis of care ethics is somewhat limited. Referencing Gilligan's work (1982), *In a Different Voice*, Macfarlane primarily introduces care ethics to illustrate that differences between researchers mean that different researchers may perceive the same ethical problems differently, taking gender differences as an example. Macfarlane (2009, p. 43) does not engage with care ethics, merely using it to suggest that we should take into consideration the gender of the researcher when evaluating the researcher's ethical decision-making and actions.

It must be stressed that the empirical correlation tentatively hypothesised between gender and approach to moral reasoning in Gilligan's (1982) early work has not been borne out by later research. It may be true to suggest that women and girls are socialised in different ways to men and boys, and that this then informs their attitudes towards rules, relationships and emotions.[2] However, while this difference in socialisation may explain why many women and girls appear better equipped for care ethics reasoning, and why many men and boys appear to appeal apparently more intuitively to rule-based reasoning, both approaches are available to us. Nor is gender the only source of such salient contextual differences between researchers. When we are considering differences between researchers to evaluate ethical decision-making, we might, as Macfarlane (2009, p. 31) suggests, consider the role accorded to individual autonomy in 'Western' culture, and contrast this with collectivism in Asian and Japanese cultures. These might result in differing interpretations of the same principle such as that of respect for persons, for example.

The connection between care ethics and virtue ethics has been widely noted. Held (2006), for example, argues that care ethics has precursors in virtue theorists from Aristotle to Hume and the moral sentimentalists. Yet, there is also a strong resistance to the idea that care ethics can be subsumed by, or merely modifies virtue ethics. This is because the notion that care is a virtue fails to grasp the relationality that lies at the heart of care ethics and its perspective on ethical issues. Virtues concern the perfection of the individual (or collective). They do not consider human persons as necessarily vulnerable and interdependent, as always in relation to and with others, or the practices required for maintaining relationships and meeting needs for living well (Tronto, 2013, p. 36). While virtue ethics has contributed to the development of the ethics of care perspective, care ethics is nevertheless distinct from virtue-based approaches. Held (2006, p. 77) ultimately argues that care and relational concerns should be understood as the 'wider network' or moral framework encompassing justice, utility and the virtues.

Carpenter's consideration of the virtues which might be used to inform his notion of the virtuous research ethics committee has great potential to provide exemplary guidance to support a research ethics committee's work without prescriptively and restrictively telling the committee exactly what to think, or how to do its job. Just as for the virtuous researchers described in Macfarlane's *Researching with Integrity*, the virtue-based approach has potential to shift the focus from the underlying values to how we should act by thinking about action guiding virtues. Carpenter's virtue ethics approach begins to responsibilise both researchers and research ethics committees for their own part in good ethical conduct and good supportive ethical guidance respectively. The virtues described are complementary and holistic in nature, which resonates with care ethics. For care ethics, taking *responsibility* for a *competent* display of virtues and practices is considered central to the *integrity* of care (Tronto, 1993, p. 136). Similarly, Macfarlane (2009, p. 45) recognises integrity as necessary for meshing the values and practices of virtuous research with the researcher's identity. Nevertheless, what appears missing in Carpenter's consideration of the virtues of the research ethics committee, and in Macfarlane's consideration of the virtuous researcher, is relationships.

RESEARCH ETHICS AND RESEARCH RELATIONSHIPS

Research ethics are of particular importance in biomedical and social studies, since research processes and research findings often significantly impact on natural persons, real human beings, whether direct research participants or not. These impacts are often more than passive external effects and, even when they are collateral consequences of the researcher's actions, they should still be considered in an assessment of the ethical impact of the research. Relationships are the loci of the research decisions and actions that we seek to ensure are ethical. These relationships include relations between researchers within the research team; between research ethics committee members; between the research team and the ethics committee; and between researchers and research institutions, funders, professional bodies, participants, gatekeepers, stakeholders and other interested or affected parties. We can recognise these relationships as sources of research and ethical obligations, interdependence and, potentially, ethical tensions.

Acting ethically requires more than careful reasoning and following rules. The virtues that Carpenter takes to underpin good ethical review includes 'intelligence', which committee members will show by trying to understand research design and its method(ology) in a sympathetic or open-minded manner. Further, the committee is expected to be sensitive to and alert to any problems that might arise from members' limited knowledge of a topic, field, or discipline. Promoting cooperation in deliberation emphasises the internal relationships of the research ethics committee, and suggests taking and sharing responsibility for competent collaborative deliberations and actions. Reflexivity suggests a continuous review of research ethics committee practice, looking for opportunities for learning and improvement, pointing towards the integrity of these virtues.

These virtues, together with the virtue of sensitivity (and empathy), towards researchers as well as potential participants suggest an engaged, open and responsive approach. Openness to the social and relational contexts in which the research occurs, enables the research ethics committee to contextualise and understand the salience of the ethical issues which might arise. In order to understand a research design intelligently, and to empathise sensitively, we need a context-informed approach. Viewing research in context allows us to intelligently discern focal factors that are relevant for appropriately understanding the situation and any arising ethical issues.

These virtues echo those described in the practices of caring. Care ethicists write about achieving good care, by taking account of various needs; the available resources; and the wishes of those receiving care. Offering a now influential set of virtues, Tronto (1993, p. 127–137) identifies attentiveness, responsibility, competence and responsiveness as essential components of good caring, which must be practiced cohesively, or with *integrity* (Tronto, 1993, p. 136). Engster (2007, pp. 30–31) suggests that care is characterised by 'an attentive, responsive and respectful manner'. There is a further point of similarity between research and caring relationships: both necessarily entail imbalances of power. In caring relationships, this is most obvious when one party is dependent on the provision of assistance and support by another. This interpretation of caring is, however, too simplistic. While any particular instance of care involves one party providing and another receiving care, we should be aware of the ongoing nature of these exchanges. Relationships of care persist over time and involve both direct and indirect reciprocity, allowing both parties to give and receive care between themselves and others. Caring relationships are sometimes described as 'nested', where care is 'paid forwards' through indirect reciprocity, rather than directly paid back (Kittay, 1999, p. 68). Likewise, research relationships have 'nested' dependencies. In research relationships, researchers rely on participant's cooperation and funder's willingness, but the research findings and the ways in which these are reported have significant consequences for participants, stakeholders and other interested parties.

It is not enough for Carpenter's virtuous research ethics committee to display one or some of these virtues. For virtuousness, the committee and its individual members must display them all. The virtues that Carpenter emphasises for research ethics committees – sensitivity, reasonableness and cooperation – implicitly recognise the interdependence with ethics committees between members, and between ethics committees and research teams. This approach leaves space for the situatedness of relationships between researchers and a variety of interested parties, and echoes the concerns of relational ethics (Austin, 2008) and care ethics (Held, 2006, p. 20). Taking a more relational approach emphasises the relational interdependence and situatedness of social research and recognises the relationships within which research takes place.

PRACTICING VIRTUE WHEN PRINCIPLES CONFLICT

Carpenter's virtue ethics approach to research ethics committee guidance has much to recommend it. However, in addition to recognising the salience of relationships, there is a further benefit to drawing on the similarities between virtue ethics and situated ethical approaches such as care and relational ethics. Relational approaches can help us to decide which features of a given situation, and which corresponding virtues, should be given priority. As Macfarlane acknowledges, the four principles offered by Beauchamp and Childress have the potential to conflict with one another. While any value pluralist approach implies that values and the principles they inform may conflict, Macfarlane identifies additional potential for conflict through the 'eclectic mix' of deontic and utilitarian ethical approaches that inform Beauchamp and Childress's principles (Macfarlane 2009, p. 28). There are, however, no rules for resolving such conflicts. Ethical decision-making therefore requires researchers to decide which principle to prioritise (e.g., respect for persons), what prioritising a principle normatively requires (e.g., respect for individual autonomy or collective concerns), and how this priority should put into practice (e.g., what, if any, limits are appropriate to individual choices in this particular context, Macfarlane, 2009, p. 29). Similarly, Carpenter's virtue-based approach may also require researchers to decide which virtue will take priority in a given situation.

While the ethics of care and relational ethical approaches are not usually characterised as rule-based systems of moral reasoning, they can, Clement (1996) argues, help us to choose between competing principles. Particular contextual information about our relationships and circumstances can help us identify which principles are important and to spot the ethically salient variables, which can help to explain and defend our decisions. By way of an example, Clement considers the provision of free school meals to underprivileged children. In this case the important issue is not just that the basic need is met and the children are fed, it is also important that the children are not stigmatised by the way in which our actions are carried out. Context and situation informs *how* we should act, not just what we should do. It provides an action guiding reason for, in this case, choosing less stigmatising practices for delivering free school meals (Clement, 1996, p. 105). A relational approach does not provide all answers but helps us to offer a defensible but defeasible account of our decisions and actions. There is scope for disagreement, but this encourages us to think critically about our choices, and offers more scope for guidance than principles alone.

Likewise, thinking about the relevant relationships, and the particular concrete contexts in which research is being, or will be, carried out, can help both the virtuous researcher and the virtuous research ethics committee to reason through the ethical implications of a particular context, and provide a principled reason for defending our choice. This encourages researchers, and research ethics committees alike, to actively take responsibility in making research ethics decisions; about which principles or virtues should be applied, and how the virtues should be practised to minimise ethical risks, rather than passively or retroactively applying a label.

CONCLUSION

Carpenter's use of virtue ethics to provide practical and actionable guidance to research ethics committees is an encouraging step. The virtues he proposes provides a clear way for committees in particular to consider what their conduct ought to be and how they should perform their ethical oversight. This shift, from what needs to be demonstrated to what needs to be done and how, helps to responsibilise both researchers and research ethics committees, for their own parts in the joint enterprise of facilitating valid ethical research. The self-direction the virtuous research ethics committee is enabled to employ offers scope to address each of the problems that Carpenter identifies with the use of checklists and codes, as used by research ethics committees:

1. That there is a confusing array of guidance;
2. that the guidance available is directed to the researcher; and
3. that the guidance is applied retroactively when used by research ethics committees, suggesting a lack of critical engagement.

Carpenter's research ethics committee virtues approach provides scope to address the core concern of reactively attaching a label after the ethics committee deliberation. Virtue ethics offers space to encouraging proactive critical engagement and reflection about what needs to be done, and how to go about it, guided by one set of virtues, as applied to research in a particular context. I have also suggested that consideration of the context and situatedness of various kinds of research relationships offers some scope for identifying and defending the use of one principle rather than another, reducing the problem of using a theoretical framework without apparent critical engagement. There are, of course, no guarantees of successfully ethically engaging research ethics committees and their members, but the opportunities for doing so will be enhanced if we take Carpenter's virtues approach and attend to relationships and context. It is however important to remember that the purpose of engaging in reflection on research ethics is not simply to identify and apply ethically perfect research practices. Eliminating all risks is not possible. Rather, our purpose is to acknowledge the potential for ethical conflict and to plan ahead and identify ways in which we can devise the best available response in terms of how researchers will deal with problems as and when they arise. Research ethics committees can support and facilitate this by similar reflexive consideration at the planning stage, but ethical reflection must continue by researchers at all stages of the project. Research ethics committee members can encourage this by taking and pursuing a virtue-informed approach towards researchers, and towards their own role. Broader reflection on the context and situation of research practices may also contribute to clearer consciousness of the nuances of the issues at hand, helping researchers and research ethics committees to provide better guidance that is tailored for practice.

ACKNOWLEDGEMENT

This chapter is developed from my contribution to an Academy of Social Sciences and British Sociological Association Symposium (Coverdale, 2015), which was presented alongside Carpenter's (2015) paper. My contribution on the day intended to provoke discussion, and this chapter has benefited enormously from the ideas raised on the day by other participants.

NOTES

1. Although see the discussion document *Generic Ethics Principles in Social Science*, published by the Academy of Social Science's Working Group on Research Ethics (2013), and republished as Dingwall, Iphofen, Lewis, Oates, and Emmerich (2017).
2. Macfarlane (2009, p. 30) separately acknowledges emotions as an important factor in moral decision-making. While Macfarlane describes Principlism's perception of emotions as 'negative', he argues that emotions cannot be disentangled and set aside easily from ethical evaluations, and that it is 'dangerous' to make moral decisions without emotional reactions.

REFERENCES

Academy of Social Sciences. (2013). *Generic ethics principles in social science.* Retrieved from https://acss.org.uk/wp-content/uploads/2014/01/Professional-Briefings-3-Ethics-r.pdf. Accessed on August 16, 2016.

Austin, W. J. (2008). Relational ethics. *The SAGE encyclopaedia of qualitative research methods* (pp. 749–750). Retrieved from http://knowledge.sagepub.com.gate2.library.lse.ac.uk/view/research/n378.xml. Accessed on May 5, 2015.

Beauchamp, T. L., & Childress, J. F. (2013). *Principles of biomedical ethics* (7th ed.). New York, NY: OUP.

Carpenter, D. (2015). *The virtuous ethics committee at virtue ethics in the practice and review of social science.* London: Academy of Social Science/British Sociology Association.

Carpenter, D. (2018). Virtue ethics in the practice and review of social science research: the virtuous ethics committee in N. Emmerich (Ed.), *Virtue ethics in the conduct and governance of social science research* (Advances in Research Ethics and Integrity, Vol. 3, pp. 105–126). Bingley: Emerald Publishing Limited.

Clement, G. (1996). *Care, autonomy, and justice: Feminism and the ethic of care.* Boulder, CO: Westview Press.

Coverdale, H. B. (2015). *Response to David Carpenter: The virtuous ethics committee at virtue ethics in the practice and review of social science.* London: Academy of Social Science/British Sociology Association. Retrieved from https://www.acss.org.uk/wp-content/uploads/2015/03/Helen-Brown-Coverdale-2015-Response-to-David-Carpenter-Virtue-ethics-in-the-practice-review-of-social-science.pdf. Accessed on August 14, 2016.

Dingwall, R., Iphofen, R., Lewis, J., Oates, J., & Emmerich, N. (2017). Towards common prin-
     ciples for social science research ethics: A discussion document for the academy of social
     sciences. In R. Iphofen (Ed.), *Finding common ground: Consensus in research ethics across
     the social sciences* (*Advances in research ethics and integrity*, Vol. 1, pp. 111–123). Bingley:
     Emerald Publishing Limited.
Engster, D. (2007). *The heart of justice: Care ethics and political theory.* Oxford: Oxford University
     Press.
Gert, B., Culver, C. M., & Clouser, K. D. (1997). *Bioethics: A return to fundamentals.* Oxford:
     Oxford University Press.
Gilligan, C. (1982). *In a different voice: Psychological theory and women's development.* Cambridge,
     MA; London: Harvard University Press.
Held, V. (2006). *The ethics of care: Personal, political, and global.* Oxford; New York, NY: Oxford
     University Press.
Iphofen, R. (2011a). *Ethical decision making in social research: A practical guide.* Basingstoke:
     Palgrave Macmillan.
Iphofen, R. (2011b). Ethical decision-making in qualitative research. *Qualitative Research, 11*(4),
     443–446.
Kittay, E. F. (1999). *Love's labor: Essays on women, equality, and dependency.* New York, NY:
     Routledge.
Macfarlane, B. (2009). *Researching with integrity: The ethics of academic enquiry.* New York, NY;
     London: Routledge.
Tronto, J. C. (1993). *Moral boundaries: A political argument for an ethic of care.* New York, NY:
     Routledge.
Tronto, J. C. (2013). *Caring democracy: Markets, equality, and justice*, New York, NY: New York
     University Press.

CHAPTER 7

A RESPONSE TO DAVID CARPENTER'S 'VIRTUE ETHICS IN THE PRACTICE AND REVIEW OF SOCIAL SCIENCE RESEARCH'

John Elliott

ABSTRACT

This article is a response to Carpenter's 'Virtue Ethics in the Practice and Review of Social Science Research: The Virtuous Ethics Committee'. While applauding his attempt to introduce the concept of 'virtue ethics' into the contemporary discourse about the practice and review of social science research, I suggest that his thinking is overly dependent on the work of Macfarlane (2009 & 2010); particularly with respect to drawing a sharp contrast between this concept and the use of principles to construct an ethical framework for research and its review. I argue that Carpenter's article would have benefited from a critique of the conceptual limitations of Macfarlane's work, particularly in a context where social science research is increasingly participatory. Following O'Neill (1996), I argue that ethical principles can be understood as universal values that orientate practical reasoning or deliberative inquiry into what constitutes virtuous action in particular cases. Such deliberative inquiry may also be guided by what Nussbaum (1990) depicts

Virtue Ethics in the Conduct and Governance of Social Science Research
Advances in Research Ethics and Integrity, Volume 3, 141–154
ISSN: 2398-6018/doi:10.1108/S2398-601820180000003008

as 'rules of thumb'; summaries of good concrete judgements and decisions that are the cumulative outcomes of past deliberations about how to realise ethical principles in action. I argue that these 'rules' do not prescribe action since they cannot be considered as ethically prior to concrete descriptions of cases. Rather, they evolve out of the deliberative process of case study itself. As Nussbaum (1990) points out, Aristotle argued for the ethical priority of concrete description over any general rule that might be applied to it. This does not, however, deny the practical significance of summaries of judgements based on a constant comparison of cases. Instead, such rules can be understood as practical hypotheses to be tested by participants in a social practice within each new concrete situation. I argue that one limitation of the dispositional frameworks that Carpenter cites as providing a basis for the practice and review of social research is their highly generic character. Much research aimed at achieving social ends is shaped by more specifically orientated professional and social practices governed by particular ends-in-view that can be conceptually linked to them. In conclusion, I suggest that, since much social research explicitly aspires to be a participatory and democratic process of knowledge construction, it should provide a starting point for ethical review, where engagement between 'the committee' and 'researchers' transcends the bureaucratic exercise of reviewing documents.

Keywords: Virtue ethics; ethics review; MacFarlane; principlism

INTRODUCTION

Carpenter's chapter in this volume interestingly attempts to extend his thinking about the relevance of 'virtue ethics', as opposed to some form of 'principlism', beyond the object of ethical review – the practice of social science research represented in research proposals – to the review process itself. In doing so he aims to 'relocate and develop' MacFarlane's work, which he used in a previous paper when making a case for *virtuous research* and the *virtuous researcher*. Carpenter's introduction of the concept of virtue into the ethical discourse about social science research practice and the work of Ethics Committee in reviewing such practice is refreshingly welcome; particularly, as I will argue, in a context where much social science research is increasingly cast in methodologically participative forms that are underpinned by a *democratic rationality* (see Elliott, 2007a). However, as in his previous paper, Carpenter displays an over-reliance on MacFarlane's work. In doing so I will argue that Carpenter fails to appreciate and address some of the conceptual limitations of this work.

Those limitations stem from the sharp contrast drawn between virtue ethics and the use of ethical principles as a basis for human conduct. While the literature is vast, it would, I think, improve Carpenter's argument if it were to draw on the wider discourse about *virtue ethics*. On this basis he could have then critically engaged with Macfarlane's text before discussing its application to the ethical aspects of social science research and the work of research ethics committees.

Certainly, Carpenter's attempt to propose a framework for the ethical review of social science research, one grounded in *virtue ethics* rather than some form of *principlism*, makes an important contribution to resolving some of the issues that have persistently dogged the discourse about the role and functions of research ethics committees. However, it arguably fails to clarify some important aspects of an ethical framework for a certain kind of social science research that is consistent with a *virtue ethics* perspective. In this response to Carpenter, I aim to clarify these issues and briefly explore their implications for the organisation of the ethical review process.

MORAL AGENCY AND THE ROLE OF PRINCIPLES IN DELIBERATIVE INQUIRY

In her book *Towards Justice and Virtue*, philosopher O'Neill (1996, p. 125) writes the following:

> Acting on universal principles does not demand uniform treatment or insensitivity to differences. Principles do not dominate or determine those who act on them or live by them. Rather agents refer to or rely on principles in selecting and steering their activities. Since principles of action are fundamental to practical reasoning, hence to ethics, so too are universal principles. To say that a principle is universal is only to say that its scope extends across the whole of some domain, and not to fix the extent of that domain ... whenever agents base their action on the assumption of connection to other agents and subjects, they must include others within the scope of their ethical consideration.

This argument challenges those who assume that action governed by universal principles represents a challenge to moral agency, or its role in ethical decision making. This seems to be the basis of MacFarlane's contrast between *principlism* and *virtue* ethics, and something that Carpenter more or less implicitly accepts. Universal principles are treated as *prescriptive rules* which prescribe behavior regardless of the perceived particularities of the situation. Instead, one should consider them to be expressions of *values* that depict connections between agents and subjects to inform judgement and decision making in relation to particular cases. As such, principles express the linguistic or conceptual form in which moral agents connect with each other to constitute a social practice in particular circumstances. Without principles to inform practice, there can be no mutual dialogue, moral agency or virtuous action. How they are to be realised in particular circumstances is a matter for deliberative inquiry, something that should be informed by Aristotle's conception of *phrónēsis* (see Section 3 of this volume). Such inquiries are, or should be, underpinned by a *democratic rationality* in which moral agents gather and interpret evidence about their practice in dialogue with each other (see Elliott, 2007a). Deliberative inquiry may also be guided by what Nussbaum (1990, pp. 68–69) depicts as *rules of thumb*, or summaries of good concrete judgements and decisions that are the outcome of past deliberations about how to realise principles of action in particular concrete situations. As such, these rules cannot be considered *ethically prior* to *concrete descriptions of cases* in the form depicted by qualitative researchers as case studies (see Elliott & Lukes, 2009). Rather, they evolve out of the process itself. As Nussbaum (1990) points out, Aristotle argues for the ethical priority of concrete description over any general rule that might be applied to it. This does not, however, deny the significance of summaries of judgements based on a constant comparison of cases. Instead, such rules can be understood as practical hypotheses to be tested by participants in a social practice within each new concrete situation. As Nussbaum (1990, p. 68) argues, rules of thumb leave room 'for recognising as ethically salient the new or surprising feature of the case before us, features that have not been anticipated in the rule, or even in principle features that could not be captured in any rule'.

Carpenter argues that when submitted for ethical review, a research proposal will tend to be 'judged as good or ethically sound insofar as it embraces the relevant principles'. He clearly understands 'principles' to refer to rules in the normative or prescriptive sense of the term. He then goes on to argue that

> this leaves little room for consideration of the role of principles in researcher conduct and, more importantly, their place in research which has a prima facie objective of achieving some social good as an end point. Other examples of research, where the conduct of the researcher is the focus of ethical consideration, rather than some sort of pre-determined design, based on principles, aim to achieve significant social impact; here, again, principles are at least partly redundant. There are numerous examples of participatory action research which sets out to achieve some social good as its primary objective; that objective might be self-evident, requiring no reference to any principles. (Carpenter, 2018)

Carpenter is clearly concerned with the ethical review of qualitative social research that aims to achieve some kind of social good. He appears to suggest that if ethical reviews of research that are aimed at achieving social ends focussed on the conduct of the researchers, it would pose issues about their moral agency and thereby embrace a virtue ethics framework rather than one based on a priori normative rules.

There are, of course, deliberative forms of social research that directly aim to develop and sustain the moral agency of researchers and research participants, particularly research that is conducted in the context of particular professional and social practices. In this paper I refer to both specific professional practices and more general social/political practices, concerned with the realization of a just and equitable social order, as contexts for participatory action research. These forms of research are often depicted in such terms as *practice-based enquiry, participatory research, action research and applied research*. Much social research in practical contexts, such as education, social work, the health professions, and community development, takes such forms and tends to be associated with *qualitative research methodology*. Carpenter acknowledges these forms of research. However, he appears to deny the relevance of ethical principles to the conduct of such research. In this respect he might have made himself more familiar with the so-called 'methodological' literature about the ethical dimensions of participatory action research, particularly in the contexts of professional and social practices. In this literature, particularly within the field of education, the relationship between principles that inform practice and virtue ethics is understood very differently to the notion that *virtues* and *principles* are in some way opposed. Indeed, action researchers working in educational contexts have tended to define the relationship between action and research in terms of the *aims* that pick out the *telos* or ends-in-view of the practice and the *procedural principles* that provide criteria for assessing the extent to which such ends are realised in practice (see Stenhouse (1975) on the *Process Model* and *The Teacher as Researcher*). When action research is cast as a form of deliberative inquiry, the nature of the ends-in-view and the means of realising them in action become joint objects of reflection. This is because the relationship between ends cast as 'values' and the means of realising them in action is a non-instrumental one; the ends are constituted and defined in action rather than as an outcome of it.

In the context of participatory action research, the *virtues* become the dispositions involved in translating the values that define the aims of a social practice into concrete actions that are constituted by a process of social interaction with significant others. The action research process maybe understood as a search for *forms of virtuous action* in which the values and principles that define a social practice are realised in particular situations. *Virtues* are those dispositions that discipline such a search. I argued earlier that, although bound to particular contexts of action, *phronesis* or deliberative inquiry should not be taken to imply the impossibility of yielding general insights into ways of realising values and principles in action via a constant comparison of cases. Such comparisons yield those rules of thumb or summaries of judgement which can function as a source of hypotheses, about how to realise principles in action to test in new situations (see also Elliott, 2015).

ETHICAL FRAMEWORKS PROPOSED BY CARPENTER

Carpenter cites MacFarlane's framework of virtues with approval. The proposed virtues – courage, respectfulness, resoluteness, sincerity, humility and reflexivity – are, or so it is suggested, involved in governing the conduct of qualitative social research. In addition, Carpenter proposes a different set of virtues – intelligence, sensitivity, discernment, perspicacity, cooperation, reasonableness, reflexivity – for governing (and assessing) the conduct of the reviewers themselves. Each virtue is accompanied by a number of guidelines for how the virtue is 'to be lived out'. For example, Carpenter suggests that *respectfulness* in the conduct of research can be lived out by

- Being respectful to others, including vulnerable individuals and communities.
- Being aware of the temptation to take advantage of organisational, social or intellectual power over others.
- Taking care not to cede too much power to others who may wish to distort the research process for their own ends.

In his framework for reviewing the conduct of ethical review Carpenter suggests that the virtue of *discernment* can be lived out by

- Careful analysis of the impact of the research – its general worthwhileness.
- Balancing of risks against benefits.
- Putting research into perspective by focussing on key aspects of context.
- Focussing on key ethical issues.
- Avoidance of paternalism.
- Endeavouring to not be distracted by trivial issues.

I would like to argue that in my view such 'lived out methods' can be understood as *procedural principles*, and placed on a par to those cited in accounts of participatory action research. It would seem, then, that Carpenter contradicts himself in claiming that a *virtue ethics* approach to the ethical review of social research tends to render the use of ethical principles redundant. This claim is based on confusion between principlism and the use of principles in a manner that is fundamental to practical reasoning across a particular domain of social practice. Such principles do not function as prescriptive rules that constrain the exercise of ethical agency. They leave necessary space for deliberating about the concrete actions to be taken and the way in which they might be realized in practice. For example, how exactly researchers, in their particular circumstances, avoid the temptation to take advantage of the organisational, social or intellectual power they have over others? How exactly does an ethical review body overcome constraints on its ability to focus on key ethical issues? The space for deliberative inquiry is not properly acknowledged by Carpenter.

One limitation of the frameworks that Carpenter cites as providing a basis for the ethical review of social research is their highly generic character. Much research aimed at achieving social ends is shaped by more specifically orientated professional and social practices governed by particular ends-in-view. These imply principles of procedure which can be conceptually linked to them. It would therefore be important to include or co-opt practitioner researchers into Research Review Panels when the conduct of participatory action research in their particular domain is the object of review. This suggests a need for a decentralised structure for research ethics committees; one that can be responsive to particular domains of social practice. Rather than as a single centralised body, they should operate in a more practical way, at a departmental level in higher education, and be constituted by the major stakeholder groups relevant to the domain or domains being researched.

Below I provide an example of an ethical framework for the conduct of *educational* research which Clem Adelman and I developed for a project funded by the Ford Foundation in the early 1970s (see Elliott, 2007b, 2015). It addressed a pedagogical aim that generally underpinned the curriculum reform movement in the 1960s and early 1970s but persistently and generally proved difficult to realise in practice; namely, that of *Inquiry/discovery learning*.

THE FORD TEACHING PROJECT

The pedagogical aim of inquiry/discovery learning was defined in terms of *independent or self-directed thinking*. This aim *was then* analysed into four

basic freedoms for students. The following formulation represents the outcome of discussions with the teachers:

1. To identify and initiate problems for inquiry.
2. To express their own ideas and develop lines of inquiry.
3. To discuss problems, ideas and evidence.
4. To test hypotheses and evaluate evidence.

The pedagogical implications of the four freedoms of inquiry learning were
then specified as a set of *negative* and *positive* procedural principles for orientat-
ing the role of teachers. The negative principles emphasized the teacher's responsibility to refrain from actions that impose constraints on students exercising
these freedoms, with a reminder also to do all in their power to protect students
from other forms of external constraint. The positive principles emphasize the
teacher's responsibility to intervene in the learning process in ways that actually enhance students' capabilities to exercise the freedoms. Implicit in the procedural principles is a distinction between the *negative* and *positive* aspects of
freedom. Students, for example, may be *free from* external constraints on their
freedom to express their own ideas and develop them into hypotheses but still be
unable to exercise this freedom because they lacked the necessary capabilities.

This clarification of the aims and principles of inquiry teaching was subsequently used by Ford T teachers as a framework for gathering and analyzing data
about the problems of engaging students in inquiry learning and testing strategies to ameliorate them. In the light of it they were able to identify the extent to
which their teaching strategies constrained or facilitated inquiry learning, and to
compare and contrast their experience across a range and variety of classroom,
school and curriculum contexts. Over time they were able to discern certain universal patterns of interaction in each other's classrooms that were problematic
for the realization of their pedagogical aim, and begin to experiment with strategies for changing them in discussion with each other. See below two examples of
hypotheses organized around particular values and procedural principles:

The Freedom to Express Ideas and Develop Lines of Inquiry

Procedural Principles

(a) Refrain from preventing students expressing their own ideas and developing lines of inquiry.
(b) Help students to develop their own ideas and lines of inquiry.

Constraint
Subject-Centered Focusing. When the teacher's questions focus students' attention solely on the subject-matter, rather than on their own ideas about it, s(he) may prevent them from initiating or developing their own ideas. Such focussing will be interpreted as an attempt to find out whether they know what s(he) expects them to know.

Constraint Removing Strategy
Refrain from framing your questions in terms which draw attention exclusively to the subject-matter rather than students' thoughts about it.

Guidance Strategy
Ask person-centered questions which focus the students' attention on their own ideas with respect to the subject-matter.

The Freedom to Discuss Problems, Ideas and Evidence

Procedural Principles

    (a) Refrain from restricting students' access to discussion.
    (b) Help pupils to learn how to discuss.

Constraint
Reinforcing Ideas. When the teacher responds to students' ideas with utterances like 'good', 'yes', 'interesting', etc., s(he) may prevent others from expressing alternative ideas. Such utterances may be interpreted as rewards for providing the responses required by the teacher.

Constraint Removing Strategy
Refrain from utterances that might imply finality, e.g., 'yes', 'good', 'right'.

Guidance Strategy
Reward students for their contributions to discussion by listening carefully to their remarks and asking others to do so.

The idea behind the construction of such a knowledge-base was to provide other teachers, who embraced a similar pedagogical aim, with a set of diagnostic and action-hypotheses to examine, test, refine and further develop in relation to their own pedagogical practices. Hence, it was hoped that other teachers might avoid constantly 'reinventing the wheel' while having space for exercising personal judgements in an ongoing process of collaborative professional knowledge construction.

The Ford Teaching Project reflected a tradition of educational action research developed initially by Lawrence Stenhouse, myself, and colleagues at the University of East Anglia. It became known as the 'British version' in comparison to earlier versions in the United States and Germany that were aimed explicitly at reconstituting the prevailing social science methodology. The 'British version' was more 'bottom up' inasmuch as it was driven by a need to address problems arising in the context of professional practice in schools in response to changes in the wider society. It is characterised by a *philosophically pragmatist* and *ethical methodology*, aimed at transforming the practice of teaching to realize *educational values* associated with a *democratic way of life*.

ETHICAL CODES OF PRACTICE GOVERNING ACCESS TO AND RELEASE OF DATA IN CASE STUDY-BASED ACTION RESEARCH

Ethical considerations are also relevant when action researchers –* participants in a social practice or those providing research support – gather data about the extent actions and interactions are consistent with the ethical aims and procedural principles of the practice. For example, a teacher may wish to record a discussion with a group of students about how a teaching strategy they use impacts on their experience as learners. This recording may then be used as evidence on which to base a judgement, in the light of a particular set of aims and procedural principles, about the extent to which the strategy needs to be changed or modified in some respect to effect an improvement in the situation. Regardless of the use of this evidence to effect an improvement, the students may be harmed by its release to others who then misuse it. In the process of securing and then releasing such evidence, the students may have been given little control. The relevant ethical considerations governing the conduct of participatory action-research in relation to *accessing and using data* about a social practice in a particular case are concerned to protect individual participants from harm. They justify the obligatory use of participant consent forms in relation to the methods of data collection and analysis when applications are made to research ethics committees.

Carpenter suggests that the use of consent forms in social research so often expresses a desire on the part of academic institutions and disciplines to protect themselves from blame. I would not disagree. However, in the context of sincerely conducted action-research, the use of a well-elaborated and detailed ethical code of practice, setting out the rights and responsibilities of individuals engaged in accessing and releasing data, is a necessary condition for enhancing the ethical agency of all participants in the social practice with respect to realising its aims and values in action. An important responsibility of an appropriate ethical review body is to monitor the extent to which procedures for obtaining participant consent are grounded in an ethical code of practice that will enable a dynamic process of participatory action research to take place.

Below I present an ethical code of practice which I have helped to develop over the years for the conduct of educational action research in schools.

Classroom Observation and Interviews with the Teacher and Pupils Concerned

1. Permission should be obtained in advance, from the teacher concerned, for opportunities to observe lessons and interview the teacher and pupils about them.
2. The focus of the observations and interviews should be negotiated with the teacher and agreed in advance of lessons.
3. Teachers should have access to all observational and interview records made about their lessons (but see 4 and 5 below).
4. Teachers should have access to observers' interviews with pupils about lessons on condition that the observer first obtains the permission of the pupils to release this data to the teacher. Pupils should be informed of this prior to being interviewed and of possible wider access to the data they provide.
5. Immediately following an interview between an observer and pupils, the latter should be given an opportunity to qualify anything they have said, to amend or add to it, and even strike it off the record.
6. All observational and interview records will remain confidential between the teacher and the observer until their use for purposes of reporting to and sharing with others has been agreed between them.
7. When pupils are interviewed by their own teacher, they should be given the same guarantees over the construction of the interview record and its subsequent use as those obtained in 5 and 6.

Access to and Release of Data by Researchers from Outside for the Purpose
of Engaging Teachers in Research

1. The focus of the research should be agreed with the in-school coordinator
   on behalf of the school.
2. Information about the aims of the research and its methodology should
   be made available to all school staff and opportunities made available for
   them to discuss it with the researcher.
3. The researcher(s) should have no automatic right to observe events and situations in the school without permission in advance from appropriate persons. This should be obtained in consultation with the in-school coordinator.
4. Teachers and pupils have the right, without prejudice, to turn down requests
   for an interview, and therefore should, whenever possible, be given advance
   notice by the researcher(s) together with relevant information about the
   focus of the interview.
5. No interview or observational data will be included in research reports,
   nor made accessible to others in any form, without the permission of those
   individuals or groups who provided it or allowed access to it.
6. Anonymity should be guaranteed to individuals whose actions and views are
   evidenced in research reports. Where anonymity is clearly not sufficient to
   mask identity the representation of relevant actions and views should be negotiated and agreed between the individuals concerned and the researcher(s).
7. Anonymity should be guaranteed to consortium schools whose activities
   are evidenced in research reports unless they jointly decide otherwise.
8. Before research reports are distributed outside the school or consortium,
   a draft should be circulated for comment and discussion to the in-school
   coordinator(s) and all those who have cooperated with the research. The
   coordinator(s) help to convene a formal meeting to discuss the draft should
   be enlisted.
9. Comment and discussion of first draft reports should be accommodated
   and incorporated into the final drafts to the satisfaction of the school(s)
   (as represented by the coordinator(s)).

Such codes of practice should, of course, be treated as provisional and open
to revision in the light of experience and shifting organisational and political
structures. They should never be regarded as fixed set of rules, but rather as a
basis for negotiating with individuals their participation in a process of research
that is designed to directly affect improvements in the quality of a social practice. Their ethical function is that of building sufficient trust to engage individuals as active participants in the transformation of their social practices.

SOME CONCLUDING REMARKS

Carpenter's paper and his extensive use of MacFarlane's work suggests to me that a starting point for developing *virtue ethics* frameworks for the ethical review of social research should be with respect to the conduct of participatory action research facilitated by academic institutions across a wide variety of professional and practical domains. In this context, ethical review should be unambiguously viewed as a participatory and democratic process, where engagement between 'the committee' and 'researchers' transcends the bureaucratic exercise of reviewing documents. Such a starting point may inform the process of developing 'virtue ethics' frameworks for social research generally. Interestingly, the British Educational Research Association has now singled out participatory action research for special consideration as an object of ethical review. This is no doubt due to the fact that such research does not easily fit into the bureaucratic format that has come to shape the ethical review process.

In this paper, by way of a response to Carpenter, I have attempted to clarify the major ethical dimensions that need to be incorporated into the design and conduct of participatory action research. Testing and further developing these as a basis for ethical review in relation to particular professional and other social domains of practice may help to clarify the ethical aspects and issues that ethical reviews of social science research more generally need to consider.

REFERENCES

Elliott, J. (2007a). Educational research as a form of democratic rationality. In D. Bridges & R. Smith (Eds.), *Philosophy, methodology and educational research* (pp. 149–166). Oxford: Blackwell.

Elliott, J. (2007b). *Reflecting where the action is: The selected works of John Elliott*, (pp. 30–61). New York, NY: Routledge.

Elliott, J. (2015). Educational action research as a quest for virtue in teaching. *Educational Action Research: An International Journal, 23*(1), 4–21. Special Issue: Value and Virtue in Practice-based Research, edited by J. McNiff.

Elliott, J., & Lukes, D. (2009). Epistemology as ethics in research and policy: The use of case studies. In D. Bridges, P. Smeyers, & R. Smith (Eds.), *Evidence-based education policy: What evidence? What basis? Whose policy?* (pp. 82–114). Hoboken, NJ: Wiley-Blackwell.

Macfarlane, B. (2009). *Researching with integrity: The ethics of academic inquiry*, Routledge: New York.

Macfarlane, B. (2010). Values and virtues in qualitative research. In M. Savin-Baden & C. H. Major, (Eds.), *New Approaches to Qualitative Research: wisdom and understanding*, Routledge: New York.

Nussbaum, M. C. (1990). *Love's knowledge: Essays on philosophy and literature* (pp. 68–69). Oxford: Oxford University Press.

O'Neill, O. (1996). *Towards justice and virtue: A constructive account of practical reasoning* (p. 123). Cambridge: Cambridge University Press.

Stenhouse, L. (1975). *An introduction to curriculum research and development* (pp. 84–97 and 142–165). London: Heinemann Educational.

CHAPTER 8

COMMENTARY ON: VIRTUE ETHICS IN THE PRACTICE AND REVIEW OF SOCIAL SCIENCE RESEARCH: THE VIRTUOUS ETHICS COMMITTEE BY DAVID CARPENTER

Jason Z. Morris and Marilyn C. Morris

ABSTRACT

David Carpenter argues in favour of Internal Review Boards taking a virtue ethics approach to their reviews of research proposals. Carpenter views principle- and code-based approaches as in competition with virtue ethics, and he describes reliance on principles and codes as neither necessary nor sufficient. We agree with Carpenter's thesis that a virtue ethics approach would be beneficial and even necessary for exemplary review of research proposals. We disagree with Carpenter, however, about the weight that should be given to principles and codes. We defend here our view that principles and regulations are indispensible to ethical review of research, in spite of the fact that principles often conflict with each other. In those

Virtue Ethics in the Conduct and Governance of Social Science Research
Advances in Research Ethics and Integrity, Volume 3, 155–160
ISSN: 2398-6018/doi:10.1108/S2398-601820180000003009

situations, the reviewer's virtue of practical wisdom is necessary to adjudicate between competing ethical claims.

Keywords: Virtue ethics; IRB; ethical review; regulations; principles

COMMENTARY

In his chapter in this volume David Carpenter describes the shortcomings of research ethics reviews based exclusively on principlism, codes, or consequentialism and lays out his vision for how virtue ethics could more fruitfully direct Internal Review Boards (IRBs in the United States), and Research Ethics Committees (RECs in the United Kingdom) in their deliberations. In a recent paper, 'The Importance of Virtue Ethics in the IRB' (Morris & Morris, 2016), we offered a somewhat different concept for the roles of regulations, principles and virtue ethics in the internal review of research proposals. We are grateful for the opportunity to continue this important discussion. For the remainder of this work, when we refer to "IRBs," we intend to indicate IRBs as well as REBs.

We agree with Carpenter's central thesis that insufficient attention is given to the importance of the virtues of IRB members in the ethics review of research involving human subjects. We also agree that a virtue ethics approach to research review facilitates collaboration between researchers and reviewers. IRBs applying a virtue ethics approach may be better able to carry out their responsibilities regarding the ethical review of research protocols and proposals. Our view differs from Carpenter's in the value that we ascribe to principle- and code-based approaches to research review. Carpenter describes non-virtue-based approaches to IRB reviews as neither necessary nor sufficient. We see them as necessary and as complementary to a virtue ethics approach. We agree that principle- and code-based approaches on their own are insufficient, in that conflicts invariably arise in which optimizing for one principle means infringing upon another. We therefore recommend viewing principles and regulations as if they were claimants in ethics disputes. Optimal adjudication of those disputes depends on the virtues of IRB members and most especially on their practical wisdom. A superficial focus on principles or consequences shifts attention away from the agent, the person conducting the ethical review, while virtue ethics focusses attention back on the IRB members. These IRB members must balance claims of relevant principles and regulations, taking into appropriate account the likely consequences of their decisions.

Carpenter sees codes as neither necessary nor sufficient for ethics review for the following two main reasons: (1) He believes that a primary function of codes is to 'protect the good standing of the profession or academic discipline responsible for its promulgation'. The fact that IRBs generally recognize the importance of lay members serving on ethics committees, he claims, runs counter to the notion that professional codes of conduct should serve as standards for review. (2) He has 'never witnessed the systematic application of a code in the course of a review', which could indicate that ethics committees cannot rely on codes to highlight important ethical concerns in research proposals.

We disagree with the proposition that codes exist primarily to protect the reputations of professions. We are not certain which codes Carpenter refers to here. For example, in the UNESCO code of conduct for social science research, researchers are called on to 'consider the effects of his/her work, including the consequences or misuse, both for the individuals and groups amongst whom they do their fieldwork, and for their colleagues and for the wider society' (UNESCO, 2017). In our view, one of the primary purposes of codes, even those originating within a professional society, is to safeguard the welfare of research subjects. We believe that in the realms of both biomedical and social sciences, IRBs, inclusive of their lay members, look to ethical codes such the Declaration of Helsinki or the Belmont Report because these documents provide well-articulated guidelines to help ensure that researchers do not lose sight of the rights and welfare of research participants.

It is difficult to estimate how often codes are systematically applied in IRB deliberations. However, drawing from our own experience, we do believe that IRB members look to professional codes to inform debate. Furthermore, whether or not it is the case that they do so, it is our contention that they ought to do so. Just as IRBs are expected and required to reject proposals that disregard or violate regulations, IRBs should reject proposals that run counter to mainstays of professional codes of conduct. For instance, it may be expedient for a researcher to enrol subjects from a vulnerable but easily accessible population (e.g. prisoners or orphans). The professional codes of conduct for research in the biomedical and behavioural sciences described in The Belmont Report serve to remind us of the need to protect vulnerable populations even when the risks and burdens of research participation are low.

We do not believe that regulations or professional codes are sufficient to ensure ethical conduct of research. Given the rapid advance of technology, codes and regulations can never address every eventuality and could never be sufficient for ethics review. Nevertheless, well-written codes that afford appropriate latitude to IRBs and researchers are indispensable to maintain a high standard of ethical review. Whilst professional codes may not play the same critical role that regulations do, we maintain that they are highly valuable in research ethics review.

Carpenter also objects to reliance on principlism. He writes that although research reviewers often refer to principles, he has 'never witnessed any systematic application of them in structuring an ethical review and providing clear feedback to applicants'. He cites Stark's (2012) ethnographic study of IRBs in support of this point. Carpenter suggests that reviewers who have already detected a likely ethical breach in a protocol simply label that breach as a violation of some principle. The principle itself is therefore seen as adding 'nothing of substance to the original intuitions of the committee'. We would want to see more empirical evidence before concluding that this treatment of ethics principles is universal, and we argue that even the exercise of labelling an intuition can be useful. A vague sense that something might be wrong gains credibility once we determine the specific principle being violated. An unnamed source of unease might be disregarded if a committee member could not articulate the basis for his or her unease. Nevertheless, such unease is not unusual in matters of moral uncertainty.

While one could argue that Beauchamp's (2009) four principles were specifically defined for application to biomedical science and have less relevance in evaluating social science research, there seems nothing intrinsically biomedical to the ideas of autonomy, beneficence, non-maleficence, and justice. We believe that Beauchamp's four principles provide a useful language for ethics debate in both biomedical and social science research review arenas.

Therefore, we disagree with Carpenter's contention that applying principles as regulatory constraints would lead IRBs to be 'less ethically responsive to particular situations'. Nevertheless, we do agree that *sole* reliance on the four principles would limit the language and substance of debate, and that a balancing influence, such as a virtue ethics approach, is warranted. The most challenging and interesting aspects of research review arise when tension exists between competing goods or principles. For instance, a population may stand to benefit significantly from the better understanding of a particular social phenomenon. IRBs are commonly asked to determine the extent to which deception, for example, is acceptable in the course of such a study. The question is not whether beneficence trumps autonomy, but whether, in this particular case, a virtuous individual or a virtuous IRB would approve the proposed research. As Beauchamp and Childress (2009) wrote: 'Principles, rules, and rights require *balancing* no less than *specification*' [emphasis in the original]. They go on to stress the importance of the agent in determining the appropriate weights to be given to the different principles, depending on the particular context. It is the role of the IRB to make these context-specific determinations.

As with principlism, we argue that Carpenter dismisses consequentialism too hastily. Again, he says 'there is no evidence of' IRBs formally applying consequentialism in the course of their deliberations, but he shows no data that would lead us to believe that consequences are generally ignored by IRBs. Certainly in the biomedical sciences, IRBs routinely approve studies in which the individual is exposed to risk without the prospect for direct benefit and do so for the greater good of society. We agree that IRBs may not readily approve studies that result in significant harm to the individual even for a significant benefit to society. However, this fact is not inconsistent with a consequentialist theory of morality. A system in which individuals were rendered entirely vulnerable to the needs of the majority would be oppressive and would not be a system that maximized benefit to those unfortunate enough to live within it.

We endorse Carpenter's suggestion to the effect that 'a review, based on virtue ethics, could be conducted by starting with an attempt to understand the research, and endeavouring to empathise with all those involved in it, most significantly the researcher and participants'. If the only role for IRBs were to protect research subjects, they could easily do so by prohibiting all research. Rather, it is the job of IRBs to facilitate quality research in a manner consistent with human research subject protection. IRBs should be cooperative and collegial and not mere gatekeepers. We therefore strongly agree with Carpenter that changing the IRB's focus from what is wrong with a research proposal to what the researchers are aiming to do, and how we can help ensure that it is done properly would have a salutary effect on ethical reviews of research.

We also appreciate the highly useful table that Carpenter composed on Reviewing Phases. IRBs are unlikely to adopt Carpenter's phases of review in a literal fashion, addressing each phase in turn. However, virtue ethics approaches generally place great emphasis on education and training in the virtues, and tools such as this table could significantly enhance the training offered to IRB members.

One interesting point of contrast between Carpenter's vision for a virtue ethics-based IRB and ours is the focus Carpenter places on the virtue of researchers. Carpenter proposes that IRB review should include efforts to discern the virtues of the researchers who submitted proposals. There are advantages and disadvantages to this approach. One of the underlying assumptions of virtue ethics is that people can recognize excellence (i.e. embodying of the virtues) in others. So in principle, it should not be impossible, given sufficient exposure, for IRBs to recognize the virtues possessed by researchers. Carpenter, however, rightly acknowledges that merely reading a proposal might not be sufficient to glean the qualities of researchers. We would add another concern to this one: IRBs are charged with approving protocols, not researchers. Though there may be some cases – where there is a history of misconduct, for example – where an IRB would be justified in taking researchers' characters into account. Personalizing IRB deliberations in the way Carpenter suggests would likely make cooperation between researchers and IRBs more contentious and could undermine the confidence that researchers have in IRBs. We agree that the virtue of researchers will determine in large part whether research is designed and carried out in an ethical manner. We believe that researchers should be trained to reflect on the virtues pertinent to conducting of ethical research and to analyze how well their research protocols reflect the ethics goals of research, but we would not recommend that IRBs should carry out such a review on behalf of the researchers who submit protocols.

In summary, we strongly endorse Carpenter's assertion that virtue ethics should guide ethics reviews of research protocols. We disagree with Carpenter when he minimizes the importance of principles, codes, and an analysis of consequences in ethical review. Rather, we believe that optimal ethics review requires that IRB members employ practical wisdom to accord appropriate, substantial consideration to principles, regulations, and the likely consequences of their decisions. We believe that institutions should train IRB members and researchers in the virtues so that they can identify and most appropriately resolve the relevant ethical issues they encounter, and we therefore particularly appreciate the tools that Carpenter has offered here for IRB members and researchers to undertake a systematic, virtue-based review of research.

REFERENCES

Beauchamp, T. L., & Childress, J. F. (2009). *Principles of biomedical ethics* (p. 18). New York, NY: Oxford University Press.

Morris, J. Z., & Morris, M. C. (2016). The Importance of Virtue Ethics in the IRB. *Research Ethics*, *12*(4), 201–216.

National Commission for the Protection of Human Subjects of Biomedical and Behavioral Research, Department of Health, Education and Welfare (DHEW) (30 September 1978). *The Belmont Report* (PDF). Washington, DC: United States Government Printing Office.

Stark, L. J. M. (2012). *Behind closed doors: IRBs and the making of ethical research*. Chicago, IL: The University of Chicago Press.

UNESCO. *Code of conduct social science research*. Retrieved from http://www.unesco.org/fileadmin/MULTIMEDIA/HQ/SHS/pdf/Soc_Sci_Code.pdf. Accessed on March 15, 2017.

SECTION 3

PHRÓNĒSIS IN THE PRACTICE/ CONDUCT AND REVIEW/ GOVERNANCE OF SOCIAL SCIENTIFIC RESEARCH

CHAPTER 9

ETHICAL REGULATION OF SOCIAL RESEARCH VERSUS THE CULTIVATION OF PHRÓNĒSIS

Anna Traianou

ABSTRACT

This chapter argues that there is conflict between the requirements laid down by the regimes of ethical regulation that have been introduced in many countries over the past few decades and what is required if social research is to be done well, not least in ethical terms. The reasons for the rise of ethical regulation are outlined along with the criticisms that have been made of it by social scientists. One aspect of this criticism has been an emphasis on the necessarily situational character of ethical judgement, the potential conflicts amongst values, and the ways in which ethical considerations are entwined with methodological and prudential ones. These points have often been formulated via the concept of phrónēsis (wise judgement). The meaning of this is outlined, as well as how the need for such judgement conflicts with the assumptions built into the operation of ethical regulation. It is suggested that these assumptions, as embedded in many official statements, amount to a form of moralism that is counterproductive if good research that is ethically acceptable is to be encouraged. It is argued that ethics committees should not exercise control over what research is done

Virtue Ethics in the Conduct and Governance of Social Science Research
Advances in Research Ethics and Integrity, Volume 3, 163–177
ISSN: 2398-6018/doi:10.1108/S2398-601820180000003010

but ought rather to serve as forums in which researchers are forced to justify
the design of proposed research studies, and to address any ethical issues
arising from research that they have already carried out.

Keywords: Phrónēsis; virtue ethics; social research; research ethics

INTRODUCTION

This chapter focusses on the sharp tension between the 'creep' of ethical regulation from the fields of medicine and psychology across the whole of social science (Haggerty, 2004) and the practical requirements of doing social research in ways that are ethically satisfactory. What is meant by 'ethical regulation' here is the operation of ethics committees, located in universities and other organisations, that decide whether or not particular research projects can go ahead, and on what terms. In the United Kingdom, and some other countries, this is a relatively new process, becoming established over the past 20 years. By contrast, in the United States, Institutional Review Boards (IRBs) have been in operation for several decades.

In part, the rise of ethical regulation reflects a now dominant feature of much public sector management: the drive for so-called 'transparent accountability' which requires members of professions continually to *demonstrate* that what they do is effective and efficient (Diefenbach, 2009; Pollitt, 1990; Power, 1997). This has been closely associated with a collapse in public trust of professionals, exacerbated by the fact that we cannot avoid reliance on strangers in an increasingly globalised world, leading to the idea that some procedural substitute for personal trust is required. Equally important, perhaps, has been increased cynicism, generated by a culture that has been strongly shaped by the falsehoods of advertisers and publicity agents, and the spin of politicians.

So, ethical regulation of social research is, to some degree, just one further example of the requirement that specialised occupational activities be subject to a mode of explicit procedural accountability. However, another major driver behind the rise of ethical regulation of social research seems to have been a concern on the part of funding bodies, in the United Kingdom principally the Economic and Social Research Council, as well as universities, that they could be open to legal prosecution and compensation claims should any research they fund, or researchers they employ, be deemed to have caused harm (Dingwall, 2008; Hedgecoe, 2016; van den Hoonaard, 2011). It is at least partly to defend themselves against this perceived threat, in an increasingly litigious society, that they have turned to the establishment of ethics committees to vet research proposals, viewing these as offering some legal defence and allowing them to deflect blame onto individual researchers where there has been deviation from laid down procedures.[1]

As already noted, moves towards ethical regulation of research initially arose in the context of medical and psychological research, including that involving animals, where, as a result of the growth of medical complaints, and of campaigns by animal rights activists, there was perceived to be an increasingly severe risk of legal challenge. However, extension of the remit of ethics committees across most social research has prompted considerable criticism: many social researchers argue that the new regulatory procedures have introduced significant barriers into the research process, as well as delays. Some have also insisted that these procedures are unnecessary, counterproductive (in the sense that, in practice, they are likely to increase the chances of unethical practice), and are themselves unethical, being an infringement of the academic freedom that is essential if sound research is to be pursued (see, for example, Dingwall, 2006; Feeley, 2007a; Hamburger, 2007; Hammersley, 2009; Katz, 2007; Schrag, 2010; Shweder, 2006; Traianou, 2015; van den Hoonaard, 2011). Discussing the US context, Zywicki (2007, p. 866) writes the following:

> Virtually all commentators who have studied the IRB system as it currently operates [...] believe that the costs of the system [...] vastly exceed the benefits, especially when the opportunity cost of researchers' and IRB panellists' time is taken into account. There is little hard evidence that IRBs, as they are currently composed, create more than trivial amounts of public value in terms of reducing the risk of dangerous or unethical research, or that less burdensome alternatives could not perform the same functions more efficiently. [...] By contrast, there are several well-known examples of IRB lapses that permitted dangerous research to occur, notwithstanding compliance with the onerous IRB process. At the same time, there are many examples of innocent researchers caught in the Kafkaesque world of IRB procedures.

Meanwhile, Coe (2007, p. 724) declares that 'the IRB movement began with a noble purpose but has degenerated into a tyranny that must be overthrown'.

One component of this criticism has sometimes been an emphasis on the essential role of phrónēsis (wise judgement) in social research, as in other professional activities (see Dunne, 1997). It has been argued that, because this is necessary if research is to be pursued well, the sort of transparency demanded by ethical regulation is impossible. More than this, there is significant potential for current attempts to regulate the ethics of research to have undesirable effects on the moral character of researchers, leading them to become primarily concerned with whether or not they are compliant with established rules or procedures rather than with making good ethical and methodological judgements; two concerns will often not be compatible. Whatever the quality of deliberation that takes place within an ethics committee, the fact that researchers are virtually forced to comply with its decisions will short-circuit any process of phrónēsis on their part – at least in the initial planning stage of the research, and perhaps later as well.

THE CONCEPT OF PHRÓNĒSIS

Aristotle argued that governance – from state decision-making to the running of a household – relies on phrónēsis. The meaning of this Greek word can, to some degree, be rendered in English by the concept of skill, especially since we talk of social as well as of physical skills. Skills are learned via lengthy periods of experience and practice, perhaps under the guidance of someone who already has them, this perhaps being accompanied by reflection on past experience that is directed towards facilitating improved performance in the future. Thus, skill does not amount to following a set of rules, even though 'rules of thumb' can be used to facilitate and refine skilful practice (see Dreyfus, 2004; Dreyfus & Dreyfus, 1986; see also Eraut, 1994). However, the notion of skill omits an important element from the meaning given to the term 'phrónēsis' by Aristotle: it is not just a matter of skill but also of virtue (see Hammersley, 2018; Macfarlane, 2009; Macintyre, 1981; Pring, 2001). What Aristotle means by an activity being done well is not just that actions are effective in achieving a goal but also that they are performed in ways that are good in a broader sense than this: that they exemplify and respect all human ideals. Furthermore, not the least part of this is that *how* the activity is performed must be good for the person engaged in it: it must form part of a good life for that person. Aristotle argues that only those who act in ways that contribute to a good life for themselves will be acting ethically. Indeed, this is in large part what the term 'ethical' means for him.

How far can this notion of phrónēsis be applied to the task of carrying out social research, and to research ethics specifically? We can think of human activities as being ranged along a dimension, or set of dimensions, of increasing complexity. It seems likely that the more complex the activity, the greater the need for phrónēsis. There are various aspects of this complexity, such as the following:

1. Interpretation may be required regarding what would count as achieving the goal(s) of the activity, and about what are the proper constraints operating on its pursuit.
2. Conflicting goals or concerns may need to be taken into account.
3. The situations faced may not conform to standard types in which standard 'treatments' can be applied.

Pursuit of activities at one end of this spectrum can be reduced to specific procedures or rules, at least to some degree. However, towards the other end, it becomes increasingly difficult to do this, and doing social research falls into this category.

Some kinds of research, especially those involving qualitative methods, display these kinds of complexity in the sharpest form. This is because they require the collection of unstructured data through open-ended interviews, and/or participant observation in 'natural' settings over which the researcher has little control. In the latter case, access may need to be negotiated if the relevant settings are to be observed, and interpersonal relations will need to be established and maintained with participants in those settings. What this will entail, and what problems may arise, cannot be anticipated with much accuracy; and judgements about what it is best to do will have to take account of particular events in the settings and of the evolving relationships of the researcher with gatekeepers and participants. Both methodological and ethical considerations are involved here. Indeed, while these two sorts of issues are analytically distinct, in practice these are closely intertwined: when researchers make decisions in the field they must take account of both these dimensions and of how they relate to one another, as well as of prudential issues such as those relating to their own safety.

In light of this, it should be clear that there are many respects in which the concept of phrónēsis captures important features of what is involved in social research. Above all, there is an unavoidable need for situational judgement: decisions have to be tailored to particular situations, involving judgements about what is more and what is less important in the circumstances, and therefore what should be foregrounded and what backgrounded (see Ebrahim, 2010; Flewitt, 2005; Simons & Usher, 2000). Equally necessary are the judgements about the likelihood of various outcomes, of what is likely to lead to success, of the probable extent of benefits, or the risks and likely severity of harms. In other words, judgements have to be made about what is proportionate and appropriate in all these respects, given the particular situations faced. Moreover, as already noted, these situations do not come in standard forms, nor are ethical issues – if what is meant by this phrase is 'what is proper in dealing with other people' – the only relevant considerations.

THE CONFLICT WITH ETHICAL REGULATION

There are two assumptions built into the process of ethical regulation that are at odds with the idea that researchers must exercise phrónēsis. First, it

assumes that ethical issues can, and should, be identified at the beginning of
the research process, with specific strategies for responding to them identified. Ethics committees will usually only give the green light to a project if
potential ethical (and indeed methodological) problems, along with ways of
dealing with them, have been spelt out in the initial proposal. In other words,
an ethical and methodological template must be set up at the beginning, and
it is expected that this will be followed in the research process itself.

However, it should be clear from what has been said above, and from even
the most superficial experience of the research process, that not all problems
can be anticipated, that some that are anticipated do not arise, and that even
when problems have been anticipated they will often take forms that require
new thinking about how to handle them in the specific circumstances in which
they occur. As already noted, this is especially true in the case of qualitative
inquiry, where research does not and cannot involve formulating a research
design, and then simply implementing it. Participant observation in natural
settings requires continual negotiation of access to data, and is therefore subject to various contingencies, over many of which the researcher has little control. Even in the case of interviews, these are usually relatively unstructured
in character, and often carried out in settings that are not controlled by the
researcher. All these features make it difficult to anticipate what will happen
at various stages of the research process and to plan in any detail how ethical
issues will be dealt with. To one degree or another, this applies to the practice
of *all* forms of social research as opposed to textbook accounts of them.

The second feature of ethical regulation which is at odds with the practical
nature of research, and its reliance on phrónēsis, is the assumption that what
is and is not the 'best practice' can be made fully explicit. This is not possible
because, like other professional activities, research necessarily depends upon
the personal capacity to make decisions in which a variety of relevant considerations must be weighed against one another and given appropriate interpretations and priority in particular circumstances. The grounds for these decisions
cannot be made fully explicit in ways that would be accessible to someone with
little experience of the kind of research involved and/or of the situation in
which it was carried out. There is a parallel here with the inability of a doctor to
explain in 'transparent' terms how she judges what particular sets of symptoms
indicate, or of a social worker to make explicit why she 'knows' that something
is wrong during a family visit even when there are no obvious signs. It is not
that these matters are beyond all expression, but rather that no formulation can
make their full significance clear to the lay person (see Montgomery, 2006).

The key problem here is that members of ethics committees, not just 'lay
members' but most members, will not have this capacity because they do not

have the relevant background knowledge and experience: they will not always have had practical experience with the methods being proposed in a particular study, and they are even less likely to have detailed substantive knowledge of the setting(s) in which the research will be carried out. As a result, most of them would not be well placed even to judge retrospective accounts of decisions that had been made in a piece of research. Yet, as already noted, in fact they are being asked to make a judgement *prospectively* on the basis of a researcher's and their own anticipations of what problems might arise and how these could best be dealt with. I suggest that it is near impossible to do this well with any reliability. This is purportedly done on the basis of various codes and procedural statements that are taken properly to govern all ethical judgements about research practice. These amount to an 'abridgement of the contingencies and vicissitudes of practice that aspires to be but can never succeed in becoming an authoritative, prescriptive guide for practice' (Gray, 2009, pp. 78–79).[2]

Moreover, very often, 'best practice' amounts to what has been called moralism: 'the vice of overdoing morality' (Coady, 2005, p. 101; Hammersley & Traianou, 2012, Conclusion).[3] In the case of ethical regulation, moralism refers to the requirement that researchers adhere to 'high', perhaps even to 'the highest', ethical standards, these being specified in terms of abstract principles whose implications for particular cases are regarded as closely determined in character – in effect, they amount to injunctions. Appeal to high, or even the highest, ethical standards is routine in the rhetoric around ethical regulation. For example, the UK Research Integrity Office (UKRIO, 2009, p. 14) states that 'we promote integrity and high ethical standards,' and recently produced a document which places emphasis on the 'training and development' of researchers in order to ensure that they meet the 'highest standards' of 'research conduct'.[4] This document is entirely about compliance, with no hint that there could be problems or disagreements about what would and would not be ethical, or what would be justifiable. For instance, one concrete requirement is that consent be obtained from research participants. But as I have argued elsewhere, written consent is not always desirable (see Hammersley & Traianou, 2014, Chapter 4), and in the context of covert research it is impossible. Amongst social science researchers, there has been much debate around whether *covert* research is ever justified and, if so, under what conditions (Bulmer, 1982; Herrera, 1999; Leo, 1995). Some commentators argue that it is virtually never legitimate (Bok, 1978; Shils, 1956; Warwick, 1982), while others insist that covert research is an acceptable and necessary strategy in particular research settings (Calvey, 2000, 2008, 2017; Douglas, 1976; Homan, 1980). These discussions have identified a range of considerations that need to be taken into account in making judgements about this issue. The discourse of ethical regulation makes it almost impossible for covert research to be pursued. In my view, however, rather than being formulated either as a general prohibition or even as a globally permissive statement, any judgement about whether or not covert research is legitimate must be made in relation to specific cases. This is because covertness can vary significantly, as too can conditions in the field that are relevant to making a judgement about its legitimacy.

In statements like those from UKRIO (2009), it is apparently assumed that we cannot be 'too ethical', and that social research involves a high risk of severe ethical dangers for the people studied so that rigorous precautions must be taken to avoid these. Yet, since there are often conflicting principles, it is by no means clear what would or would not be ethical, or more rather than less ethical, in some cases. Furthermore, there is very often a tension between ethical considerations relating to the people being studied and the methodological requirements of the research, so that some sort of trade-off is required between the two. Once again, this must necessarily be done in a way that takes account of the distinctive features of the particular situation faced. For reasons already explained, this is not the sort of judgement that ethics committees can make.

It is also necessary to recognise that in the world in which researchers must operate, the other parties with whom they have to deal may well be committed to ideals and interests that are at odds with the requirements of social research in one respect or another. One of the problems with the kind of moralism being criticised here is that it is premised on an unrealistic view of human nature and society. Conflicting ideals and interests, and struggles over these, are endemic in social life; and, as a result, the use of coercion, manipulation and deception is widespread. Given this, moralism is not a viable basis for carrying out any activity, including qualitative inquiry (Douglas, 1976; Duster, Matza, & Wellman, 1979; Littrell, 1993). If researchers are to get their work done in *the world as it is* and produce reliable knowledge, they will often have to engage in actions that fall short of 'the highest standards'.

In short, what can reasonably be expected of social researchers is *not* adherence to the highest standards but rather that their behavior is *acceptable* in terms of practical values, *taking account of the constraints operating in the situations concerned*. It is also important to remember that social scientists are members of a profession operating *within* societies and that all they can distinctively aspire to is a high commitment to a specific goal and to the values associated with this, not some general ethical superiority. Perhaps it is necessary to emphasise that this does not amount to a recommendation of expediency, even less to the conclusion that 'anything goes'. In fact, adopting a more realistic conception of what research ethics entails ought to lead to more careful and realistic judgements about what can and should be done in the field.

Interestingly, all this suggests a slightly different approach to the notion of phrónēsis from that characteristic of Aristotle, one that takes in Machiavelli's rather different conception of 'virtue'. Contrary to what is sometimes assumed, Machiavelli did not propose that rulers and other political agents should pursue evil ends. Rather, he argued that they will often have to use means that are regarded as morally questionable, such as deception, and even sometimes those that are abhorrent, such as war, *in order to pursue effectively ends that are good.* According to Strauss (1987, p. 84), Machiavelli was the first of the early modern political philosophers whose ethical thinking starts not from 'how people ought to live', in the manner of the ancients, but rather from 'how people actually live'. In Max Weber's terms, Machiavelli rejected an 'ethics of ultimate ends' in favor of an 'ethic of responsibility' (see Bruun, 2007, pp. 250–259). It seems to me that there is scope for applying this argument in the context of research (Hammersley & Traianou, 2011). However, the contrast between this Machiavellian approach and the Aristotelian notion of phrónēsis should not be exaggerated: in both cases the emphasis is on the need to develop wise and skilful judgement in dealing, in the best way possible, with the contingencies that arise, taking account of all the considerations that are relevant, including those that conflict with one another. This is not a matter of the end justifying the use of any means but rather that both ends and means must be ranked in terms of desirability (on various grounds), with phrónēsis being deployed to 'weigh' the relative desirability of achieving a particular end against the use of means of varying degrees of likely effectiveness and desirability.

CONCLUSION

The demand for transparent accountability is understandable. There are genuine, and potentially serious, ethical dangers involved in the pursuit of some kinds of research; and, where these arise, regulation will certainly be necessary. More generally, the second half of the twentieth century witnessed a gradual erosion of public trust in claims made by professionals to be devoted solely to carrying out their tasks well, and thereby in their capacity to regulate themselves. Indeed, some sociologists and economists came to view professionalism as an ideology designed to enable occupations to increase their power over clients, over other occupations, and in relation to other organisations, including nation-states (see, for example, Larson, 1977). In this context, it might be argued that use of the concept of phrónēsis amounts to little more than an appeal to professional mystique, allowing bias in the service of self-interest.

Moreover, in the context of large, complex, and, to a large degree, globalised societies, we are forced to rely on anonymous others, where there can be no personal trust. While professional status and expertise at one time provided a substitute for this, in a world where status hierarchies are increasingly under challenge, and where trust has been eroded by fraudulent advertising and political spin, this kind of trust is undercut. As a result, there have been increasing demands for 'transparent accountability', in other words, that the basis for professional judgements be made explicit so as to be open to judgement by others. This was, of course, a central theme in the evidence-based practice movement (Wieringa, Engebretsen, Heggen, & Greenhalgh, 2017). While such accountability may not be possible, the concerns lying behind the call for this are by no means all misguided, some are genuine.

At the same time, we must not allow this to blind us to the problems involved in doing research well, and the necessary reliance of this on situational judgements, albeit guided by principles. I have spelt out the implications of this for research ethics. There is no form of transparency that will allow others to see, or to be completely assured, that what is being done by professionals, including researchers, conforms to 'best practice', in the sense of what it would be best to do in the specific circumstances faced. And pretending that there is some means of doing this, by enforcing procedures relying on this assumption, for instance, in the form of ethical regulation, damages the practice involved. Any attempt to deal with the ethical dangers associated with research must be proportionate, and should respect the limits of what is possible – rather than simply assuming that transparent accountability must be achievable, and that it will eliminate all uncertainty and risk. The risks associated with most social research are very different from, and arguably less severe than, those involved in testing medical treatments, which is where the pressure for ethical regulation originally arose. Furthermore, non-experimental research, and especially that involving the collection of unstructured data in the field, is much less open to prospective, procedural control than experimental work. Indeed, attempts to achieve this will almost always be counterproductive.[5]

It is also worth emphasising that researchers have never been free to do as they wish, contrary to what often seems to be assumed about the past. Prior to the spread of ethical regulation, they nevertheless operated in situations where legal rules applied; where other agents, notably gatekeepers but also sometimes research participants, had considerable power over the research process; and where there was always the prospect that colleagues would bring what they regarded as unethical behaviour to public attention, resulting in reputational damage for the researcher concerned, at the very least.[6] Any justification put forward for ethical regulation needs to demonstrate that these curbs were, and are, inadequate in the case of social research. It also needs to show that ethical regulation works in minimising, or at least reducing, unethical behaviour on the part of researchers. Yet, there is little evidence that it does; indeed, determining this is fraught with difficulties because of the variable judgements that can be made about what is and is not ethical. These judgements are rarely a matter of the straightforward application of a single principle, and as a result there is considerable scope for reasonable disagreement about what would and would not be ethical. This is precisely why phrónēsis is required, and that's why the attempt to achieve 'transparency' is unrealistic, while *efforts* to achieve it will very often have damaging consequences.[7]

It is perhaps necessary to emphasise that even if research necessarily depends upon phrónēsis, this does not rule out the desirability of guidelines, such as the 'codes' developed by professional associations. However, these must recognise that ethical considerations – specifically those relating to how researchers deal with the people they study – are multiple and potentially in conflict, and that they are not the only considerations that must be taken into account in doing research. Above all, codes must acknowledge that researchers have an obligation to pursue worthwhile knowledge effectively, and in a way that is *prudent*, for instance, keeping any risk of serious harm to themselves below an acceptable threshold. Furthermore, the pressure built into the specification of guidelines towards treating these as rules that should *govern* research activity must be resisted. Yet, this is precisely the tendency that ethical regulation institutionalises.

The role of phrónēsis does not eliminate all the functions of ethics committees, but they should no longer be regulatory bodies determining whether or not research projects can go ahead. Instead, they ought to be forums in which researchers are required to outline and defend their research proposals, or to defend research they have already carried out where this has generated ethical concerns.[8] In this way ethics committees could play an important role in facilitating the development of phrónēsis on the part of researchers, since they would force greater attention to methodological and ethical issues, and expose individual researchers to diverse views about these. At present, the regulatory function of ethics committees seriously inhibits this process, and thereby damages social research.

NOTES

1. Even though it is external funding bodies that instituted the requirement of ethical approval, most universities require almost all social research to go through an ethics committee, even that which is not externally funded, or not funded by an external agency that requires a research proposal to be approved by an ethics committee.

2. Gray is here discussing philosopher Oakeshott's (1962) critique of what he labels "rationalism."

3. There is a parallel between moralism and the religious enthusiasm that Locke (1975, Chapter 19) and others objected to in the seventeenth century as part of their defence of political liberalism.

4. See http://ukrio.org/wp-content/uploads/UKRIO-Code-of-Practice-for-Research.pdf. Accessed on June 23, 2017.

5. In addition, Stark (2011, p. 2, and *passim*) has shown that in medicine ethical regulation "has served to enable research as much as to restrict it," including some that many would regard as unethical.

6. For examples of cases where colleagues have called one another to account in the context of social research, see Hammersley and Traianou (2012, Chapter 1).

7. The case of medical research, and indeed any experimental research that involves treatments that carry with them substantial risks of harm, as well as potential benefit, is different from that of most social research. Here the potential dangers of ethical regulation may be outweighed by the risks carried by the research. However, it is important to note that even here regulation cannot deliver transparent accountability, nor does it necessarily prevent harm. Of course, ethical regulation can have beneficial consequences in terms of prompting researchers to take more account of ethical considerations, to recognise problems that they had overlooked, etc. However, it seems likely that these benefits could be gained in other ways.

8. For various other proposals for reform, usually less radical, see Carpenter (2007), Feeley (2007b), Hyman (2007), Marlow and Tolich (2015), Stark (2007), and van den Hoonaard and Hamilton (2016).

REFERENCES

Bok, S. (1978). *Lying: Moral choice in public and private life*. Hassocks Sussex: Harvester Press.

Bruun, H. H. (2007). Science, values, and politics in Max Weber's methodology. Aldershot: Ashgate.

Bulmer, M. (ed.). (1982). *Social research ethics: An examination of the merits of covert participant observation*. London: Macmillan.

Calvey, D. (2000). Getting on the door and staying there: A covert participant observational study of bouncers. In G. Lee-Treweek & S. Linkogle (Eds.), *Danger in the field: Risk and ethics in social research* (pp. 43–60). London: Routledge.

Calvey, D. (2008). The art and politics of covert research: Doing "situated ethics" in the field. *Sociology*, *42*(5), 905–918.

Calvey, D. (2017). *Covert research: The art, politics and ethics of undercover fieldwork*. London: Sage.

Carpenter, D. (2007). Institutional review boards, regulatory incentives, and some modest proposals for reform. *Northwestern University Law Review*, 101(2), 723–733.

Coady, C. A. J. (2005). Preface. *Journal of Applied Philosophy*, 22(2), 101–104.

Coe, F. (2007). The costs and benefits of a well-intended parasite: A witness and reporter on the IRB phenomenon. *Northwestern University Law Review*, *101*(2), 723–733.

Diefenbach, T. (2009). New public management in public sector organisations: The dark side of managerialsm "enlightenment." *Public Administration*, *87*(4), 892–909.

Dingwall, R. (2006). *Confronting the anti-democrats: The unethical nature of ethical regulation in social science.* Summary of Plenary Address to British Sociological Association Medical Sociology Group Annual Conference, Edinburgh, September 2006. Retrieved from https://www.academia.edu/1184594/Confronting_the_anti-democrats_The_unethical nature_of_ethical_regulation_in_social_science

Dingwall R. (2008). The ethical case against ethical regulation in humanities and social science research. *Twenty-First Century Society (Contemporary Social Science)*, *3*(1), 1–12.

Douglas, J. (1976). *Investigative social research.* Beverly Hills, CA: Sage.

Dreyfus, S. (2004). A five-stage model of the activities involved in teaching skills. *Bulletin of Science, Technology & Society*, *24*(3), 177–181.

Dreyfus, H., & Dreyfus, S. (1986). *Mind over machine: The power of human intuition and expertise in the era of the computer.* New York, NY: The Free Press.

Dunne, J. (1997). *Back to the rough ground: Practical judgment and the lure of technique.* Notre Dame, IN: University of Notre Dame Press.

Duster, T., Matza, D., & Wellman, D. (1979). Fieldwork and the protection of human subjects. *American Sociologist*, *14*, 136–142.

Ebrahim, H. (2010). Situated ethics: Possibilities for young children as research participants in the South African context. *Early Child Development & Care*, *180*, 289–298.

Eraut, M. (1994). *Developing professional knowledge and competence.* London: Falmer Press.

Feeley, M. (2007a). Legality, social research, and the challenge of institutional review boards. *Law & Society Review*, *41*(4), 757–776.

Feeley, M. (2007b). Response to comments. *Law & Society Review*, *41*(4), 811–818.

Flewitt, R. (2005). Conducting research with young children: Some ethical considerations. *Early Child Development and Care*, *175*(6), 553–565.

Gray, J. (2009). *Gray's anatomy: Selected writings.* London: Allen Lane.

Haggerty, K. (2004). Ethics creep: Governing social science research in the name of ethics. *Qualitative Sociology*, *27*(4), 391–414.

Hamburger, P. (2007). Getting permission. *Northwestern University Law Review*, *101*(2), 405–492.

Hammersley, M. (2009). Against the ethicists: On the evils of ethical regulation. *International Journal of Social Research Methodology*, *12*(3), 211–225.

Hammersley, M. (2018). Is PHRÓNE–SIS necessarily virtuous? In Ibhophen, R. (Ed.), *Advances in Research Ethics and Integrity* (pp. 179–198). Emerald Publishing Ltd, Bingley: UK.

Hammersley, M., & Traianou, A. (2011). Moralism and research ethics: A Machiavellian perspective. *International Journal of Social Research Methodology*, *14*(5), 379–390.

Hammersley, M., & Traianou, A. (2012). *Ethics in qualitative research.* London: Sage.

Hedgecoe, A. (2016). Reputational risk, academic freedom and research ethics review. *Sociology*, *50*(3), 486–501.

Herrera, C. (1999). Two arguments for "covert methods" in social research. *British Journal of Sociology*, *50*(2), 331–343.

Homan, R. (1980). The ethics of covert methods. *British Journal of Sociology*, *31*, 46–59.

Hyman, D. (2007). Institutional review boards: Is this the least worst we can do? *Northwestern University Law Review*, *101*(2), 749–773.

Katz, J. (2007). Toward a natural history of ethical censorship. *Law & Society Review*, *41*(4), 797–810.

Larson, M. S. (1977). *The rise of professionalism*. Berkeley, CA: University of California Press.

Leo, R. (1995). Trial and tribulations: Courts, ethnography and the need for evidentiary privilege for academic researchers. *American Sociologist*, *26*(1), 113–134.

Littrell, B. (1993). Bureaucratic secrets and adversarial methods of social research. In T. Vaughan, G. Sjoberg, & L. Reynolds (Eds.), *A critique of contemporary American sociology* (pp. 207–231). Dix Hills, NY: General Hall.

Locke, J. ([1689] 1975). *An essay concerning human understanding*. Edited by P. H. Nidditch. Oxford: Oxford University Press.

Macfarlane, B. (2009). *Researching with integrity: The ethics of academic inquiry*. London: Routledge.

Marlow, J., & Tolich, M. (2015). Shifting from research governance to research ethics: A novel paradigm for ethical review in community-based research. *Research Ethics*, *11*(4), 178–191.

Montgomery, K. (2006). *How doctors think: Clinical judgment and the practice of medicine*. Oxford: Oxford University Press.

Oakeshott, M. (1962). *Rationalism in politics and other essays*. London: Methuen.

Pollitt, C. (1990). *Managerialism and the public services: The Anglo-American experience*. Oxford: Blackwell.

Power, M. (1997). *The audit society: Rituals of verification*. Oxford: Oxford University Press.

Pring, R. (2001). The virtues and vices of an educational researcher. *Journal of Philosophy of Education*, *35*(3), 407–421.

Schrag, Z. M. (2010). *Ethical imperialism: Institutional review boards and the social sciences, 1965—2009*. Baltimore, MD: The Johns Hopkins University Press.

Shils, E. (1956). *The torment of secrecy*. London: Heinemann.

Shweder, R. (2006). Protecting human subjects and preserving academic freedom: Prospects at the University of Chicago. *American Ethnologist*, *33*(4), 507–518.

Simons, H., & Usher, R. (2000). *Situated ethics in educational research*. London: Routledge.

Stark, L (2007). Victims in our own minds? IRBs in myth and practice. *Law & Society Review*, *41*(4), 777–786.

Stark, L. (2011). *Behind closed doors: IRBs and the making of ethical research*. Chicago, IL: University of Chicago Press.

Strauss, L. (1987). 'Machiavelli.'' In L. Strauss & J. Cropsey (Eds.), *History of political philosophy* (3rd ed.) (pp. 296–317). Chicago, IL: University of Chicago Press.

Traianou, A. (2014). The centrality of ethics in qualitative research. In P. Leavy (Ed.), *The Oxford handbook of qualitative research methods* (pp. 62–80). New York, NY: Oxford University Press (Stonehill College).

Traianou, A. (2015). The erosion of academic freedom in UK higher education. *Ethics in Science and Environmental Politics*, *15*(1), 1–9.

UK Research Integrity Office (UKRIO). (2009). *Code of practice for research: Promoting good practice and preventing misconduct*. Retrieved from http://ukrio.org/wp-content/uploads/UKRIO-Code-of-Practice-for-Research.pdf. Accessed on October 16, 2016.

van den Hoonard, W. C. (2011). *The seduction of ethics: Transforming the social sciences*. Toronto: University of Toronto Press.

van den Hoonaard, W. C., & Hamilton, A. (Eds.). (2016). *The ethics rupture: Exploring alternatives to formal research-ethics review*. Toronto: University of Toronto Press.

Warwick, D. (1982) Types of harm in social research. In Beauchamp et al. (Eds.). *Ethical Issues in Social Science Research* (pp. 230–250), London: Johns Hopkins University Press.

Wieringa, S., Engebretsen, E., Heggen, K., & Greenhalgh, T. (2017). Has evidence-based medicine ever been modern? A Latour-inspired understanding of a changing EBM. *Journal of Evaluation in Clinical Practice*. Retrieved from http://onlinelibrary.wiley.com/doi/10.1111/jep.12752/epdf

Zywicki, T. (2007). Institutional review boards as academic bureaucracies: An economic and experiential analysis. *Northwestern University Law Review*, *101*(2), 861–895.

.

CHAPTER 10

IS PHRÓNĒSIS NECESSARILY VIRTUOUS?

Martyn Hammersley

ABSTRACT

This chapter examines the role of phrónēsis in the context of research ethics, noting how it is often contrasted with the proceduralist approach associated with ethical regulation. The meaning of the term in the writings of Aristotle is outlined. This is followed by an examination of some of the ways in which the concept has been applied more recently, for example in relation to professionalism and professional ethics. Here, it is often combined with similar ideas, such as Polanyi's notion of tacit knowing. These more recent applications of the concept involve some deviation from the original sense of the term, but it is argued that there are good reasons for this, arising from changes in prevailing values and social conditions since the time of Aristotle. Furthermore, there are complexities with which he did not deal, notably the Machiavellian idea that in some circumstances unethical actions may be necessary to achieve desirable goals. The chapter ends by considering whether phrónēsis always leads to good ethical judgements. This seems to be true by definition on Aristotle's formulation, but he assumes a greater degree of harmony amongst virtues or values than seems to be the case. And this is a particular problem in the case of social research, since its goal is in dispute.

Keywords: Phrónēsis; virtue ethics; social research; Aristotle

Virtue Ethics in the Conduct and Governance of Social Science Research
Advances in Research Ethics and Integrity, Volume 3, 179–195
Copyright © 2018 by Emerald Publishing Limited
All rights of reproduction in any form reserved
ISSN: 2398-6018/doi:10.1108/S2398-601820180000003011

INTRODUCTION

The concept of phrónēsis is an important component of virtue ethics, an approach that is gaining increasing attention in the literature on social research ethics (Macfarlane, 2009, pp. 36–37; Pring, 2001; see other chapters in this book). Generally translated from the Greek as 'practical wisdom', phrónēsis is at odds with the idea that ethical conduct amounts simply to the observance of explicit rules or principles that specify what would and would not be ethical. For this reason, today it is often treated as in conflict with ethical regulation, in the form of ethics committees which decide whether or not particular research projects are ethical, whether they can go ahead, and on what terms (see Traianou, 2018). The basic argument is that, properly understood, ethical conduct is not a matter of compliance but must instead be based on practical reasoning that is rooted in virtues, and that takes account of contingent circumstances and competing considerations. Whilst Aristotle is usually treated as the originator of virtue ethics, appeal is also sometimes made to others, including Socrates, Plato, and Aquinas, as well as to more recent philosophers who draw on these sources, notably Anscombe (1958), Foot (1978), MacIntyre (1981), and Hursthouse (1999). In fact, though, as we shall see, recent usage of the concept of 'phrónēsis' has been sometimes only very loosely based on ancient philosophical sources – and perhaps for good reasons.

In suggesting that ethical judgement is essentially phrónētic in character, there is a danger that the default assumption will be that compliance with rules, procedures, or commands rarely produces good judgements, except by chance, whilst phrónēsis automatically does so. However, this is open to question. Here I want to examine the role of phrónēsis, and to consider whether it should be treated as *necessarily* virtuous, particularly in the context of social research.

ARISTOTLE, VIRTUE, AND PHRÓNĒSIS

Whilst Aristotle's writings on ethics and politics do not provide us with an unequivocal understanding of the meaning of 'phrónēsis', it is nevertheless clear that he regarded it as a virtue, an intellectual virtue – 'the excellence of practical intellect'. He identified it as the form of wisdom, or capacity for practical reasoning, that is required for well-directed engagement in governing a household and participating in the policymaking of a city-state. However, part of Aristotle's argument was that, contra Plato, virtue is not simply a matter of knowledge. He draws a sharp distinction between 'the virtues of character' and the intellectual virtues; and he argues that the virtues of character can only be acquired through practice, modelled on the actions of others who are virtuous. These provide the framework within which phrónēsis, as an intellectual virtue, operates: its task is to make sense of the implications for action of the virtues of character in particular situations.[1]

Aristotle distinguishes between 'phrónēsis' and 'technē', the latter being conceived as what is required in the pursuit of well-defined, relatively standard tasks, albeit ones that require considerable skill, such as medicine or shipbuilding, or the kind of mastery we may associate with carpentry or pottery. By contrast, phrónēsis amounts to the capacity to find the right course of action in social situations that involve uncertainties and exigencies. It is the art of reasoning required in reaching sound conclusions about what can and should be done, and especially about what would be the best course of action in particular circumstances; where the goal is to achieve and, in so doing, simultaneously to display excellence in a particular human activity or, more generally, qua human being. In short, it is an essential requirement if human beings are to flourish or live well.

Many interpreters of Aristotle believe that phrónēsis covers the ability to determine what are good ends as well as what are good means. Others regard it as restricted to the latter, insisting that for Aristotle ends are not a product of intellect but of character, of 'habituation' (Moss, 2011). However, at the very least, for Aristotle phrónēsis involves interpretation of what would be required in the pursuit of a particular virtuous goal in a particular situation, *against the background of all the other virtues that must also be taken into account.* It also involves assigning appropriate priority amongst the different virtues. Furthermore, in relation to any specific virtue, Aristotle portrays phrónēsis as involving discovery, for a particular situation, of the appropriate mean between opposing vices. Thus, what would be courageous lies somewhere between cowardice and foolhardiness; what would be generous lies between miserliness and extravagance, and so on. However, just where that line is to be found will vary across situations. Phrónēsis is the ability reliably to find that mean in practice.

THE REVIVAL OF INTEREST IN PHRÓNĒSIS

For much of the nineteenth and early twentieth centuries, Aristotle's ideas about virtue and phrónēsis were rather neglected, in favour of other approaches to ethics, notably consequentialism and deontology. However, in recent decades there has been a revival of interest in these concepts, in both the field of philosophical ethics and much more widely.

The concept of phrónēsis has become particularly influential in attempts to understand the nature of professionalism and, more specifically, in discussions of professional ethics. Krajewski (2011, p. 8) reports that: 'One can find scholarly articles that map phrónēsis on to educational and business leadership, medical training, urban planning and political science, giving the impression of a renaissance in the past 100 years of Aristotle's terms'. However, Kristjánsson (2015, p. 317) points out that

> a cynical interpretation [...] would be that at least some of the authors using 'phronesis' simply latch on to a term that sounds to them like a fancy way of saying 'professional judgement'. They then pack into it whatever they happen to think 'professional judgement' means, without much awareness of the background thinking around the concept.

Whilst there may be some truth to this criticism, several key features of the original sense of the term have usually been retained in more recent work. In particular, the typical contrast has been with claims that professional work can be reduced to following well-defined rules, recipes, or procedures that specify what should be done in standard types of situation (an approach that would fall under Aristotle's heading of technē). Instead, phrónēsis is taken to involve the exercise of judgement in dealing with uncertain, complex, and often difficult situations, in which great reliance is placed upon local knowledge and skill, along with deliberation informed by reflection on past experience (see Swartwood, 2013). Thus, contemporary arguments for phrónēsis have often been mobilised to resist attempts to impose technical or ethical regulations of various sorts on the work of the professions. It has been argued that these are incompatible with the very nature of professional work, properly understood, and that attempts to impose them will necessarily distort it (see Dunne, 1997; Traianou, 2018).

Furthermore, whilst we should certainly be aware that the concept of phrónēsis has been interpreted in ways that depart from the meaning given to it by Aristotle and other ancient writers, we ought not to overlook the possibility that there may be good reasons for this deviance. After all, our present social context has changed dramatically from that of the ancient world. For Aristotle, phrónēsis was the capacity required by those running households and participating in the governance of city-states. Today it tends to be applied to the knowledge and skill demanded by occupations that form part of a complex and diverse division of labour: modern societies involve a much wider range of occupational tasks than was characteristic of Ancient Greece, each characterised by distinctive obligations and forms of license. Furthermore, these operate within a socio-political context that has changed at a fundamental level: both everyday life and the form that democracy took in ancient

Athens were very different from today. This has raised questions about the viability of any distinction between technē and phrónēsis or, at least, about the relationship between them. Indeed, the occupation where most extensive use has been made of the concept of phrónēsis – medicine – was, as I noted earlier, regarded by Aristotle as demanding technē. Of course, medicine and medical ethics have developed considerably since his time, indeed in ways that may seem to confirm this. However, even today, neither can be simply reduced to the application of craft rules.[2]

Another reason for changes in the meaning given to 'phrónēsis' is that most of us are unlikely to share Aristotle's assumption that the task of governance is to rule others, and to do so in such a way as to instil virtue in them. Furthermore, he took it for granted that state government should be the prerogative of a small and relatively closed elite of men, whilst the duty of the mass of human beings, including all women, whether free or slaves, was to perform their allotted tasks with due deference to the existing socio-political order (see Pellegrin, 2013). He did not believe that they were capable, psychologically and/or socially, of achieving what he outlined as the ethical good life, in its highest form. Thus, for Aristotle, phrónēsis was self-evidently the property of a male elite.

In applying the concept of phrónēsis to the case of social research we face a further problem, over and above those arising in its application to other modern professions. This is that Aristotle also contrasted phrónēsis with 'epistêmê', a term that refers to the intellectual virtues required for *theoretical*, as opposed to practical, inquiry. Given this, it might be concluded that it is *these* virtues, rather than those that fall under the heading of phrónēsis, that are most appropriate to social research; after all, his conception of a 'practical science' of politics was very different from what passes for social, or even political, science today.[3] Indeed, Aristotle did not believe that there could be *theoretical* inquiry into human social life; in other words, inquiry of a kind that is similar in character to that of natural philosophy. Furthermore, in spite of his engagement in empirical biological inquiries, Aristotle seems to have taken philosophy as the exemplar of *theoria*, and, similar to Plato, to have regarded it as a process of contemplation. Thus, it is not clear that his concept of epistêmê can even be applied to the natural sciences as they are practised today, and it certainly does not match social science very well.

In short, then, social research does not fit straightforwardly into Aristotle's typology of forms of activity, and as a result its relation to phrónēsis is uncertain.[4] Of course, it could be argued that there is no doubt that he regarded the latter as central to ethical judgements so that its relevance to social research *ethics* is clear. However, I have suggested that Aristotle viewed ethics as integral to practical decision making, regarding the form of life open to the Athenian citizen as the highest form; he was not outlining an ethical life that was open to all members of society. Equally important, social research ethics is not concerned with how people should treat one another per se, but rather with how members of a particular occupation should deal with those with whom they come into contact as part of their work. Here, too, ethical considerations cannot be separated off from other practical matters; yet, at the same time, the form of activity involved was unknown to Aristotle, and very different from what he had in mind.

We must also see Aristotle's ideas about ethics in the context of his broader philosophy, which puts forward a teleological view of the world, in which each type of thing has its place; and either has, or tends to acquire, what it needs to perform its distinctive role.[5] In the case of human beings, whilst we are not born with the virtues we need, he assumes that we do a natural inclination, and perhaps also a facility, to acquire the knowledge, skills, and sensibilities required. Thus, he draws parallels between *eudaemonia* (happiness or flourishing) and health, implying that in the former, as in the latter, there is a natural although not an invariable tendency towards it.[6] He also appeals to an analogy between the beauty of objects produced by technē, where they exemplify the skill or craft knowledge that went into their production, and the noble character of good conduct, especially in difficult circumstances. This indicates something of the teleological conception of virtue on which he relies.

So, for Aristotle, ethics is concerned with what is excellent for human beings in terms of the role that they are destined to play in the world, with judgements about what is excellent hinging on the exercise of reason. Furthermore, as already noted, Aristotle was no egalitarian: he saw some people, a minority, as superior to others (and, one might add, as potentially exemplifying the highest expression of human being). He took their superiority to be closely associated with the social roles that they performed and were destined to perform. He identifies two superior forms of life: that of politics and philosophy, each pursued by an elite.[7] Below these, there are lower-level occupations in which specialised skills are deployed, thereby meeting various human needs; and beyond this there is the great mass of humanity who are engaged in activities that require very basic skills and intensive labour. Perfecting the superior forms of life demands the exercise of leisure, and this is one reason why these are not open to most people. Nevertheless, he also believes that few have the natural capacities required to engage in these activities. The form of governance implied is therefore one of elite rule: in the case of each household by a single patriarch, who rules in a way that is concerned to direct subordinates to lead virtuous lives *appropriate to their station in life*.

Not surprisingly, Aristotle seems to take this background for granted, without any idea that there either could or should be any change that would allow *all* human beings to pursue the highest forms of excellence, or to decide for themselves what this involves. Furthermore, we should note that, in the case of politics, excellence relates to the governance of others; and this is to be done, not in the interests of all, but in those of the household or the state, in a way that attracts honour, and facilitates the achievement of what is taken to be human excellence on the part of members of the elite.[8]

In short, then, the fact that the concept of phrónēsis was originally embedded in, and shaped by, a social and intellectual context that was politically very different from that of today means that it can now only be used in a relatively selective and analogical fashion. And, indeed, this is what has happened. Furthermore, whilst Aristotle may have thought that phrónēsis was necessarily good, today we are unlikely to regard the form of society it was designed to serve in that way, in key respects. Nevertheless, we should take care not to turn our own assumptions into prejudices.

NEW ELEMENTS IN RECENT USAGE OF PHRÓNĒSIS

Contemporary use of the term phrónēsis has been shaped by some more recent ideas. One is the notion of 'tacit knowledge' (or, better, 'tacit knowing') developed by Michael Polanyi (1962) in thinking about the practice of natural scientists. One example of such 'knowledge' is skills, and Polanyi (1962, p. 50) insists that these cannot be reduced to rule following. He writes that

> rules of art can be useful, but they do not determine the practice of an art; they are maxims, which can serve as a guide to an art only if they can be integrated into the practical [i.e., tacit] knowledge of the art. They cannot replace this knowledge.

To take an example, my native ability to speak grammatical English (much of the time) does not come from my having learned the propositions laid out in books about English grammar – indeed most native English speakers do not have this propositional knowledge! Nor can that capacity be based on learning propositional knowledge of this kind alone. As an illustration of his conception of tacit knowing, Polanyi (1966, p. 2) draws on the work of the gestalt psychologists, who emphasised the essential background that must be taken for granted if we are to make sense of what is in the foreground of our attention: 'focal' awareness depends upon 'subsidiary' awareness. In some cases, this background can itself be foregrounded through a shift in focus, and perhaps even turned into propositional knowledge. However, much tacit knowledge is closer in character to 'knowing how' rather than to 'knowing that', in other words to being a learned skill, and therefore cannot be spelt out in explicit propositional terms.

Tacit knowing is an essential resource in many kinds of activity, but as I noted Polanyi (1966, p. 1) is concerned specifically with natural science. He writes that

> no rules can account for the way a good idea is found for starting an inquiry; and there are no firm rules either for the verification or the refutation of the proposed solution of a problem. Rules widely current may be plausible enough, but scientific enquiry often proceeds and triumphs by contradicting them. Moreover, the explicit content of a theory fails to account for the guidance it affords to future discoveries.

In short, at many points, the work of scientists relies on tacit knowledge of various kinds. Polanyi emphasises that, to a large extent, this has to be acquired through practice. It is not hard to see how this line of thinking would extend to other activities outside of natural science, including ethical reasoning, and especially that in the context of social research.

Consistent with the notion of phrónēsis, Polanyi's argument suggests that some activities, and perhaps all activities to some degree, cannot be exhaustively formulated in terms of a set of rules or recipes to be followed. Indeed, it is often argued that following a set of rules necessarily relies upon some background capability that is not, and could never be, spelt out within those rules: rules never simply apply themselves, they do not contain exhaustive instructions for their own application. Polanyi (1966, p. 18) writes that 'any attempt to gain complete control of thought by explicit rules is self-contradictory, systematically misleading and culturally destructive'. Rules must themselves be interpreted; and the situations to which they are to be applied must also be interpreted. If what were involved here were rules formulated in a perfectly clear and formal language, and the cases to which they were to be applied corresponded exactly to standard types, the work involved would be minimal. However, this is rarely true, indeed it can be argued that this situation is a limit case that, at best, can only be *approximated*. Moreover, it should be noted that this argument opens up space for variation in the degree to which activities depend upon distinctive forms of tacit knowing: the application of some rules in relation to some range of situations may demand little interpretative work, whereas others may require a great deal, necessitating reflection and deliberation. This is the basis on which arguments about the distinctiveness of professional occupations have been founded, and these extend to the practice of research (Emmerich, 2016).

Whilst Polanyi's focus was natural science, this sort of argument has often been seen as having particular force in relation to the study of social phenomena. It is claimed that, whereas physical phenomena are sharply differentiated into types with measurably variable characteristics, and are controlled by exact laws, social phenomena can at best only be grasped through fuzzy categorisation and measurement, and are subject to probabilistic laws at most. An extreme version of this sort of argument, ruling out even the latter possibility, is put forward by ethnomethodologists (see Heritage, 1984; Sharrock and Anderson, 1986). They emphasise the context-sensitive character of the meanings that constitute social actions: these cannot be derived from some set of semantic, or indeed pragmatic, linguistic rules. It is argued that the kind of indexicality that has long been recognised in the case of words such as 'I', 'me', 'here', 'there', and so on, actually applies to all language use in social life. Whilst most of the time this does not generate problems for native speakers operating in relatively familiar contexts, and therefore does not demand conscious interpretation or deliberation, it is emphasised that 'work' is always involved in making sense of what is meant and what is going on. And this 'work' is necessarily 'artful' or 'ad hoc', in other words context-sensitive. Ethnomethodologists argue that this has radical implications for how we go about understanding social phenomena: both the facts of situations, and any evaluative characteristics assigned to them or to particular actions, are constituted entirely in and through processes of local social interaction rather than having any independent existence.

Along somewhat similar lines, and this time specifically in relation to ethics, Dreyfus and Dreyfus (1991) have argued that it is important to recognise the role of what they refer to as 'everyday ethical skills'. They insist that these are essential to enable us to know how to make ethical sense of situations. Critical here is the contextualisation of any rules: expertise is required to know when and how rules apply, in other words what they mean in particular situations. Dreyfus and Dreyfus (1991) criticise the way in which thinking about ethics and morality tends to focus immediately on deliberation and decision making, forgetting what necessarily underpins these. They outline a stage-model of the development of 'ethical expertise', a concept that bears important similarities with phrónēsis. They quote Dewey (1960, p. 131) summarising Aristotle to the effect that 'it takes a fine and well-grounded character to react immediately with the right approvals and condemnations' (Dewey, 1960, p. 237); although they also criticise Dewey for lapsing into treating ethics primarily as a matter of problem-solving, yet, of course this was the focus for Aristotle.

Another relevant kind of argument developed in the field of philosophical ethics is 'particularism'. This challenges the idea that ethical judgements are produced by *applying* ethical principles, indeed it denies any role for such principles. According to Dancy (2004, p. 1), a key exponent of this position, 'particularists think that moral judgement can get along perfectly well without any appeal to principles, and indeed that there is no essential link between being a full moral agent and having principles'.[9] Dancy's argument is that in making ethical judgements we are often faced with a range of 'contributory reasons' on each side, *and that the 'weight' and even the direction in which these point will vary depending upon the features of the situation concerned, rather than being fixed independently*. Less radical versions of this sort of position have been put forward under the headings of 'situationist' and 'casuistic' approaches to ethics (see Hammersley and Traianou, 2012, pp. 24–27).

Along with changes in intellectual and socio-political context, these and other sorts of arguments have led to significant departures from Aristotle's notion of phrónēsis. In particular, it is now often seen as being involved in setting goals and not simply pursuing them. Furthermore, whereas Aristotle appears to assume that, in principle at least, virtue and the good represent a unified whole, today phrónēsis is often regarded as essential precisely because we face conflicting goals in making ethical judgements and practical decisions, a point that will be developed later.

VARIATIONS IN THE INTERPRETATION OF PHRÓNĒSIS

Kristjánsson (2015, pp. 309–310) identifies several important divergences in the recent literature on phrónēsis from the ancient meanings given to the word, particularly in the work of Aristotle. He notes, for example, that whilst Aristotle tends to see virtues and phrónēsis in universalistic terms, albeit allowing for some situational variation in the priority given to different virtues, others, notably MacIntyre (1981), adopts a relativistic position – he treats the virtues, and thereby phrónēsis, as varying across traditions or cultures. More radically, MacIntyre (1981) goes on to argue that phrónēsis is impossible in the modern world because the framework of virtues that was widely accepted in the Middle Ages has disintegrated, producing incoherence.

There is also variation between generalist and particularist readings of Aristotle, these differing in the degree of emphasis they give to the virtues of character on the one hand, which are general, and the process of interpreting the implications of these in particular situations on the other. As Kristjánsson (2014) notes, there has been a strong tendency in recent usage of 'phrónēsis' in the context of professionalism and professional ethics to adopt a particularistic view, largely as a result of opposition to attempts to impose general procedural codes and regulations on professional activity (see also Dunne, 1997). This parallels similar disputes about the role of principles in ethical judgements relating to research involving human subjects (Hammersley, 2015).

Finally, phrónēsis is sometimes regarded as a matter of intuition, or as an ability or skill that, once learned, is deployed for the most part effortlessly, and with little in the way of deliberation or hesitation. By contrast, other commentators present it as a much more reflective or even agonising process. And this is closely related to variation in the nature of the problems that are being addressed: these can be regarded as difficult but not intractable, *or* as 'wicked' – in the sense that there is no 'solution' to them so that there could be several equally reasonable but incompatible judgements about what is appropriate in the same situation (Churchman, 1967).

There is also variation in the literature regarding how sharp a distinction is made between phrónēsis and technē. In much discussion of professional work and ethics, the boundary between the two has become very weak if not erased altogether: as already noted, doctoring was a form of technē for Aristotle and, therefore, did not involve phrónēsis. This is, perhaps, because he saw medicine as concerned with a single goal rather than as focussing on how an overall form of excellence or flourishing is to be achieved. However, there is a complication here: If phrónēsis is what is required of those engaged in politics, then it too concerns a specialized form of life, even if an unusual one in that, in Aristotle's view, it involves the responsibility to try to bring about appropriate types of excellence within a community. This signals a curious feature of Aristotle's concept, hinted at earlier: whilst it is generally taken to refer to what is required for *any* human being to live well, in fact it related primarily to the way of life of an Athenian citizen, the member of a political elite engaged in both domestic and civil governance; in other words, to a very specific set of activities rather than to human life in general.

This raises broader questions about the sorts of consideration that phrónēsis takes into account. In discussions of research ethics there is a tendency to focus on the notion of 'ethical conduct', so that phrónēsis would be concerned with the capacities and virtues required to engage in this. As a result, what is and is not 'ethical' is often interpreted narrowly, as relating to how researchers should deal with the people they study or from whom they obtain information. It focusses on considerations such as minimising harm, respecting autonomy, preserving privacy, and so on. However, this is at odds with most uses of 'phrónēsis', both ancient and more recent, where it is taken to relate to practical decision making as a whole; and the need to take into account, and 'weigh' against one another, *all* relevant considerations, not just specifically ethical ones. And, indeed, this seems to be a more sensible perspective.

IS PHRÓNĒSIS NECESSARILY GOOD?

Having outlined the meaning of phrónēsis in Aristotle's writings, and some of the ways in which the concept has subsequently changed, along with a few of the ideas influencing this, I now want to turn back to the question in my title. For Aristotle, phrónēsis is good by definition: he treats practical reasoning that is not governed by the virtues of character as mere cleverness. So, phrónēsis is virtuous not just because it is itself an intellectual virtue but also because it is tied to clarifying and specifying the implications of the virtues of character in particular situations.

There is circularity here: It appears that what is good can only be determined on the basis of phrónēsis; yet phrónēsis is itself defined as producing good living. Moreover, what is good, and what counts as phrónēsis rather than cleverness, can only be decided by those who already have the capacity for phrónēsis. It seems likely that, for Aristotle, this was a matter of praxis, to be resolved through learning – in other words, he saw no logical conundrum. This was perhaps encouraged by his assumption that the virtues form a unity. Whilst he recognises that acting well sometimes involves reconciling the implications of two or more virtues, he seems to assume that, ultimately, the virtues of character form a harmonious whole. This was, of course, underpinned by his political assumptions and teleological conception of the world.

There is a correspondence here with some recent uses of the concept of 'integrity' in the field of research ethics, the literal meaning of this term being 'wholeness'. Banks (2018) notes that a distinction needs to be drawn between 'research integrity' and 'researcher integrity', the first frequently implying 'thin, conduct-focussed' conceptions, in effect amounting to compliance with rules and procedures, whilst the second refers to 'thicker' characterisations that treat integrity as a virtue, in a sense that is closely related to phrónēsis. As an example of the latter position, Macfarlane (2009, p. 45) treats it as 'the integration of a person's true self and a linking of their values and identity as a person with their practice as a researcher'.[10] However, this raises some difficult questions. Even leaving aside the problematic notion of a 'true self', implying some concept of authenticity (Guignon, 2004), there may sometimes be conflict between what is demanded by the role of researcher and the beliefs, preferences, interests, etc. of particular researchers. For instance, there is an interesting question, here, as to whether researchers have an obligation to exercise more tolerance than they would when acting in other roles, and about what are the proper limits to this (Hammersley, 2005).

Perhaps even more importantly, there can be conflict amongst the various considerations that should be taken into account in doing research.

There are no sound reasons to assume that these form a harmonious unity. To the contrary, the potential for conflict between ethical considerations, narrowly defined as relating to researchers' treatment of the people studied, and the methodological requirements of good research, is the very reason why a commitment to research ethics has been thought necessary. Equally important is the fact that conflicting implications can be derived from different ethical principles, or even from a single ethical principle as it relates to different people (Hammersley & Traianou, 2012). These forms of conflict carry the possibility that, in maximising one value, we lower the chances of realising another, thereby generating dilemmas (Cassell & Jacobs, 1971, Chapters 3 and 4). This implies the prospect that one ethical consideration may sometimes need to be compromised, or traded off, against others, or against non-ethical considerations.

There is a parallel here with political philosophy. For the most part, Aristotle left it to later writers, notably Machiavelli, to underline the fact that pursuing the interests of the state may require a ruler to engage in 'unethical' actions. This is not a matter of the end justifying the use of *any* means, but rather that both ends and means must be coordinated, and ranked in terms of desirability (on various grounds). In this context phrónēsis can be thought of as being deployed to 'weigh' the relative desirability of achieving a particular end against the use of means that have varying degrees of likely effectiveness and undesirability. I suggest that this function of phrónēsis must also be applied in the case of social research (Hammersley & Traianou, 2011).[11]

A key question arises: how is phrónēsis to be distinguished from mere expediency or adhocery? The obvious answer is that this is avoided when it operates within a framework set by the goal of research and by reliance on ethical principles. This may seem to work against the very point of phrónēsis, this often being seen – as in the case of particularist approaches to ethics – as incompatible with reliance on principles, methodological or ethical. However, there is no necessary incompatibility here: I suggest that this problem can be overcome if we recognise that what is involved in the proper deployment of a principle is the use of an ideal-typical exemplar (or a set of these) with which particular cases can be compared, and judged to conform or deviate in various respects, thereby indicating what may and may not be the most appropriate course of action in the circumstances according to this principle. If this approach is accepted, we do not have two contrasting positions – compliance with rules or principles versus free judgement – but rather two ways in which judgement can deviate from a proper mean: towards an oversimplification or distortion that seeks to force particular cases into a standard form and derive implications for action from this on the one hand, and judgements of particular cases that involve no strain towards overall consistency in the resolution of the issues involved in those cases on the other. So, there is no conflict between phrónēsis and a reliance on principles, *where the latter are seen as providing guidance rather than serving as commands or absolute rules.*

From this, I think we can conclude that phrónēsis is an important and necessary capacity in the context of social research, as in other professional activities. However, we cannot assume that the conclusions reached when it is exercised will always be good. And, indeed, there may be genuine uncertainty in particular cases about the soundness of these conclusions. At the same time, there is no remedy for this problem: *sole* reliance on explicit rules and procedures is even less likely to generate good outcomes.

CONCLUSION

In this chapter I have explored the meaning of 'phrónēsis', in both the work of Aristotle and more recent usage, and the implications of this for its value in thinking about the practice of social research and research ethics. I have argued that today it cannot be applied in its Aristotelian form because much of the original intellectual and socio-political context has been abandoned or has disappeared. At the same time, detaching it from that context opens up various further problems.

One of these is the question of what goal or value complex should act as a framework for the exercise of phrónēsis in the context of social research. In the case of many occupational practices, the goals to be pursued are fixed or given to a considerable extent. Thus, the goal of medicine is to promote the health of the patient. Whilst this does not rule out the possibility of conflicting considerations, and contrasting practical judgements, most of the time it does provide a framework, along with bio-ethics, within which decisions can be made and defended. However, the case of social research is more problematic in this respect. After all, its goal is far from clear or consensual. In recent decades, along with questions about whether it can produce genuine scientific knowledge, or indeed knowledge of any kind, there have been demands that the social sciences should pursue various practical and/or political goals as well as, or instead of, aiming to produce factual knowledge (Hammersley, 1995, 2008). This means that there is considerable scope for disagreement regarding what the goals of social research are and, therefore, what would be involved in pursuing them well. Moreover, it is rare for a clear distinction to be drawn between these goals and ethical considerations. In the case of social research, then, there seem to be even fewer grounds for assuming that the exercise of phrónēsis by researchers will necessarily be virtuous, or that there will be agreement about what this entails.

Rectifying this situation would require determining what is and is not the proper goal of social research, what are the tasks of different types of social inquiry, and in what terms these are themselves justified; and doing so in a way that commands general agreement amongst social researchers, and amongst relevant stakeholders, publics, and audiences. It may also be necessary to clarify the rationale for the ethical restraints that ought to operate on the pursuit of these goals, and for any license that is allowed in relation to these if they render the pursuit of research too difficult or impossible. It has been argued that all professional occupations legitimately claim some license of this kind, but does this apply to social research, if so what does it imply (Hammersley & Traianou, 2012, pp. 50–51)?

Unfortunately, the prospects for reaching agreement on any of these matters are currently very poor. Meanwhile, government policies and institutional initiatives are seeking to impose various procedurally defined and enforced notions of ethicality and 'research integrity', these undercutting the exercise of phrónēsis by researchers. In the face of this, it may be tempting to suggest, along with Aristotle, that phrónēsis is by its very nature virtuous. However, unfortunately, for the reasons I have outlined, this argument cannot be sustained. Nevertheless, this concept does point to a capacity that is essential in doing social research, and specifically in making good ethical judgements in that context; and it is one for which there is no substitute.

ACKNOWLEDGEMENT

I am grateful to Nathan Emmerich for detailed comments on an earlier draft of this paper, and for references to relevant literature.

NOTES

1. He mentions quite a large number of 'virtues of character', and it is not clear that even this list is exhaustive, or that it is a systematically structured set. For an interesting, much more recent, discussion of 'the great virtues', see Comte-Sponville (2003).

2. For a useful discussion of the complexities of Aristotle, and other ancient philosophers, conceptions of technē, particularly in relation to epistēmē', see Parry (2014, Fall).

3. There is a link here with the recently developed notion of "epistemic virtues," see Greco and Turri (2015).

4. Flyvbjerg (2001) argues that social research should be phrónētic, but what he means by this is significantly different from what Aristotle had in mind (Hammersley, 2007).

5. On the complexities of this, see Johnson (2005).

6. The concept of eudaemonia is complex: in ancient Greek it literally implied having a happy life because misfortune is kept at bay by a good demon, see McMahon (2006). However, later it came to be interpreted as the kind of flourishing that results from leading one's life in such a way as to achieve the full potential of human being.

7. The relative status of these forms of life has been a persistent area of dispute in interpretations of Aristotle.

8. In my view, the distance in political perspective between Aristotle and Nietzsche is less than often thought.

9. Particularism can take a variety of forms, but here I will focus for the sake of argument on Dancy's radical particularism, perhaps its most influential version.

10. There is a different, modern, sense of 'integrity' that is close to 'objectivity' in meaning, and that also bears a close parallel with Aristotelian thinking: taking into account all of what is relevant, and only what is relevant, in making a decision; where 'relevance' is determined by the task and its associated principles, specifically excluding self-interest along with other extraneous considerations.

11. Dingwall (2007, pp. 788–789) provides an example of what can be involved here, which, ironically, relates to "being economical with the truth" in dealings with an ethics committee.

REFERENCES

Anscombe, G. E. M. (1958). Modern moral philosophy. *Philosophy*, *33*(1), 1–19.

Cassell, J., & Jacobs, S.-E. (Eds.). (1971). *Handbook on ethical issues in anthropology.* Washington, DC: American Anthropological Association. Retrieved from http://www.americananth ro.org/LearnAndTeach/Content.aspx?ItemNumber=12912

Churchman, C. W. (1967). Guest editorial: Wicked Problems. *Management Science*, *14*(4), B-141–2.

Comte-Sponville, A. (2003). *A short treatise on the great virtues: The uses of philosophy in everyday life.* London: Vintage. (First published in French in 1996.)

Dancy, J. (2004). *Ethics without principles.* Oxford: Oxford University Press.

Dewey, J. (1960). *Theory of the moral life.* New York, NY: Holt, Rinehart and Winston.

Dingwall, R. (2007). Turn off the oxygen…: Comment on the presidential address. *Law & Society Review*, *41*(4), 787–795.

Dreyfus, H., & Dreyfus, S. (1991). Towards a phenomenology of ethical expertise. *Human Studies*, *14*(4), 229–250.

Dunne, J. (1997). *Back to the rough ground: Practical judgment and the lure of technique.* Notre Dame, IN: University of Notre Dame Press.

Emmerich, N. (2016). Reframing research ethics: Towards a professional ethics for the social sciences. *Sociological Research Online*, *21*(4), 7. Retrieved from http://www.socresonline. org.uk/21/4/7.html

Flyvbjerg, B. (2001) *Making Social Science Matter*. Cambridge: Cambridge University Press.

Foot, P. (1978). *Virtues and vices.* Oxford: Oxford University Press.

Greco, J., & Turri, J. (2015, Fall). Virtue epistemology, In E. N. Zalta (Ed.) *The Stanford ency-clopedia of philosophy*. Retrieved from https://plato.stanford.edu/entries/epistemology-virtue/ And insert Accessed 30/11/2017 There are no page numbers

Guignon, C. (2004). *On being authentic.* London: Routledge.

Hammersley, M. (1995). *The politics of social research.* London: Sage.

Hammersley, M. (2005). Ethnography, toleration and authenticity: Ethical reflections on field-work, analysis and writing. In G. Troman, B. Jeffrey, & G. Walford (Eds.), *Methodological issues and practices in ethnography.* (pp. 37–55) Amsterdam, the Netherlands: Elsevier.

Hammersley, M. (2007). Phrónēsis and phrónētic social science. In G. Ritzer (Ed.), *Blackwell encyclopedia of sociology.* Oxford: Blackwell.

Hammersley, M. (2008). *Questioning qualitative inquiry.* London: Sage.

Hammersley, M. (2015). On ethical principles for social research. *International Journal of Social Research Methodology*, *18*(4), 433–449.

Hammersley, M., & Traianou, A. (2011). Moralism and research ethics: A Machiavellian per-spective. *International Journal of Social Research Methodology*, *14*(5), 379–390.

Hammersley, M., & Traianou, A. (2012). *Ethics in qualitative research.* London: Sage.

Heritage, J. (1984). *Garfinkel and ethnomethodology.* Cambridge: Polity.

Hursthouse, R. (1999). *On virtue ethics.* Oxford: Oxford University Press.

Johnson, M. (2005). *Aristotle on teleology.* Oxford: Oxford University Press.

Krajewski, B. (2011). The dark side of *phrónēsis*: Revisiting the political incompetence of phi-losophy. *Classica* (Brasil), *24*(1/2), 7–21.

Kristjánsson, K. (2014). *Phronesis* and moral education: Treading beyond the truisms. *Theory and Research in Education*, *12*(2), 151–171.

Kristjánsson, K. (2015). Phronesis as an ideal in professional medical ethics: Some preliminary positionings and problematics. *Theoretical Medicine and Bioethics*, *36*, 299–320.

Macfarlane, B. (2009). *Researching with integrity: The ethics of academic inquiry.* London: Routledge.

MacIntyre, A. (1981). *After virtue.* London: Duckworth.

McMahon, D. (2006). *The pursuit of happiness: A history from the Greeks to the present.* London: Penguin.

Moss, J. (2011). "Virtue makes the goal right": Virtue and *phrónēsis* in Aristotle's *Ethics. Phrónēsis*

Parry, R. (2014, Fall). Episteme and techne. In E.N. Zalta (Ed.), *The Stanford encyclopedia of philosophy*. (pp. 204–61) Retrieved from http://plato.stanford.edu/archives/fall2014/entries/episteme-techne/. Accessed on November 30, 2017.

Pellegrin, P. (2013). Natural slavery. In M. Deslauriers & P. Destrée (Eds.), *The Cambridge com-panion to Aristotle's politics* (pp. 92–116). Cambridge: Cambridge University Press.

Polanyi, M. (1962). *Personal knowledge.* Chicago, IL: University of Chicago Press.

Polanyi, M. (1966). The logic of tacit inference. *Journal of the Royal Institute of Philosophy*, *XLI*(155), 1–18.

Pring, R. (2001). The virtues and vices of an educational researcher. *Journal of Philosophy of Education*, *35*(3), 407–421.

Sharrock, W., & Anderson, B. (1986). *The ethnomethodologists.* London: Tavistock.

Swartwood, J. (2013). Wisdom as an expert skill. *Ethical Theory and Moral Practice*, *16*, 511–528.

CHAPTER 11

FROM PHRÓNĒSIS TO HABITUS: SYNDERESIS AND THE PRACTICE(S) OF ETHICS AND SOCIAL RESEARCH

Nathan Emmerich

ABSTRACT

This chapter questions the way virtue ethics is being drawn into debates about the ethics of social research. In particular, it suggests that discussion of virtue may be motivated by a desire to counter existing, largely principlist, approaches to the ethics of research and its associated administrative structures; virtue ethics has a prima facie appeal for those who are seemingly in need of an alternative moral philosophy. In addition, I argue that, as it stands, the complexity of virtue theory is not fully reflected in, or acknowledged by, debates about the ethics of social research. In the light of these remarks I suggest that the resources of social research can be drawn upon to generate critical theoretical insights into the ethics of social research. I discuss how a normative understanding of practices, and the concept of synderesis understood in a broadly Bourdieuan framework,

Virtue Ethics in the Conduct and Governance of Social Science Research
Advances in Research Ethics and Integrity, Volume 3, 197–217
Copyright © 2018 by Emerald Publishing Limited
All rights of reproduction in any form reserved
ISSN: 2398-6018/doi:10.1108/S2398-601820180000003012

could provide a starting point for such critical insights. I conclude that this perspective might be taken to suggest that the ethical stance most appropriate to the culture of social research is one of ongoing critical engagement.

Keywords: Phrónēsis; habitus; social research; research ethics; synderesis; practice

INTRODUCTION

As the increasingly vast literature on the topic makes clear, there is extensive dissatisfaction with the way in which research ethics and associated modes of governance have developed over the past two decades, particularly in the social sciences (Dingwall, 2006, 2012; Hammersley, 2009, 2010; Sleeboom-Faulkner, Simpson, Burgos-Martinez, & McMurray, 2017; van den Hoonaard, 2011). Whether implicitly or explicitly, the response of social researchers to burgeoning ethical governance of their activities has involved a rejection of the 'biomedical' or 'bioethical' model of research ethics, at least as it has come to be applied to the social sciences. sst there remains some degree of antagonism, the majority of commentators seem in favour of some kind of reform (Dingwall, Iphofen, Lewis, Oates, & Emmerich, 2017; Hammersley & Traianou, 2014; van den Hoonaard & Hamilton, 2016). Various strategies for effecting change have emerged. These include engaging with the creation and design of research ethics bureaucracies (Macdonald, 2010); recreating the ethics of social science research via the pursuit of a 'bottom-up' process (Emmerich, 2017; Iphofen, 2017); and, as in the case in this volume, considering the implication of virtue ethics.

Whilst it is certainly the case that the advent of 'applied ethics' can and should be linked to casuistry, an approach to ethical analysis that emerged in the medieval period (Jonsen & Toulmin, 1992), it is also clear that it is a distinctively modern phenomena, and directly linked to what Anscombe (1958) called modern moral philosophy. Standing in stark contrast to virtue ethics, modern moral philosophy objectifies and externalizes morality, disconnecting it from both the social life and the moral psychology of human beings. Regardless of whether one prefers to think of morality in terms of duty or consequences, or whether one is a Kantian or a Utilitarian, modern moral philosophy renders ethics a matter of rational argumentation, a matter of applied ethics. Whilst there are examples of virtue ethics being 'applied' to moral problems (cf. Austin, 2013; Axtell & Olson, 2012), and a long tradition of virtue ethics being used to inform discussion of professionalism and professional ethics (Pellegrino, 2007), it remains a – perhaps the – heterodox position within the discourse of applied (bio)ethics.

This is also the case in research ethics. Not least because of its particular history, i.e., the fact that the biomedical and organizational context of its emergence meant that it could not be represented as a kind of professional ethics (Emmerich, 2016; Schrag, 2010; Stark, 2011), virtue ethics has not influenced the development of research ethics to any great degree. Whilst contemporary advances in the topic mean that this is changing – as some of the chapters in this volume show, virtue ethics complements the current turn to integrity – the impact virtue ethics might have is not yet clear. In this context, it is unsurprising to find social scientists – who are, on the whole, dissatisfied with the current regime of ethics governance – turning to virtue ethics. The hope is that in virtue ethics they will find philosophical and theoretical tools that might be used to rethink the ethics of social research and, in the longer term, reform the administrative structures that, for many, are a particular source of concern.

At least to some degree, this hope is being met. There are, of course, some troubling questions that we might pose. For example, both Clifford (2014) and Kwiatkowski (2018) caution that virtue ethics might be a convenient tool for the preservation of professional autonomy for social scientists to effectively counter external oversight of the ethics of their research activities. However, to my mind, what is worth considering further is the degree to which virtue ethics can be legitimately thought of as an appropriate perspective for understanding the ethics of social sciences. As pointed out by both Hammersley (2018) and Traianou (2018), the theory is a product of Ancient Greek thought. It is, of course, true that following MacIntyre's (1981) *After Virtue*, a good deal of contemporary philosophical work has addressed the topic, and virtue ethics has since undergone something of a renaissance. Nevertheless, regardless of the degree to which current *neo-Aristotelian* virtue ethics can be thought of as bringing such thought up-to-date, significant questions remain. Virtue ethics still seems to be an inherently conservative moral philosophy which, as we shall see, implies some should be normatively understood as (moral) authorities if only in a structural sense. More specifically, the situationist critique calls into question some of the basic assumptions regarding the durability or reliability of an individual's moral character (Doris, 2002).

Of course, neo-Aristotelians have replied to such critiques but the point remains. Whilst philosophical methodology might be such that the socio-historical, cultural, and political roots of a particular theory or theoretical perspective can be overlooked, or otherwise placed to one side, the same cannot be said of social theory. In contrast, most social theorists think that the history of an idea is of direct relevance to those ideas and their socio-political viability. Given that the turn to virtue in the ethics of social research has socio-political, and not just ethical, ends, the politics of virtue theory would seem to be relevant to any use that we might want to make of it. The question is, then, where should social scientists look if they are to both *understand* and *engage with* the ethical dimensions of their discipline? If the matter at hand was an attempt to understanding the morality or ethics of any other form or mode of social life, one would not expect the social scientist to make use of moral philosophy. Or, at least, not to do so without significant critical engagement of the kind that we can find in the currently resurgent sociology of morality (Abend, 2014; Hitlin & Vaisey, 2010) and anthropology of ethics (Fassin, 2012; Laidlaw, 2013).

Whilst the motivation for making use of virtue ethics might be to 'push back' against a perspective and mode of governance intimately connected to the discourse of applied ethics, it may well be that, at least in part, the problem stems from the external or 'top down' nature of such work. If this is the case, then virtue ethics may also be problematic. Rather than looking to moral philosophy for solutions, we might look to social theory and, in so doing, social researchers might effectively stand their ground. Certainly, the particular social theory that I intend to discuss, that of Pierre Bourdieu, can be thought of as related to the Aristotelian worldview. In particular, the concept of habitus can be seen as a particular distinct point of contact between Aristotle and Bourdieu. Furthermore, the manner of my discussion might be thought of as further promoting, exposing, or developing these connections – possibly to a degree that is without precedent or, at least, without obvious precedent. Nevertheless, not least because Bourdieu does not make reference to Aristotle, there are good reasons not to think of Bourdieu as an Aristotelian or neo-Aristotelian. Furthermore, the Bourdieuan and, one might add, modern conception of society (or social fields), culture, and human being (Chernilo, 2016) is very different from that of Aristotle.

Whilst there might be something to be said for the idea that MacIntyre's (1981) neo-Aristotelianism can be taken as a form of practice theory – or, at least, something of a precursor to practice theory, properly understood (Schatzki, Knorr-Cetina, & von Savigny, 2000) – it is nevertheless the case that MacIntyre's (1981) conception of practice (or 'tradition', a term he prefers) differs in significant respects from that espoused by Bourdieu. This can be seen in Bourdieu's view that practice results from the interaction of habitus and social structure or, better, the interaction of habitus and the particular location one occupies within the structure of a particular social field.

In what follows, further differences between the moral philosophy of Aristotelian virtue ethics and my largely Bourdieuan approach to social theory will, no doubt, become apparent. The most obvious of these will be the nature, or location, of normativity and the critical role that particular practices, such as reflection and dialogue, have to play. However, I first turn to a discussion of phrónēsis, a concept that plays a central role in virtue ethics but, or so I suggest, should be seen as problematic from the more critical perspective adopted by social researchers.

PHRÓNĒSIS

The notion of phrónēsis is usually translated as prudence or wisdom, both of which are what we might call a complex or meta virtues. As Banks (2018) suggests in relation to integrity, complex virtues coordinate or otherwise mediate between other non-complex virtues. From a theoretical perspective, phrónēsis introduces a contextual or situational sensitivity to virtue ethics. So understood, it would seem that phrónēsis can take on various guises or, to put it another way, it can be realized in a variety of ways. For example, a great number of individuals can be thought of as acting with prudence or with a certain degree of wisdom. This might range over various professional occupations, such as doctor, lawyer, journalist, civil servant or architect. It might also be applied to more everyday activities, such as raising children or 'parenting'. These latter two activities are endeavors that the majority of people engage in and, furthermore, something that can be done in a great variety of ways. Both within and across cultures, the way in which children are raised is highly variable. Nevertheless, at least in principle, such variation and attendant idiosyncrasies do not introduce a barrier to parenting with wisdom; phrónēsis is not, and cannot be, considered a fully determinative concept. Indeed, it is introduced to facilitate certain pluralism or flexibility in deciding what is and is not the ethical course of actions. Or, at least, that is how it is treated in contemporary virtue theory.

Such pluralism, however, reflects certain modern presumptions that would not sit well within Aristotelian or neo-Aristotelian thought. As both Hammersley and Traianou have pointed out (2018) the original conception of phrónēsis is loaded with certain socio-political and cultural assumptions. For Aristotle phrónēsis was something that could only be contemplated in relation to men of a certain social standing. Furthermore, phrónēsis was not generally seen as something that was present in everyday life or activities. Rather, it was primarily related to decisions regarding matters of state, community, and household; decisions regarding the way in which the community or polity was to be organized and, therefore, the way in which life was to be led. At least in part, this is because phrónēsis relates to the notion of eudaimonia or human flourishing. With perhaps the exception of the purely contemplative or philosophical life (of, presumably, the type led by Aristotle), men of a certain social standing were taken to be the fulfilment of eudaimonia, and part of their responsibility was to ensure the proper flourishing of all human beings.[1] Others could, of course, flourish. However, eudaimonia, in the fullest sense of that term, was not available to all. Similar thinking applies to the notion of phrónēsis. It was inconceivable to think that women, slaves, and other non-citizens could embody phrónēsis, wisdom in its fullest sense.

The highly diverse and stratified nature of our present form (or modes) of (social) life was not, of course, something the Ancient Greeks encountered or could have conceived of. Thus, the variety with which phrónēsis is currently understood requires embracing a broader conception of eudaimonia, or human flourishing, than is found in Aristotle. Whilst some contemporary thinking in this area can be understood as insufficiently recognizing this point, movement in this direction can be clearly perceived in some neo-Aristotelian thinking. MacIntyre's (1981) notion of tradition and practice is a particular case in point. Regardless of the particulars of such accounts, it is clear that what was once predicated on the telos of a singular philosophical account of human being must now be taken in relation to various modes of social life.[2]

To broaden phrónēsis in such a way that it can be realized in relation to a variety of human activities that can be pursued with wisdom in a similar variety of ways means that we must reconstitute eudaimonia in such a way that it can be articulated in relation to each of these activities, modes of social life or ways of being (human). The present socio-political milieu means that both eudaimonia and phrónēsis need to be rearticulated in relation to such activities. Nevertheless, we might think that what constitutes the proper flourishing of social science research – or, better, what constitutes the proper flourishing of social science researchers – cannot be given any simply definition. Rather, it is a complex phenomenon, one that might vary both over and, possibly, within particular (sub) disciplines. Furthermore, the need for phrónēsis in the proper pursuit of such ends remains and, in each case, will require some degree of reconstruction. Whilst one could argue that this endeavor lies at the heart of many of the essays in this volume, and much of the contemporary effort to make use of virtue ethics in relation to various activities, including those of the professions and character education more broadly, it is not clear that the complexity of the task – and the theoretical implications of this complexity – has been fully grasped.

It is not, of course, my intention to dismiss such efforts out of hand. Nor do I wish to suggest that ethical conduct is necessarily predicated on understanding some complex moral philosophy, at least not in the way that the quality of research depends on understanding some complex methodological issues. Nevertheless, there is value in developing a proper grasp of the matter at hand. Certainly, a great deal of effort has been expended in relation to modernizing virtue ethics and character education. That it has found traction in a variety of domains also seems clear. At minimum, this can be taken as indicating that virtue ethics has found some degree of cultural acceptance. Furthermore, as suggested, one can understand MacIntyre's (1981) project to be motivated by a similar impetus; the need to broaden the teleological basis of eudemonia and, therefore, the scope of flourishing to dictate ethics or 'the good'. As Higgins (2010) put it, MacIntyre's (1981) notion of tradition can be thought of as defining worlds of practice, and creating something to which professions in particular can appeal to when defining the good that they pursue and, therefore, the ethics that should inform, shape, and constrain the pursuit of that good. Nevertheless, social research cannot be considered a unitary institution; Social research embodies a variety of concerns, aims, and objectives, as well as a certain degree of methodological pluralism; considering it a unified world of practice may not be entirely sustainable.

The concept of phrónēsis – that seems bound to a fairly narrow account of moral wisdom – seems similarly troubling. Indeed, both Hammersley (2018) and Traianou (2018) seem to be reluctant to embrace it fully. It may be that they intuit something of the problems outlined above and, given the moral culture and socio-political context we currently inhabit, it may also be the case that they are somewhat skeptical of the very idea of 'moral wisdom'. The normative dimension of phrónēsis seems to appeal to a paternalist figure of both embodied and theoretical morality. Whilst the structural diversity of modern society pulls contemporary neo-Aristotelian thought away from this configuration, and whilst the idea of the phronemos, at least as a unitary phenomenon, is unsustainable and can be rejected, the concept of phrónēsis as a whole remains tainted by association.

In the final analysis, phrónēsis can be perceived as a kind of moral, normative or philosophical 'ghost in the machine'. It suggests that some kind of normative or action-guiding wisdom is out there, waiting to be found, but provides little in the way of concrete or substantive guidance. Thus, we are left with certain ideas about phrónēsis about which we are rightly be ambivalent; the concept of phrónēsis necessarily promulgates certain presumptions about moral wisdom being the preserve of a certain type of individual or individuals who occupy certain locations within particular social fields.

As such, we are left with the impression that it appeals to, or justifies appeals to, (moral) authority and those within a particular field who occupy positions of (moral) authority. This perspective connects to the charge that, as a moral philosophy, virtue ethics is an inherently conservative theory. More often than not virtue ethics appears to maintain the status quo, to reproduce the existing moral order; it tends to justify existing social arrangements often by making them appear as a matter of natural order. This is not, of course, to say that no proponent of virtue ethics has ever called for change or against entrenched interests or existing distributions of power. Certainly, they have. Nevertheless, when virtue theory provides the basis for a call to re-establish the 'knightly virtues'[3] as the basis for character education in the United Kingdom and beyond, it seems hard to repudiate the charge of moral conservatism.[4]

Equally, the notion of phrónēsis seems hard-pressed to explain how certain individuals who occupy subaltern social locations might exemplify moral wisdom. Consider the following example. In the late 1950s/early 1960s two individuals – Dr Henry Beecher in the United States and Dr Maurice Pappworth in the United Kingdom – advanced arguments to the effect that medical doctors should stop using patients to teach students various kinds of medical procedures without their knowledge or consent. Beecher was a member of the American medical establishment and could advance his point of view whilst remaining secure in his position and, indeed, drawing on it to further his ends. In contrast, Pappworth was not a member of the UK medical establishment. Rather, he was something of an outsider and the way in which he was able to advance his point of view was correspondingly different and more than a little combative. From the point of view of phrónēsis, whilst both had very similar core ethical insights into certain problematic medical practices, only one can be said to have acted with wisdom, namely, Henry Beecher. From the point of view of phrónēsis, the way Pappworth undertook his endeavors look decidedly unwise and imprudent. This view strikes me as deeply troubling. In first instance we should note that Pappworth's actions, and the degree to which the medical establishment was prepared to listen to him, were decidedly constrained by his social and professional position (themselves arguably a result of anti-Semitic discrimination). As such, it seems that Pappworth is effectively barred from acting in accordance with phrónēsis. The implication of this would seem to be that phrónēsis is the preserve of those who occupy privileged positions in particular social field.

However, it often seems to be the case that critical ethical insights originate from those who occupy subaltern positions or who are in some way outsiders. Such individuals are able to cast a critical eye on practices that are accepted or otherwise taken for granted. However, it seems to me that if phrónēsis is to be stretched so as to encompass the insights of individuals such as Pappworth, then it is simply becoming a term that covers all sins, that is to say, all virtues or all those things that we currently identify as right and, therefore, virtuous. If so, one might wonder how informative discussion of particular virtues might be. After all, how much agreement might we expect there to be, both about substantive virtues but about who, precisely, can be taken as embodying the good and, therefore, those virtues that we should seek to emulate. At the very least, such discussion must be informed by a proper understanding of the practices we are concerned with.

THE NORMATIVITY OF PRACTICE(S)

For the time being, then, we can put talk about phrónēsis and virtue to one side and instead simply speak of morality and ethics as practices, or as an ineliminable dimension of social life and, therefore, as being an aspect of all practices. Furthermore, given that virtues are held to be dispositions, it is not difficult to (re)conceive of them in relation to habitus or, more specifically, a moral habitus – something that is structured by moral and/or ethical dispositions, produced in relation to the (or a particular field's) ethical structure or moral order.[5] Indeed, Meisenhelder (2006) argues that habitus ought to be understood as the conceptual heir to character in contemporary sociology and social theory. I will return to the idea of moral habitus. However, before doing so, I now turn to a brief consideration of normativity and its connection to social practice.

Part of the problem for social researchers who would adopt virtue ethics is the question of normativity and its sources. At least for the most part, this is something that social researchers have, generally speaking, failed to engage with. Whilst there is, certainly, interesting work out there (Turner, 2010), Chernilo (2014, 2016, pp. 1–10) points out that sociology and, by extension, social research as whole has a poor track record when it comes to engaging with the normative dimension of social life.[6] For the present purposes the deeper recesses of this debate need not concern us. All that need concern us is the analysis presented by Rouse (2001, 2007) regarding two different ways of understanding practice: as regularities or as normative phenomena.

Understood as regularities, practices are a feature of social life, one that social researchers can attempt to detect or discern and, subsequently, make them the subject of social analysis or critique. They might do so in a purely descriptive manner or might adopt a more critical approach. However, on the view that both descriptive and critical social research can be considered practices, it would seem that practices can have normative – or, perhaps better, *crypto-normative* (Kolodny, 1996) – implications. Such normativity is not, however, reserved for social researchers. It is clearly possible, at least in principle, for anyone to adopt a critical standpoint *qua* some feature of social life. As such, some form of normativity is clearly a feature of the social world inhabited and promulgated by human beings. This thinking can be taken further if we reflect on the fact that there would be no point in offering a critical perspective were it not the case that the targets of such criticism – the social world, or particular practices – had the potential to change.[7] As it concerns how we might intervene in the process of social reproduction, such thinking is predicated on the question of how social life is reproduced. According to Rouse (2001) – and, indeed, to many other theorists – social practices should be understood as an inherently normative phenomena and, therefore, as playing a central role in the process of social reproduction. Thus, if we focus on a specific practice, we find that:

> [W]hat a practice is, including what counts as an instance of the practice, is bound up with its significance, i.e., with what is at issue and at stake in the practice, to whom or what it matters, and hence with how the practice is appropriately or perspicuously described. (Rouse, 2001, p. 202)

Thus, when a particular individual attempts to understand or engage in a particular practice, they encounter it as a normative phenomenon. For example, consider the difference between playing the piano as a practice and simply 'playing' the piano by bashing the keys. Whilst, at root, playing the piano consists in pressing the keys, it is nevertheless the case that not everyone who happens to do so can be considered to be 'playing the piano'. Rather, certain additional conditions must be met. However, precise expression of what those conditions might be is not a simple task. As Rouse (2007, p. 54) says:

> [T]he normativity of practices is expressed not by a determinate norm to which they are accountable but instead in the mutual accountability of their constitutive performances to issues and stakes whose definitive resolution is always prospective.

Practices are always subject to change and, one might say, innovation. Thus, for example, one might think that the advent of jazz altered the practice of piano playing, and expanded it to include something new. A similar thought can be extended to the 4'33 by the *avant-garde* composer John Cage. Here Cage can be understood as having expanded the practice of piano playing in such a way that it includes not playing the piano at all. However, this cannot be taken to mean that all those who do not play the piano can, in fact, play the piano. Rather, Cage's composition draws attention to performance as an aspect of (professional) piano playing and concert going. Thus, as normative phenomena, practices are more than the activity (piano playing) itself. If it is properly understood knowledge of a a practice will encompass the conditions of its performance. Furthermore, in some cases, such conditions can be pushed to the forefront of the practice and, at least temporarily, take centre stage.[8]

The idea is, then, that practices are inherently normative. Indeed, they are the source or basis of normativity in social life. This has implications from broader critical practices, such as ethics. Rouse (2007, p. 55) suggests that:

> Critical reflection on meaning, knowledge, or social life instead arises from within our practices of communication, understanding, production and exchange, and governance, that is, from the midst of our complex causal intra-actions in partly shared circumstances.

Practices, therefore, contain and create the conditions for their own ethical critique. However, whilst ethics is, first and foremost, a feature of social life, in contemporary society ethics has also become a practice unto itself. Nowhere is this clearer than in the discourse of applied ethics, a discourse that plays a large role within debates on research ethics, and is related to the difficulties social researchers have with the ethical governance of their work. Thus, whilst applied ethics has undeniably become a practice in its own right, practice theory suggests that there is something distinctly troubling about this fact. In particular, we might be concerned with the way in which the analytic perspectives offered by applied ethics are unmoored from the particular modes of social life upon which comment is sought. The problem or, at least, part of the problem is the degree to which applied ethics, as a matter of methodology, discounts or disregards the normative reality of social life, and the way in which those involved in a particular practice are mutually accountable to each other, as both part of that practice and a condition of success – something that is defined by that same accountability.

Such thinking reflects something of the criticisms social researchers have leveled at the ethical governance of research – that it does not seem accountable to those it subjects to scrutiny or, indeed, to the practice with which it is ostensibly concerned. However, the following question remains: On what basis might we proceed?

SYNDERESIS AND THE (MORAL) HABITUS OF SOCIAL RESEARCHERS: AN ALTERNATIVE TO PHRÓNĒSIS

At first blush the term synderesis – the notion that human beings have an innate moral sense or habit[9] that is oriented towards the good – might not seem to be a promising candidate for building a social theory of morality.

It is a somewhat arcane term and is rooted in scholastic philosophy; a medieval intellectual activity that can be thought of as a mode of Christian theology that seeks to reconcile itself with, and thereby incorporate, Aristotelian thought. Whilst scholasticism continues to be pursued today, it is a relatively niche activity, and I do not intend to discuss it in any detail. Rather, I wish to appropriate the idea of synderesis and use it to name or speak about the innate moral sense of human beings. Whilst its origins would connect this sense with natural law and the first principles of theological morality, these can be replaced with secular alternatives. Thus, the claim that human beings have an innate moral sense might be considered in Chomskian terms (Mikhail, 2016), or it might be taken to amount to the claim that pro-sociality or, simply, sociality, is an innate part of human condition. This is something that Bauman (1993) uses as the basis of his sociology of morality. Regardless, it can be thought of as a basic facet of our being, and the precondition for our social ability to perceive directly normative states (Zahle, 2013, 2014).

Construed in this way, the concept of synderesis is being offered as part of a philosophical anthropology built upon, or within Bourdieu's social theory. As such, synderesis can be taken as a basic fact of our form of life. Whilst synderesis relates to our moral sense, we need to go beyond this if we are to speak of our moral or ethical *sensibility*. One way to do this is to consider it in relation to habitus, particularly the way in which it can be developed and conditioned through processes of moral socialization and ethical enculturation (Emmerich, 2015). In the same way, we can train our other senses However, such process of development do not leave the sense itself untouched. Indeed, at a certain point it will become undesirable to consider our innate moral sense (synderesis) as fully distinct from the moral sensibility or (moral) habitus it makes possible. As such, like the body itself, synderesis becomes a foundational facet or a priori commitment of habitus.[10] In the final analysis, one cannot speak of habitus without an acknowledgment of its normativity or, perhaps better, its sensitivity to the normativity of social practices; the idea of synderesis is conceived as the heart of this normativity or our sensitivity to the normativity of social practices. In the light of Rouse's (2007) analysis, discussed above, this creates the conditions for ethics, and for moral reflection and (self) criticism understood as an explicit feature of certain social practices. The notion of a profession is one such example of this. Understood from a sociological point of view, self-avowed ethical commitments are essential to the emergence development and institutionalization of a profession (Freidson, 1970, 2001; Macdonald, 1995).

A potentially more problematic aspect of synderesis is the fact that, unlike phrónēsis, it is not predicated upon 'the good'. If we are to fully perceive the moral dimension of the situations we encounter – what Zahle (2013, 2014) calls the 'normative states' of our social contexts – then synderesis must, of course, attend to good and bad, right and wrong. It cannot, therefore, be orientated towards the good alone. As such, synderesis itself does not offer any guarantee that we will do the right thing. Of course, given that we often do the wrong thing, even when we know it is wrong to do, this has the virtue of reflecting reality. This has the potential to place us in a problematic position of moral relativism. What the right or wrong thing to do can be understood in one of the two ways: first, as some (set of) transcendental truth(s)[11]; or second, as related to a particular set of social or cultural norms.

Given the fact that some sets of cultural norms, not least those of racism and anti-semitism, are clearly ethically objectionable, both in themselves and with regard to their consequences, one might think that proceeding without some transcendental commitments is problematic. Whilst there is not the space to go into it in any detail, we need not think this is the case. Rather, from a social scientific point of view, we might note that 'the only reasonable notion of transcendence available to humans [is] the ability to move beyond our current habits of thought and action to creatively remake some aspect of ourselves and our world' (Johnson, 2014, p. xii). Such thinking connects with the normative account of practice discussed above. Social and cultural norms are not monolithic, or beyond question and critique. They can, of course, weigh more or less heavily, and such weight may be more or less obvious. Consider the differential perception of, for example, the normative weight exerted by totalitarian societies on the one hand and gender norms on the other. Nevertheless, none are beyond challenge or change.

We must, however, acknowledge that any challenge or critique will itself be produced within a particular socio-cultural, political, and intellectual context. Furthermore, certain historical antecedents will always circumscribe the possibilities of change. All this is, however, to say little more than we have no choice but to start from where we are, and to proceed with the tools at our disposal. The inclination to seek external foundations reflects the philosophical hopes of enlightenment thinking. On the one hand we might argue that, in the era of post-modernity, such hopes have met their limit. However it is, perhaps, enough to note that whilst such hopes might be maintained with certain cultural formations, such as the intellectual culture of moral philosophy, there seems little reason to think that they should be taken up more generally. Furthermore, the nature of social research is such that one cultural formation – that of an intellectual discipline – is being brought to bear on another – the object of study. Since each of these fields contain normative practices, practices that provide conditions for their own explication, the ethics of social research needs to find a way of engendering ethical dialogue between moral actors who may have differing moral perspectives, perceptions, and standpoints.

Unlike phrónēsis, synderesis does not involve privileging a particular moral perspective, usually those in positions of social authority, over the views of others. However, the collapsing into extreme, or naive, relativism – where all points of view are treated as independent and equally valid – is belied by practice theory. Not only is no man an island, but no 'world of practice' or culture is entirely independent of any other. Interestingly, MacIntyre's (1981) philosophy of the social sciences can be understood as making a similar point (Blakely, 2013). Adopting a Wittgensteinian position similar to that of Winch, MacIntrye (1981) nevertheless points out the flaws and contradictions of the former's radically relativist conclusion.[12] At least in part, he rejects this conclusion because it is not possible for a social science to be purely descriptive; it always has an evaluative component. One cannot understand a 'tradition' or 'practice' without having some interpretative understanding, meaning that one must have some grasp of its normative dimension. In the light of this we might conclude that the 'moral and social sciences are not nearly so far apart as many today assume' (Blakely, 2013, p. 460). Whilst social scientists have tended to disavow the normative dimension of their work, another way is possible.

CONCLUSION: PRACTICING ETHICS

In her contribution to a review symposium, Arpaly (2005) advances the view that, in his book *Lack of Character* (2002), Doris (2005, p. 643) can be understood as suggesting 'that there exist no such thing as Global Character Traits (or, as Gilbert Harman calls them, One-Word-In-English Character traits)'.[13] Doris' work and the 'situationist critique' of virtue theory more generally have prompted a great number of responses and theoretical reconstructions by those of an Aristotelian inclination. In this context, Snow's (2009) account of virtue as social intelligence is, perhaps, of particular note.[14] In the context of these criticisms and related developments in virtue theory, it is not clear whether naming particular virtues has much to recommend it. Certainly, many of those who now seek to do so, including some of the contributors to this volume, tend not to speak of global character traits per se. Rather, they tend to discuss the character traits that might be relevant to particular tasks or situations. Nevertheless, it seems legitimate to consider what it is that discussions of particular substantive and normative virtues might hope to achieve. It seems to me that what virtue ethics has to offer those who are concerned with the way in which certain tasks or practices are pursued is a way to under-stand how ethics is – or should be – pursued as a part of those activities or practices. It also seems to me that the perspective offered by Bourdieu's social theory is better placed to accomplish this task. Certainly, a Bourdieusian perspective is accompanied by far less normative baggage than that of (neo) Aristotelians. However, it is the degree to which Bourdieusian social theory represents the (re)production of habitus and social structure as intertwined that makes the largest contribution to this preference. The view that habitus and the structures of a social field (or 'situation') interact in the production of practice is another significant point in its favour.

It could, of course, be argued that MacIntyre's (1981) conception of tra-dition could be used to frame an Aristotelian ethics of social research. As Higgins (2010) suggests, MacIntyre's (1981) neo-Aristotelianism implies that there are worlds of practice, and that such worlds condition the ethics of the practices that take place within them in important ways. Such thinking clearly reflects something of the perspective I have set out, but would preserve a notion of phrónēsis and, therefore, a certain normative ideal based on the teleology of a particular social world, its traditions and practices. Whilst I have nothing against such a reconstruction, my view is that as yet this project has not been properly pursued. In addition, it can only be properly pursued as a philosophical project. If, as seems to be the case, the current impetus is one in which social researchers are motivated to engage with the mode of ethi-cal thinking and governance of their research, it would seem better to draw on the tools they have at hand, and are sufficiently familiar with. Strathern (2000) provides an example of this in an essay that draws on the notion of audit cultures.[15]

Furthermore, I am somewhat sceptical that social research can be thought of as constituting a world of practice in a MacIntyrian (1981) sense. The activities of social research are relatively diverse'; they range from the positiv-ism of quantitative psychology, epidemiology, etc., the qualitative activities of sociologists, and the ethnographic ambitions of anthropologists, to name only the most obvious. One could, of course, suggest the same of something that is normally accepted as a candidate for constituting a world of practice. The medical profession, for example, might be thought of as consisting of a diverse range of specialisms, such as emergency medicine, general practice, surgery, paediatrics, etc. Nevertheless, from a socio-historical point of view, there is a collective, institutional, and organizational consistency – a certain degree of internal cohesion – to the medical profession. This is not something that can be said of social research. Indeed, one might argue that a certain lack of cohesion is entailed if particular areas of social research are considered to be flourishing. The ends of social research are served by conflicting views on matters of philosophical, methodological, and substantive importance. Unlike the natural sciences, the social sciences do not seem to have periods of what Kuhn (1996, p. 23) called 'normal science'. This is not to say that the social sciences consistently proceed under revolutionary conditions. Rather, it is to acknowledge that the notion of a scientific paradigm does not provide a good account of social scientific knowledge. Instead, like social reality more generally, the endeavour of social research is marked by an inherent interpretative pluralism.

It is in this context that we must consider the ethics of social research. Furthermore, we might add further layers of interpretive pluralism by considering, first, the ethical perspectives of research participants – both as individuals and as social groups with collective interests – and, second, the frameworks and analysis we find in the literature on research ethics as well as those expressed in processes of ethics review.[16] Thus, I would suggest that if we are to move forward then we should not focus our concern on the ethics of practice but, instead, consider the practice of ethics. Of course, this is not something that has previously gone unaddressed. Carpenter's (2018) concern for the ethics of ethical review can be taken as a case in point. However, this chapter has taken a different approach. My aim has been to promote an understanding of ethics as a part of broader social practices, and a social practice in its own right. My suggestion is that we abandon notions such as phrónēsis – and the idea that some individuals might possess moral wisdom – and promoting the adoption of synderesis – the idea that human beings have a (universal) moral sense and a (culturally specific or contextually relative) moral sensibility. In so doing, I am aiming to provide a social understanding of morality that promotes a mutually informative dialogue regarding matters of ethics – in both general and the more specific case of social research.

It seems to me that, if anything, wisdom involves realizing that one's own moral perspectives may be misguided and incomplete. It involves considering and evaluating the perspectives of others, particular those with whom we are involved. Such activities involve, I would suggest, the exercise of synderesis and a normative or evaluative understanding of particular practices that concern us. As such, the term synderesis does not merely name our moral sense – our ability to directly perceive normative states. It should also be taken to include our moral sense of other people's moral sense or perspective. Indeed, the fact that they also have moral senses and perspectives is something that deserves to be shown proper consideration, as part of what it means to treat people with respect. Herein lies a (ethical) criticism of existing approaches to the governance of research and, indeed, an ethics for the conduct of social research.

NOTES

1. Whilst I will not discuss it further, the term 'proper' in this sentence covers a multitude of Ancient Greek, and therefore Aristotelian, sins. For example, it is more than conceivable that the proper flourishing of slaves, and other subjugated groups, was something that could be overseen with phrónēsis or wisdom.

2. Indeed, one could argue that this is the minimum that is required. It may be that virtue theory must also embrace diversity in our theoretical self-understanding (Chernilo, 2016). The first nature of human beings is to have a second nature. This second nature encompasses the way we understand ourselves and, therefore, is able to condition the way we actually are. We inhabit a world that is not only practically diverse but is also theoretically diverse. It is not clear that a singular conception of flourishing and eudaimonia can encompass such diversity.

3. See the Jubilee Center for character and virtues, particularly: http://www.jubilee-centre.ac.uk/1576/projects/previous-work/knightly-virtues (accessed on July 13, 2017).

4. For a rejoinder to the myth of virtue ethics predisposition towards conservativism, see Kristjánsson (2013, pp. 280–281). As this article acknowledges, virtue ethics is additionally charged with being paternalistic, old fashioned, quasi-religious, anti-intellectual, and anti-democratic. As with the charge of conservativism, there are replies to each of these points, and Kristjánsson's points are well made. Nevertheless, given part of the point being made not only concerns virtue ethics in theory but also its practical uses, such concerns deserve to be kept in mind.

5. On the notion of moral order, see Smith (2009, Chapter 2).

6. The recent developments in research that fall under the rubric the sociology of morality/the anthropology of ethics provide some evidence that this is currently changing. However, the very fact that such interest is both recent and without significant historical precursors bears out the point that Chernilo is making; sociology, anthropology, and social research, more generally, have not fully engaged with or properly grasped the normative dimensions of social life. The intellectual paucity of much of the work that passes under the banner of 'empirical ethics' provides additional confirmation of both the difficulty of doing so and the fact that neither applied ethics and 'analytic' nor 'modern' moral philosophy can provide the required intellectual resources.

7. My point here is not, of course, that any and all social researchers are engaged in such criticism. Merely that they must be open to the possibility of change, including changes brought about as a result of their work, even if that work is 'descriptive'.

8. Here one might think of those, like contemporary composer and pianist Hauschka, who play 'prepared piano', i.e., those who contrive to play the piano in ways other than pressing the keys. In addition, one also thinks of the stand-up comic Stewart Lee, whose act often simultaneously involves its own deconstruction. Both activities challenge, but nevertheless reiterate, the underlying normativity of the relevant practices, i.e., the way in which a piano ought to be played, and the way in which explaining a joke usually ensures that it will no longer be found humorous. Finally, one might also consider the way Les Dawson contrived to play the piano badly as part of his comedy routine. This is something that is made possible by, on the one hand, his not inconsiderable ability to play the piano, and on the other, the comedic setting in which the performance takes place. The example shows how practices can be intertwined.

9. On the complexities of the term habit, something that is too often treated simplistically, see Carlisle (2010), Ravaisson (2008), and Sparrow and Hutchinson (2013).

10. One could think of conatus in similar terms (Fuller, 2008).

11. These could take the form of theological, teleological (virtue, eudemonia), or otherwise philosophical (Kantian or utilitarian) commitments.

12. Notably in his *Idea of the Social Sciences in Relation to Philosophy* (Winch, 1990) and *Understanding Primitive Society* (Winch, 1964).

13. In his reply, Doris (2005, p. 666) confirms that he shares this view.

14. The reason being that what else could synderesis – both in the sense of a universal moral sense and culturally specific or contextually relative moral sensibility – be, other than a kind of social intelligence?

15. Indeed, anthropologists seem to be leading the way in this regard (cf. Meskell & Pels, 2005).

16. It would be easy to read my work as dismissing the legitimacy of external analysis of the ethics of social research. My intent is, certainly, to challenge its dominance. However, in the final analysis, my hope is that it can be brought into a more productive dialogue with the full range of pertinent ethical perspectives. My aim is to provide a shared understanding on which this dialogue can be taken forward.

REFERENCES

Abend, G. (2014). *The moral background: An inquiry into the history of business ethics*. Princeton, NJ: Princeton University Press.

Anscombe, G. E. M. (1958). Modern moral philosophy. *Philosophy*, *33*(124), 1–19.

Arpaly, N. (2005). Comments on lack of character by John Doris. *Philosophy and Phenomenological Research*, *71*(3), 643–647. Retrieved from https://doi.org/10.1111/j.1933-1592.2005.tb00477.x

Austin, M. W. (2013). *Virtues in action: New essays in applied virtue ethics*. Basingstoke, UK: Palgrave.

Axtell, G., & Olson, P. (2012). Recent work in applied virtue ethics. *American Philosophical Quarterly*, *49*(3), 183–204.

Banks, S. (2018). From research integrity to researcher integrity: Issues of conduct, competence and commitment. In Emmerich, N. (Ed.), *Virtue Ethics and Social Science Research: Integrity, Governance and Practice*. Bingley: Emerald Group Publishing.

Bauman, Z. (1993). *Postmodern ethics*. Hoboken, NJ: Wiley-Blackwell.

Blakely, J. (2013). The forgotten Alasdair MacIntyre: Beyond value neutrality in the social sciences. *Polity*, *45*(3), 445–463. Retrieved from https://doi.org/10.1057/pol.2013.13

Carlisle, C. (2010). Between freedom and necessity: Félix Ravaisson on habit and the moral life. *Inquiry*, *53*(2), 123–145.

Carpenter, D. (2018). Virtue ethics in the practice and review of social science research: The virtuous ethics committee. In Emmerich, N. (Ed.), *Virtue Ethics and Social Science Research: Integrity, Governance and Practice*. Bingley: Emerald Group Publishing.

Chernilo, D. (2014). The idea of philosophical sociology. *British Journal of Sociology*, *65*(2), 338–357. Retrieved from https://doi.org/10.1111/1468-4446.12077

Chernilo, D. (2016). *Debating humanity: Towards a philosophical sociology*. New York, NY: Cambridge University Press.

Clifford, D. (2014). Limitations of virtue ethics in the social professions. *Ethics and Social Welfare*, *8*(1), 2–19. Retrieved from https://doi.org/10.1080/17496535.2013.804942

Dingwall, R. (2006). Confronting the anti-democrats: The unethical nature of ethical regulation in social science. *Medical Sociology Online*, *1*, 51–58.

Dingwall, R. (2012). How did we ever get into this mess? The rise of ethical regulation in the social sciences. In Love, K. (Ed.), *Ethics in social research* (Vol. 12, pp. 3–26). Emerald. Bingley: Emerald Group Publishing.

Dingwall, R., Iphofen, R., Lewis, J., Oates, J., & Emmerich, N. (2017). Towards common principles for social science research ethics: A discussion document for the Academy of Social Sciences. In R. Iphofen (Ed.), *Finding common ground: Consensus in research ethics across the social sciences* (Vol. 1, pp. 111–123). Bingley: Emerald Publishing Limited. Retrieved from http://www.emeraldinsight.com/doi/full/10.1108/S2398-601820170000001010

Doris, J. M. (2002). *Lack of character: Personality and moral behavior*. Cambridge: Cambridge University Press.

Doris, J. M. (2005). Replies: Evidence and sensibility. *Philosophy and Phenomenological Research*, *71*(3), 656–677. Retrieved from https://doi.org/10.1111/j.1933-1592.2005.tb00479.x

Emmerich, N. (2015). Bourdieu's collective enterprise of inculcation: The moral socialisation and ethical enculturation of medical students. *British Journal of Sociology of Education*, *36*(7), 1054–1072.

Emmerich, N. (2016). Reframing research ethics: Towards a professional ethics for the social sciences. *Sociological Research Online*, *21*(4), 7.

Emmerich, N. (2017). Remaking research ethics in the social sciences: Anthropological reflections on a collaborative process. In Iphonfen, R. (Ed.). *Finding common ground – Consensus in research ethics across the social sciences* (p. 125). Bingley: Emerald Group Publishing.

Fassin, D. (Ed.). (2012). *A companion to moral anthropology*. London: Wiley-Blackwell.

Freidson, E. (1970). *Profession of medicine. A study of the sociology of applied knowledge*. Chicago, IL: University of Chicago Press.

Freidson, E. (2001). *Professionalism, the third logic: On the practice of knowledge*. Chicago, IL: University of Chicago Press.

Fuller, S. (2008). Conatus. In Grenfell (Ed.), *Pierre Bourdieu: Key concepts*. Stocksfield: Acumen: Durham, UK.

Hammersley, M. (2009). Against the ethicists: On the evils of ethical regulation. *International Journal of Social Research Methodology*, *12*(3), 211–226.

Hammersley, M. (2010). Creeping ethical regulation and the strangling of research. *Sociological Research Online*, *15*(4), 16.

Hammersley, M. (2018). Is Phrónēsis necessarily virtuous? In Emmerich, N. (Ed.), *Virtue Ethics and Social Science Research: Integrity, Governance and Practice*. Bingley: Emerald Group Publishing.

Hammersley, M., & Traianou, A. (2014). An alternative ethics? Justice and Ccre as guiding principles for qualitative research. *Sociological Research Online*, *19*(3), 24.

Higgins. (2010). Worlds of practice: MacIntyre's challenge to applied ethics, worlds of practice: MacIntyre's challenge to applied ethics. *Journal of Philosophy of Education*, *44*(2–3) 237–273. Retrieved from https://doi.org/10.1111/j.1467-9752.2010.00755.x

Hitlin, S., & Vaisey, S. (Eds.). (2010). *Handbook of the sociology of morality*. London: Springer.

Iphofen, R. (2017). *Finding common ground – Consensus in research ethics across the social sciences*. Bingley: Emerald Group Publishing.

Johnson, M. (2014). *Morality for humans: Ethical understanding from the perspective of cognitive science*. Chicago, IL: University of Chicago Press.

Jonsen, A., & Toulmin, S. (1992). *The abuse of casuistry: A history of moral reasoning*. Berkley, CA: University of California Press.

Kolodny, N. (1996). The ethics of cryptonormativism: A defense of Foucault's evasions. *Philosophy & Social Criticism*, *22*(5), 63–84.

Kristjánsson, K. (2013). Ten myths about character, virtue, and virtue education: Plus three well-founded misgivings. *British Journal of Educational Studies*, *61*(3), 269–287.

Kuhn, T. S. (1996). *The structure of scientific revolutions* (3rd ed.). Chicago, IL: University of Chicago Press.

Kwiatkowski, R. (2018). Questioning the virtue of virtue ethics: Slowing the rush to virtue in research ethics. In Emmerich, N. (Ed.), *Virtue Ethics and Social Science Research: Integrity, Governance and Practice*. Bingley: Emerald Group Publishing.

Laidlaw, J. (2013). *The subject of virtue: An anthropology of ethics and freedom*. Cambridge: Cambridge University Press.

Macdonald, K. M. (1995). *The sociology of the professions*. London: Sage.

Macdonald, S. (2010). Making ethics. In M. Melhuus, J. P. Mitchell, & H. Wulff (Eds.), *Ethnographic practice in the present* (pp. 80–94). Berghahn Books: Oxford, UK.

MacIntyre, A. (1981). *After virtue: A study in moral theory*. London: Duckworth.

Meisenhelder, T. (2006). From character to habitus in sociology. *The Social Science Journal*, *43*(1), 55–66. Retrieved from https://doi.org/16/j.soscij.2005.12.005

Meskell, L., & Pels, P. (2005). *Embedding ethics*. Oxford: Berg.

Mikhail, J. (2016). *Chomsky and moral philosophy*. SSRN scholarly paper No. ID 2759924. Rochester, NY: Social Science Research Network. Retrieved from http://papers.ssrn.com/abstract=2759924

Pellegrino, E. D. (2007). Professing medicine, virtue-based ethics, and the retrieval of professionalism. In R. L. Walker & P. J. Ivanhoe (Eds.), *Working virtue: Virtue ethics and contemporary moral problems* (pp. 113–134). Oxford, UK: Oxford University Press.

Ravaisson, F. (2008). *Of habit* (C. Carlisle & M. Sinclair, Trans.). London: Continuum.

Rouse, J. (2001). Two concepts of practices. In T. R. Schatzki, K. Knorr-Cetina, & E. von Savigny (Eds.), *The Practice Turn in Contemporary Theory* (pp. 189–198). New York, NY: Routledge.

Rouse, J. (2007). Social practices and normativity. *Philosophy of the Social Sciences*, *37*(1), 46–56. Retrieved from https://doi.org/10.1177/0048393106296542

Schatzki, T. R., Knorr-Cetina, K. D., & von Savigny, E. (Eds.). (2000). *The practice turn in contemporary theory*. Abingdon: Routledge.

Schrag, Z. M. (2010). *Ethical imperialism: Institutional review boards and the social sciences, 1965–2009*. Baltimore, MD: The Johns Hopkins University Press.

Sleeboom-Faulkner, M., Simpson, B., Burgos-Martinez, E., & McMurray, J. (2017). The formalisation of social-science research ethics: How did we get there? *Journal of Ethnographic Theory*, *7*(1), 71–79. Retrieved from https://doi.org/10.14318/hau7.1.010

Smith, C. (2009). *Moral, believing animals: Human personhood and culture*. New York, NY; Oxford: Oxford University Press.

Snow, N. E. (2009). *Virtue as social intelligence: An empirically grounded theory*. New York, NY: Taylor & Francis.

Sparrow, T., & Hutchinson, A. (Eds.). (2013). *A history of habit: From Aristotle to Bourdieu*. Lanham, MD: Lexington Books.

Stark, L. (2011). *Behind closed doors: IRBs and the making of ethical research*. Chicago, IL: University of Chicago Press.

Strathern, M. (2000). New accountabilities: Anthropological studies in audit, ethics, and the academy. In M. Strathern (Ed.), *Audit cultures: Anthropological studies in accountability, ethics and the academy* (pp. 1–18). London: Routledge.

Traianou, A. (2018). Ethical regulation of social research versus the cultivation of Phrónēsis. In Emmerich, N. (Ed.), *Virtue Ethics and Social Science Research: Integrity, Governance and Practice*. Bingley: Emerald Group Publishing.

Turner, S. P. (2010). *Explaining the normative*. Cambridge, UK: Polity Press.

van den Hoonaard, W. C. (2011). *The seduction of ethics: Transforming the social sciences*. Toronto: University of Toronto Press.

van den Hoonaard, W. C., & Hamilton, A. (Eds.). (2016). *The ethics rupture: Exploring alternatives to formal research-ethics review*. Toronto: University of Toronto Press.

Winch, P. (1964). Understanding a primitive society. *American Philosophical Quarterly, 1*(4), 307–324.

Winch, P. (1990). *The Idea of a social science and its relation to philosophy* (2nd ed.). London: Routledge.

Zahle, J. (2013). Practices and the direct perception of normative states: Part I. *Philosophy of the Social Sciences, 43*(4), 493–518. Retrieved from https://doi.org/10.1177/0048393112454995

Zahle, J. (2014). Practices and the direct perception of normative states: Part II. *Philosophy of the Social Sciences, 44*(1), 74–85. Retrieved from https://doi.org/10.1177/0048393112462517

INDEX